London's Pleasures

A politician thinks of it merely as the seat of government in its different departments; a grazier, as a vast market for cattle; a merchantile man, as a place where a prodigious deal of business is done upon 'Change; a dramatick enthusiast, as the grand scene of theatrical entertainments; a man of pleasure, as an assemblage of taverns, and the great emporium for ladies of easy virtue. But the intellectual man is struck with it, as comprehending the whole of human life in all its variety, the contemplation of which is inexhaustible.

Dr Johnson

London's Pleasures

From Restoration to Regency

DAVID KERR CAMERON

SUTTON PUBLISHING

First published in the United Kingdom in 2001 by
Sutton Publishing Limited · Phoenix Mill
Thrupp · Stroud · Gloucestershire · GL5 2BU

British Library Cataloguing in Publication Data
A catalogue record for this book is available from the British Library.

ISBN 0-7509-2448-9

Typeset in 11/15pt Ehrhardt MT.
Typesetting and origination by
Sutton Publishing Limited.
Printed and bound in England by
J.H. Haynes & Co. Ltd, Sparkford.

Contents

Acknowledgements

The author acknowledges a deep debt of gratitude to all those who helped him to locate the images that illustrate this work. His thanks are particularly due to Jeremy Smith and his colleagues at the Guildhall Library, and to David Taylor of the National Maritime Museum's picture library; their assistance and unfailing courtesy far exceeded the call of duty.

CHAPTER I

Introduction: a Return to Merriment

The year 1660 was a good one; a turning point in England's history. The capital shrugged off the shroud of Puritanism's dolour and took to the streets; there was a lifting of the spirits, a joy in the heart as the city prepared itself for a return to its old roguish ways and waited to greet its new monarch, Charles II. He entered, he processed and was wildly applauded, a man at the peak of regal achievement, wrenching back, at last, his father's throne from the deadening Cromwellian grasp. He came, triumphantly, over London Bridge, the ancient gateway to the capital, in a magnificent panoply of noise and colour, 300 gentlemen in cloth of silver riding with him and escorted by troops, trumpeters, the Lifeguards and a further 300 soldiers in velvet. Accompanying him, and basking in his glory, was a phalanx of the city's dignitaries. Charles had landed at Dover on 25 May to a tumultuous welcome of cheering and church bells. John Evelyn, that most diligent of diarists and chronicler of capital events, watched his monarch's arrival in the Strand. It was dazzling; he would confide to his now-famous *Diary* for 29 May 1660:

> This day came in his majestie Charles II to London, after a sad and long exile and calamitous suffering both of the king and church, being seventeen years. This was also his birthday, and with a triumph of above 20,000 horse and foot, brandishing their swords and shouting with inexpressible joy; the ways strew'd with flowers, the bells ringing, the streets hung with tapestry, fountains running with wine; the mayor, aldermen, and all the companies in their liveries, chains of gold, and banners; lords and nobles clad in cloth of silver, gold, and velvet; the windowes and the balconies all set with ladies; trumpets, music, and myriads of people flocking even from so far as Rochester, so as they were seven hours in passing the City, even from two in the afternoon till nine at night. I stood in the Strand and beheld it, and bless'd God. And all this without one drop of blood shed, and by that army which rebelled against him; but it was the

Lord's doings, for such a restoration was never seen in any history, ancient or modern, since the return of the Jews from Babylonish captivity; nor so joyful a day and so bright ever seen in this nation, this happening when to expect or effect it was past all human policy.

The future seemed secure; it would be another country. England was about to enter an era of elegance and unrestrained indulgence. There would be capital amusement, every diversion that could entice the human spirit, a hedonism the city had not seen before. The Merry Monarch himself would lead the way, the welcome herald of a new age, a man at ease with his crown and his kingdom, accessible, urbane and witty; 'a prince', according to Evelyn, 'of many Virtues & many greate Imperfections, Debonaire, Easy of access, not bloody or Cruel' who would embrace culture and the arts, license the theatre and move comfortably in the new ambience of the times, free of that frigidity that had so recently kept society in an iron grip of denial and restraint. Given his example, morals would become noticeably relaxed, not to say non-existent.

Perhaps that day – indeed it is most likely – amid the mood of pomp and celebration, his thoughts as he approached Whitehall clouded for a moment to reflect on the sorrow of that January day in 1649 when his father Charles I had stepped out from the Banqueting House on to the scaffold prepared for him, where his stubbornness had led him. There was speculation still about the identity of the axeman who, that grey, chill day, would cleave the head from its royal shoulders. Out from the Palace had come the fateful pageant, his escort a guard of halberdiers, with colours dancing in the wind and drums beating. 'This day,' reported one observer, 'about one o'clock, he came from St James's in a long black cloak and grey stockings. The Palsgrave came through the Park with him. He was faint, and was forced to sit down and rest in the Park . . . He walked twice or thrice about the scaffold, and held out his hands to the people. His last words, as I am informed, were, "To your power I must submit, but your authority I deny." He pulled his doublet off, and kneeled down to the block himself. When some officer offered to unbutton him . . . he thrust him from him. Two men, in vizards and false hair, were appointed to be his executioners. Who they were is not known. Some say that he that did it was the common hangman; others that it was one Captain Foley, and that the hangman refused.' A proclamation that succeeded the dire event had unequivocally warned 'that no man shall presume to proclaim his son Prince Charles as King'.

The brutal warrant for the king's execution had specifically ordered that his death should publicly take place 'in the open street before Whitehall'. The majesty with which he died – some said he walked to the scaffold with a cheerful face and a steady step and behaved 'wonderfully bravely' – impressed Andrew Marvell, whose verse famously immortalised the moment and the royal demeanour:

> While round the armed bands
> Did clasp their bloody hands,
> He nothing common did, or mean,
> Upon that memorable scene,
> Nor called the gods, with vulgar spite,
> To vindicate his hopeless right;
> But with his keener eye
> The axe's edge did try;
> Then bowed the kingly head
> Down, as upon a bed.

His usurper's death at Whitehall nearly a decade later was longer drawn-out and more painful. He exited at the height of a violent storm, symbolic perhaps of the tumult he had caused. By contrast his circumstances were pitiful, his end affectingly unheroic. During his illness he became slightly deranged and took against barbers so that his beard growth extended all over his face. None the less, the honours of his burial in Westminster Abbey were offensively regal. Evelyn again, in his *Diary* entry for 2 October 1658, would record the Lord Protector's 'superb' funeral. 'He was carried from Somerset House in a velvet bed of State drawn by six horses.' His effigy lay in royal robes and crowned with a crown, sceptre, and globe, like a king.

The pendants, and guidions were carried by the officers of the army; and the imperial banner, achievement, etc, by the heraulds in their coates; a rich caparizon'd horse, embroider'd all over with gold; a knight of honour arm'd cap-a-pie, and after all, his guards, soldiers, and innumerable mourners. On this equipage they proceeded to Westminster; but it was the joyfullest funeral that ever I saw, for there were none that cried but dogs, which the soldiers hooted away with a barbarous noise, drinking and taking tobacco in the streets as they went.

Cromwell, looking on the scene, would have been distraught. It could hardly have been the solemn farewell he would have foreseen for himself. And with the Restoration, his rest was soon to be violently disturbed. Society would take a macabre revenge.

At the end of his seven-hour procession through the capital's streets, the son of the martyred monarch would mark the Restoration in the hall of the same building that had witnessed his father's execution, giving a moment of astonishing symmetry to one of the bloodiest episodes in England's history. Samuel Pepys, that other revealing diarist of the time, was just fifteen when he saw Charles I beheaded. Remarkably, a decade or so later, as a minion of the navy, he would be among those who fetched his son back from Holland to claim the throne. With the fleet had gone a small, precautionary sweetener of £50,000. Still on duty at Dover, Pepys missed his monarch's entry into his capital on his birthday, 29 May; he was there, however, for the coronation the following year, on 23 April, a day of bunting and bravura, and, most appropriately, St George's Day. The day previously there had been a royal procession through the city, from the Tower to Westminster, a cavalcade that glittered and dazzled with the dancing glints of silver and gold. The following day, having cozened himself a coign of vantage, Pepys reports:

> About four I arose and got to the Abbey, where I followed Sir J. Denham, the surveyor, with some company he was leading in. And, with much ado, by the favour of Mr Cooper, his man, did get up into a great scaffold, across the north end of the Abbey, where, with a great deal of patience, I sat from past four till eleven, before the King came in. And a pleasure it was to see the Abbey raised in the middle, all covered with red, and a throne (that is a chaire) and footstools on the top of it. And all the officers of all kinds, so much as the very fidlers, in red vests. At last comes in the Deane and prebends of Westminster with the bishops (many of them in cloth-of-gold Copes), and after them the nobility, all in their parliament robes, which was a most magnificent sight. Then the Duke and the King, with a scepter (carried by my Lord Sandwich) and Sword and mond [orb] before him, and the crowne too. The King in his robes, bare-headed, which was very fine. And after all had placed themselfs, there was a sermon and the service. And then in the quire of the high altar, he passed all the ceremonies . . . which, to my very great grief, I and most of the Abbey could not see. The crowne being put on his head, a great shout begun . . .

For the diarist, as for many others, the day ended drunkenly.

The king's return had been orchestrated by, among others, the Duchess of Albemarle, working on the sensibilities of her turncoat husband General Monck, commander-in-chief of the army. Some said she terrified him into acquiescence. It may well have been the case, for the duchess was the granddaughter of one of the capital's five women barbers – and a lady apparently not only of vulgar habits but plain and alarmingly ill-favoured. She was known, generally, as 'Dirty Bess', and Pepys, who sometimes dined with the duke, tells us why: 'I find the Duke of Albemarle at dinner with sorry company, some of his officers of the Army – dirty dishes and a nasty wife at table – and bad meat; of which I made but an ill dinner.' But low-born or not, the duchess was loyal to the class she had moved into, working on Monck and finally persuading him into organising the Restoration and putting himself at the head of the campaign. In February 1660 the general, with his troops in control of the capital, declared for a free Parliament. The long-repressed capital went wild. Bonfires raged everywhere and joyous bells gave tongue to the message. At the gate of Westminster Hall on 8 May Charles II was proclaimed as king. Whatever the sombre memories stirring amid the mirth and feasting that May day of his triumphal return, nothing would cloy the capital's – or the king's – appetite for joy.

The capital he had come into, like his Stuart inheritance, was one that had survived the tumult of history. How it rose from the ooze of the Thames foreshore is charted, still, with some uncertainty, but undoubtedly it was functioning and even flourishing as a trading entity before Tacitus set eyes on it around the year AD 67. The Romans took what they found there, inhabited it and methodically exploited it, calling their city Londinium. That they civilised it, refining its lifestyle, has been proved by the artefacts found in the excavating digger's wake. (It would be 1,500 years after they left before central heating again became a feature of city life.) They threw a bridge over its undisciplined river, where London Bridge spans it today, and walled it, allowing access only by its city gates.

In the sixth century the Saxon invaders inherited it, but did little to enhance it. They were not city folk. Successive kings from Ethelbert, the Kentish king and a Christian, raised St Paul's to the glory of God, and created a palace at Aldermanbury, wisely, to emphasise the monarch's pre-eminence. The Conqueror came and saw – and built the Tower, the gem and centrepiece of much of London's story, to keep watch on its approaches; shrewdly, he was careful not to antagonise the population by driving a coach and horses through their traditional rights. Subsequent kings conferred further privileges, including the right to appoint those who would govern the city. In 1215 Magna Carta gave a boost to London's status, confirming its 'ancient liberties' and appointing a mayor whose processions from the Guildhall would become (and remain) one of its most momentous events of celebration, still undiminished. Out of the example the capital set would grow the country's system of government as it is still exercised at the start of the twenty-first century.

London Bridge, rebuilt of stone in 1209, sitting squat and narrow, with an overweening confidence in its nineteen arches, and lined on either side by the habitations of citizens and merchants, impeded the natural flow of the river, ensuring down the centuries that a severe winter would result in a petrified river and the efflorescence of the capital's infamous frost fairs. They were naughty occasions; the merry king himself would enjoy them. More importantly, the bridge was the sole southern approach, funnelling a never-ending stream of continental merchants and potentates, pilgrims and the medieval wandering classes, into the capital. The city they entered was a trading hub, the country's premier port into which flowed goods from all corners of the world. Men of the arts chronicled and depicted its rise and expansion and in some cases deeply influenced them. By the late eighteenth century it would be 'the greatest Emporium in the known world'. Defoe, less flatteringly, saw it as a place 'that sucks the vitals of trade in this island to itself'. Beyond the bounds of Holborn and Tower Hill lay the English countryside: still, green and pastoral.

The capital was indeed a *mélange* of trades. Society was closely knit, cohesive, with the master's fine house adjoining the habitations of the underclass who manned his mill or workshop. It may have been shrewd psychology, but society had not as yet segregated itself into divisive social groupings. Wealthy and deprived would mingle indiscriminately too in such arenas as the capital's pleasure gardens, like those of Vauxhall, where whores and pimps plied their trade in the shadier avenues. Each city trade had its own governing body for its craft – and today's names, such as Cornhill, Poultry, Ironmonger Row, Bread Street and so on, are a reminder of the quarters of the city they collectively colonised, leaving their history in the ancient streets. Goldsmiths congregrated in Cheapside, butchers sought a necessary propinquity with the source that supplied them, Smithfield, and made Newgate their own, slaughtering their meat in the street and tossing the entrails into the communal gutter to the peril of the populace, who were periodically ravaged by fevers and disease and sometimes burned in their beds as their straw-roofed hovels took alight. The air was putrid with the stench of hide- and skin-dressing – among other things. Brew-wives made their hasty ale to slake the thirsts such conditions undoubtedly engendered, drawing their water from the Thames, the river into which the city simultaneously slopped its waste. Men and women drank immoderately; drink would always be a problem.

Above all, what London's people loved was a procession, and the riot of colour it brought into their drab lives for a day. Then the civic fathers, the clergy and the noblemen and their ladies paraded themselves to the public view – and public approval or ridicule. May Day was a like excuse for excess – and more. Theatre took to the streets, at that early time in the performances of the miracle and mystery plays staged by the craft guilds on carts that came to almost every street corner, in a movable, cultural feast.

Six years into the Restoration devastation struck in 1666 (after the great pestilence of only the year before), when a baker's oven caught alight in Pudding Lane – and took two-thirds of the City with it, including the cream of its architectural gems. The Great Fire took the heart out of the capital, the residences of the wealthy merchants along with their neighbouring warehouses, from the Tower to the Temple, but without impinging on the 'liberties' clinging to its fringe, which contained the greater part of its half-million population, in slums such as Lambeth, Westminster, St Giles and Cripplegate. Fortuitously, it also took the rats that had spread the plague.

But always it was the Mecca, the lodestone, the place that men (and women) came to, to fulfil their destinies and their dreams; hopefully, to make their fortunes. They descended from all compass points of the land, drawn by its clamour and its excitement, its capacity to surprise and provide adventure; in the face of plague and every pestilence they came, adventurers (and adventuresses) of every colour and nationality to populate the gilded palaces or pollute their souls in the sour tenements and stews of what the wise and ancient Bede called 'the mart of all nations'. And so it was, sucking dry the eastern ports that dared to oppose it to take its place as the gateway between the nation's commerce and the landmass of Europe.

For nearly half the year the roads that led into London were a quagmire of deep, glutinous mud that could suck the boots off a wandering pedlar and make the route all but impassable; for the rest of the time they were deep-rutted tracks on which wagons lurched and skewed their way in a cloud of choking dust. Into the putrid squalor of its main market, where the weekly horse sale kept its link with the Norman past, were driven livestock of every kind to sustain its tables, in a droving ritual that ended only in 1855. Down its converging roads, too, came those men *in extremis*, summoned in chains to their nemesis, to their last act of public greatness – on the gibbet at Tyburn Green, on the plainstones of Tower Hill, or the martyrs' plaza under the dark shadow of Smithfield's Elms – reckless men who had dared too far or forgot to curb their fiery tongues. The hoi polloi flocked to hear their final words to posterity and witness their last appearance on the stage they had strutted so bravely, if ill-advisedly. Some died with a riposte on their lips; most came sombrely to the gallows and composed themselves for the end.

Men approached it, this diverse city, if they had sense, with circumspection. Up the Dover road they came from their foreign lands, to catch their first glimpse of its sprawl beyond its single bridge and the uncongenial clutter of Southwark, prolific with stews and jails. Before them spread a capital where glorious history lay thick and embedded under the carapace of its shimmering image. It was a violent Mecca; a tinderbox for ever waiting to ignite, and always at the mercy of the unpredictable mob, conjuring itself suddenly out of the night and sometimes dispersing as quickly as it had appeared. It formed from the disparate elements of society but mainly from the working class (not the riff-raff), stung by some perceived injustice, and at other times law-abiding citizens. Such mobs made damaging attacks on property and almost always had a poor-versus-rich undertow, whatever the issue that inflamed them. In its history the capital had been host to riots of every hue and denomination: political, social and economic. The spark could ignite from an execution procession (always a drunken and highly charged event), an increase in the cost of gin or the price of a theatre ticket, even the closure of a favourite brothel. Fairs were a flashpoint for mindless and recurrent mischief. One post-Restoration eruption of 1668 involved the city's apprentices (the students of their day); Pepys again was around to record their Moorfields rampage as they took 'the liberty of these holidays to pull down bawdy houses'. It was time to call out the cavalry: 'Presently . . . forthwith alarmes were beat by drum and trumpet through Westminster, and all to their colours and to horse, as if the French were coming into the town.'

Newgate prison ablaze in 1780 as mobs claimed the streets during the Gordon Riots. (By courtesy of the Guildhall Library, Corporation of London)

The focus of unrest constantly shifted, from the weavers and the powder-keg of Spitalfields to the coal-heavers, the watermen – even tailors. All trades and crafts in turn (or in violent association) would parade their grievances. And there were the more serious ripples of contention in religion and in politics – the latter exploited and magnificently manipulated by the dissident MP John Wilkes in 1768, a hero to the mob. His tussle with the Establishment turned the city to turmoil and terror as his gangs trailed the streets with the slogan 'Wilkes and Liberty', breaking the windows of important personages and demanding that all house-holders show allegiance to their cause by placing a light in their windows.

Wilkes was bad news, though his cause led to a greater care for democracy. The Pope-hater and MP Lord George Gordon was a fanatic intent on nothing less than the repeal of the Roman Catholic Relief Act, a measure that enabled long-suffering Catholics to come out of their closets but led to the much more destructive Gordon Riots of 1780 as the Protestant lord lost control of his forty thousand followers after Parliament contemptuously threw out their petition. Chapels were targeted, the homes of known adherents attacked and pillaged (their possessions made a bonfire in the street), and priests beaten up (one died from his injuries). Irishmen were vulnerable, but even more to the mob's liking was the destruction of a Holborn distillery. Many of the rioters were so drunk by the time they set it ablaze that several of them perished in the flames.

But increasingly the spark would be political. In 1831, in the disturbances of the Reform and later Clerkenwell riots, was rooted the challenge of the Chartists, which came to a head on Kennington Common in 1848, when the campaigners, subdued by a massive police presence, took their petition quietly to the Commons – by cab. In 1866 nothing less than full-blown revolution was feared in the Hyde Park Reform riots as the mob tore out the park's railings to use as weaponry and went looting in the West End. 'This mighty mob of famished, diseased and filthy helots is getting dangerous, physically, morally, politically dangerous,' wrote one fearful commentator – and was proved right a year later when the Bloody Sunday protesters filled Trafalgar Square in a mass sit-in of the jobless, setting a pattern for our own time. They would be brutally crushed by both police and military force.

Then as now the rabble clung to the coat-tails of the mob for the rich pickings it provided – the cutpurses, footpads, pickpockets, harlots and the highwaymen who haunted the city and the heaths and commons that surrounded it. Crime was endemic, flourishing in relative safety in a metropolis as yet inadequately policed. The young Boswell, shaken on his way south when the horse yoked in the chaise bolted and overturned the vehicle and its occupants, was far more concerned as he neared the capital and 'a good deal afraid of being robbed'. Danger thrived in the smog that so frequently swaddled the city, though robbers hardly needed its cover and preyed blatantly on the unwary in the broadest daylight and in the busiest thoroughfares: George II, walking alone in Kensington Gardens, was robbed of his purse, his watch and his buckles by a solitary highwayman, who, having dared to climb the wall, showed a suitable deference in the commission of the deed. George IV, as the Prince of Wales, and the Duke of York were held up and robbed in Hay Hill, near Berkeley Square. Horace Walpole, who seems to have been singularly unfortunate (or perhaps because he was such a constant gadabout), returning late from an evening with Lord Holland at his country house, was stopped in Hyde Park by that daring duo Plunket and Maclean and narrowly escaped death when Maclean's pistol went off by accident and the shot 'razed the skin under my eye, left some marks of shot on my face and stunned me'. They took his watch and eight guineas. But it was, he later told friends, an incident conducted 'with the greatest good breeding on both sides'. For many, perhaps because he robbed mainly the rich, the highwayman was a romantic figure, a hero to the hoi polloi. But not all encounters were so polite and Walpole concluded 'one dare not stir out after dinner but well-armed'. Ruffianly behaviour was indeed widespread: at Snow Hill, before Holborn Viaduct was built, young scoundrels-about-town amused themselves by 'capturing' old ladies, thrusting them into barrels, and rolling them down the steep hill.

But the spectrum of pleasures was wide: hangings apart, at Tyburn and elsewhere, there was the ever-popular sport of bull- or bear-baiting; the heady risks of the gaming tables; the brutish, bare-knuckle prize-fights; the bonhomie of the coffee-houses, the city's taverns and tea gardens, the beckoning bordellos and the louche pleasures of such precincts as the Haymarket, Bankside, Covent Garden and the unspeakable Lambeth Marshes. The capital did not stint. It seethed with every temptation. For two centuries, without let or hindrance, it would give itself up to an orgy of gratification, a broad-minded bawdiness that ran through the classes. Unerringly, its mysteries drew men and women seductively under its spell.

Samuel Johnson, advising his young Scots devotee that the essence of London was not 'in the showy evolutions of buildings', believed that it was rather 'in the multiplicity of human habitations which are crowded together, that the wonderful immensity of London consists'. Boswell, destined to explore the labyrinthine capital, concurred in his mentor's view that the capital (for a man of pleasure) was 'an assemblage of taverns, and the great emporium of ladies of easy virtue'. His countryman Byron, on his first visit in 1807, had the time of his life in 'a perpetual vortex of dissipation . . . routs, balls and boxing matches, cards, crim cons, aquatic races, love and lotteries'. He was enchanted by Mayfair where, besides his pugilistic training, he 'clareted and champagned till two' at the Cocoa

Hampstead Heath in 1745, still a scene of pastoral innocence and tranquillity. (By courtesy of the Guildhall Library, Corporation of London)

Tree 'then supped, and finished with a kind of regency punch composed of madeira, brandy, and green tea, no real water being admitted therein . . . I have also, more or less, been breaking a few of the favourite commandments.' Felix Mendelssohn on his first visit in 1829 wrote home: 'It is fearful! It is mad! I am quite giddy and confused. London is the grandest and most complicated monster on the face of the earth . . .'

Johnson, coming from Lichfield to lodge, full board, in Exeter Street in a staymaker's house for the princely sum of fourpence-halfpenny a day, was himself still besotted, believing that there a 'man of curious enquiry might see . . . such modes of life as very few could even imagine'. Boswell responded, almost child-like, to its wonders. Indeed, it might be said of him that his first visit to the capital changed his character. His initiation into the ultimate pleasure (for a young man) was joyously accomplished and the shy retiring boy returned to his northern roots a confident young blade with but one ambition:

to get back to the capital's fleshpots at the earliest opportunity. He behaved like a bewitched tourist. Walking in St James's Park with the actor Thomas Sheridan, he would learn of the important seismic shift the Restoration had triggered: 'In Oliver Cromwell's time they were all precise, canting creatures. And no sooner did Charles the Second come over than they turned gay rakes and libertines.'

Edward Gibbon, the historian, just up from Hampshire in his twenties, thought the capital 'a perpetual and astonishing spectacle' affording many amusements. Every 'taste, every sense, may be gratified,' he circumspectly observed. His own confessed daily routine of pleasure was 'from the tavern to the play, from the play to the coffee-house, from the coffee-house to the Bagnio'. Bath-houses, one should say, had a somewhat sullied reputation.

William Cobbett's hatred of the capital was encapsulated in his condemnatory epithet, 'the great wen'. It sapped the kingdom. Arthur Young, a man out of rather the same mould, was aware of the temptations it held for the country boy in the 1770s. In his *Farmer's Letters* he regretted:

> Young men and women in the country villages fix their eyes on London as the last stage of their hope. They enter into service in the country for little else but to raise money enough to go to London, which was no easy matter when a stage-coach was four or five days in creeping an hundred miles. The fare and the expenses ran high. *But now!* a country fellow, one hundred miles from London, jumps on a coach box in the morning, and for eight or ten shillings gets to town by night, which makes a material difference; besides rendering the going up and down so easy, the numbers *who have seen London* are increasing tenfold, and of course ten times the boasts are sounded in the ears of the fools to induce them to quit their healthy clean fields for a region of dirt, stink, and noise.

For one Scots physician, indeed, the capital was a microcosm of hell, if not the genuine article. You lived there at your peril. Thomas Carlyle would have agreed, calling it, as he did, the 'heart of the universe' before going on to categorise its appalling atmosphere. Ruskin, not unexpectedy, railed against it, and Henry James, quitting Rye for its hubbub, was ambivalent. It was, he averred, neither pleasant, nor agreeable, nor cheerful, nor 'exempt from reproach', only magnificent. Foreigners in fact found it 'not a polite place' and its crowds 'insolent and rowdy'. Encountered in the streets they were likely to find

Point of arrival: numerous inn yards like this were the capital's stage-coach termini. (By courtesy of the Guildhall Library, Corporation of London)

themselves jeered at or 'bespattered by mud . . . but as likely as not dead dogs and cats' would be thrown at them. Another foreign pilgrim complained of its 'crowds and clatter'. But all that said, its lure was incontestable:

> Assemblies, parks, coarse feasts in city halls,
> Lectures and trials, plays, committees, balls,
> Wells, Bedlam, executions, Smithfield scenes,
> And fortune-tellers' caves and lions' dens,
> Taverns, Exchanges, Bridewells, drawing-rooms,
> Instalments, pillories, coronations, tombs,
> Tumblers and funerals, puppet-shows, reviews,
> Sales, races, rabbits and (still stronger) pews.

Thus, extravagantly trumpeted, were the capital's amusements comprehensively categorised. Hogarth would immortalise its grosser pleasures as well as its manners *à la mode* in a lurid *oeuvre* without equal. Yet he loved its capriciousness. For all its dangers, its crimes and congested slums, he found it mesmerising. At its Restoration epicentre, the Merry Monarch, the arbiter of current morals and fashions, took the air almost daily with one or other of his mistresses (all of them conveniently installed nearby) and mingled with his people. His accession had restored to the aristocracy their former place in society and they were suitably grateful. Never would the Court have such flamboyance, be so accessible, so much the focus of capital life. As Pepys puts it: 'Everybody now drinks the King's health without any fear, whereas before it was very private that a man dare do it.' Pepys, as Clerk of the Acts, a senior-ranking civil servant in the country's naval administration, would stay close to the action, observing it at close quarters. He was in Whitehall Palace frequently, almost a courtier, but not quite, though he would talk directly to the king and be thanked by his majesty for his considerable services to the state. He would be one of the most entertaining of the capital's chroniclers as it launched itself into a mad social whirl, a crowded two-centuries-long party of uninhibited pleasure to which fashionable society and hoi polloi alike assembled as to a Restoration rout, that occasion of noise and heat that had the ladies fainting in its claustrophobic excitement. 'Yet all rejoice,' said one shrewd Teutonic observer of this popular entertainment, 'at being so divinely squeezed.' Truly, England's capital city was an enchantress; in the words of the Scots poet William Dunbar,

> . . . the flower of cities all!
> Gemme of all joy, jasper of jocundite!

CHAPTER II
Moving in Fashionable Circles

Innocence was under constant siege in the Merry Monarch's kingdom. In a brittle, shallow society riven by a mocking cynicism – as delightfully conveyed in the letters of the wit Horace Walpole – every woman was seen as a challenge to the predatory amorist, regardless of her station; indeed, no less was expected of him. At the theatre, the opera house, the assembly rooms with their masquerades and masked balls, at the spas and in the pleasure gardens of the time, there was an open and tantalising mingling of the sexes and endless opportunity for intrigue. Ladies of fashion sought lovers at the rout with an extraordinary freedom, coquettish but with unambiguous intent. Maids were coerced to oblige their masters and may perhaps have willingly acquiesced – to their pecuniary advantage; young footmen, almost certainly, were similarly co-opted when his lordship lost interest or the vigour of youth. Men of influence regularly abused their power to enjoy the sexual favours of the wives and mistresses of lower-ranking colleagues complaisant that the favour they allowed would be returned in their career advancement.

The Court hardly set a good example. Charles II's first night back from exile in the capital was spent, it is said, in the bed of Barbara Villiers in Whitehall. Her understanding husband Mr Palmer was soon Lord Castlemaine. Besides his favourites, the king was rumoured to have clean but rougher trade from the streets admitted by the back stairs. Indeed, the king's peccadilloes caused raised eyebrows and considerable comment, from Pepys among others; on 25 April 1663 he made this entry in his famous *Diary*: 'I did hear that the Queene is much grieved of late at the king's neglecting her, he not having supped with her once this quarter of a year, and almost every night with Lady Castlemaine, who hath been with him this St George's Feast at Windsor.' The ladies at Court were no less negligent in their behaviour than the courtiers. Thus Macaulay: 'In that Court a maid of honour who dressed in such a manner as to do justice to a white bosom, who ogled significantly, who danced voluptuously, who excelled in pert repartee, who was not ashamed to romp with lords of the bedchamber and captains of the guards, to sing sly verses with a sly expression, or to put on a page's dress for a frolic, was more likely to be honoured with royal attentions, more likely to win a rich husband . . .' Or at least a protector.

Gallantry and gambling were the continuing diversions of the rich, habits that percolated down to the hoi polloi. Ladies before noon would receive men callers in their boudoirs while in bed, or still *en déshabillé*. And at Gore House's masquerades, where fancy costume disguised the identities of those who had come to flirt or satiate desires in uninhibited company, the mask offered a welcome protection of the reputation. The lustful Regency pleasure-seeking society of the *bon ton* would be satirised by Gillray, Rowlandson and the Cruikshank brothers with a freedom that today seems astonishing. Much of their work was obscene – yet it was openly displayed in booksellers' windows. But the hedonistic mood of the time is best captured in the works of Hogarth, whose brush provides a record of the dissolute and debauched, the capitulation of the capital to a gross enjoyment that regularly transcended the barriers of class. In the sage Swiftian lines:

> Now here and there a hackney coach
> Appearing, shows the ruddy morn's approach.
> Now Betty from her master's bed had flown,
> And softly stole to discompose her own.

Gambling was a fever in the blood of both sexes; gaming was incessant. Men bet on trifles for the highest stakes, and fortunes and reputations were routinely won and lost overnight. One of the descendants of Horace Walpole, the author incidentally of that famous romance of terror, *The Castle of Otranto*, lost the Berkeley Square house that the MP and novelist had once lived in (No. 11) to the banker Henry Baring on the turn of a card. In that gambling heyday of the eighteenth century, while they were strolling along Bond Street, the politician Charles James Fox, orator, rake and darling of the House of Commons but an inveterate gambler, struck a wager with the then Prince of Wales on the number of cats that would be seen on either side of the street; choosing the sunny side, he won the bet with a show of thirteen cats to nil. Fox, who kept a mistress in South Street, lost £140,000 in three years of steady gaming at loo and hazard. His friend Georgiana, the young Duchess of Devonshire, a member of the fast set, an addict all her life and always in debt, on one occasion arranged the drawing-room of Devonshire House as a gaming parlour. Her mother, Lady Spencer, also gambled wildly, pitching her rings on to the faro table when she ran out of cash. The gambling sessions at Devonshire House continued into the morning light – and sometimes well beyond it. At Chatsworth the cost to a female gambler might be £500, even £1,000 a night. Such losses had to be borne stoically.

The gaming clubs – White's, Boodle's, Brooks's, all in St James's Street – were awash with lordly money. White's, the recognised haunt of card-sharpers and 'noble cullies' [dupes], was founded in White's Chocolate House by an Italian in 1693 and rapidly became a 'gambling hell'; here Lord Masham once lost £3,000 in three hours at hazard. It was at White's, a club that was strongly Tory, that Hogarth found the inspiration for *A Rake's Progress*. At the Cocoa Tree Chocolate House in Pall Mall, suspected during the 1745 rebellion of being a Jacobite headquarters and later notorious for its wild gambling, thousands of pounds were nightly wagered at hazard, and when William Almack in 1674 started Brooks's (later to be established in St James's Street), the gaming in what was a Whig stronghold was heavy – so heavy that, as Walpole put it, 'a thousand meadows and cornfields are staked at every throw'. Here Fox, when hit by a losing streak, would borrow from the waiters. Edward Gibbon loved Brooks's, and said of it: 'This is the only place which still invites the flower of English youth. The style of living is extremely pleasant although somewhat expensive: and notwithstanding the rage of play I have found more entertainment and even rational society here than in any other club to which I belong.' Gibbon was a fervid clubman and the Duke of Devonshire was just as enthusiastic. Having escorted his young wife to the opera, he then took himself to Brooks's, where his supper was always blade-bone of mutton. He then played cards till six in the morning. Even in 1822, when he was elected to it, the then Lord Chancellor John Campbell believed the club's membership consisted 'of the first men of rank and talent in England'.

White's would have disputed any such claim. It too gathered a galaxy of distinguished members, including the witty Walpole himself and his oddball friend George Augustus Selwyn, who never married but, as they say, had a lifelong interest in young girls; it could boast admirals, premiers and ex-premiers, Clive and Wellington, Gibbon and Beau Brummell. It initially moved premises with some frequency and was the kind of place, one wag observed, where 'young noblemen were fleeced and corrupted by fashionable gamblers and profligates'.

One room was named Hell and the establishment had an inner clique, the Old Club. After dinner at seven the gaming continued until dawn. Fortunes were squandered in its hothouse atmosphere: in 1755 Sir John Bland lost £32,000 in one evening – and then promptly shot himself. Brummell, often in debt to the tune of £500, and his dandy friends preened daily at its famous bow window. Successive owners would make a fortune from men's folly; it was Harriette Wilson, sometime comforter of the Duke of Wellington, who said that the club would accept any gentleman capable of tying a good knot in his neckerchief and who could remember to keep his hands out of his breeches' pockets. She may have exaggerated. (The club, with a fine irony, would be bought eventually by a man it had once black-balled, a former omnibus driver.)

The fever for gaming would make one Temple Bar fish merchant a millionaire. William Crockford, an East End lad, set up his gaming house for the 'chief aristocracy of England' about 1828 in St James's Street. At an 'entrance' fee of thirty guineas it was the most expensive club in town. Wellington was a member here, too, presumably for the quality of the company and the food, since he did not gamble. Crockford did not stint in the personnel relations department, paying his renowned chef Louis Eustace Ude a well-publicised £1,200 a year, a shrewd move, perhaps, since the food at Brooks's close by was considered atrocious. Hazard was the game at Crockford's, according to the old soldier Gronow, who would add:

> No one can describe the splendour and excitement of the early days of Crockey. A supper of the most exquisite kind, prepared by the famous Ude, and accompanied by the best wines in the world, together with every luxury of the season, was furnished gratis. The members of the club included all the celebrities of England, from the Duke of Wellington to the youngest Ensign of the Guards; and at the gay and festive board, which was constantly replenished from midnight to early dawn, [were heard] the most brilliant sallies of wit, the most agreeable conversation, the most interesting anecdotes . . .

When Crockford died in 1844, stigmatised as the 'keeper of Hell Gaming House', his club rivalled White's as a Mecca for the real and committed gambler.

In such a society – and especially during Regency times – the quality expected of a young blade was 'bottom' (what today we might call 'bottle'). When his luck ran out at the tables he was expected to show the character of his class. Walpole, in 1770, would be an interested observer: 'The young men lose five, ten, fifteen thousand pounds in an evening. Lord Stavordale, not one and twenty, lost eleven thousand last Tuesday, but recovered it by one great hand at hazard . . .' On the conduct of the losers, he says: 'When they had lost, to show that they were undaunted, they went peacefully to sleep with their heads on the table beside the dicebox.'

Gamblers have always been superstitious. In Walpole's time, at Almack's they donned special costume to play: 'They began by pulling off their embroidered clothes, and put on frieze greatcoats, or turned their coats inside outwards for luck. They put on pieces of leather such as are worn by footmen when they clean the knives, to save their laced ruffles; and to guard their eyes from the light, and to prevent tumbling their hair, wore high-crowned hats with broad brims, and adorned with flowers and emblems.'

Money was laid on anything: on horses, cocks, wrestling, prize-fighting, cricket, on whose father would be the first to die (no doubt of some financial concern); on the length of the vicar's sermon; on who would hang and who wouldn't; and even on who would be the first to seduce a lady aloft in a balloon. About 1754 the *Connoisseur* magazine reported a wager struck between the Lords Lincoln and Winchilsea, the former betting one hundred guineas to fifty that the Duchess of Marlborough would survive the Duchess of Cleveland. Walpole's nephew Lord Orford and Lord Rockingham wagered £500 on the outcome of a race between five turkeys and five geese from Norwich to London. One day Lord Arlington staked £3,000 on which of two raindrops would first reach the bottom of the pane. One man bet that he would jump out of his drawing-room window into the next barouche that came along and kiss its occupant. No doubt in the name of valuable publicity, Mr Henry Hunt of Hunt's Matchless Blacking took £100 off a 'noble lord' in 1826 by driving one of his vans with its team of four across the ice of the Serpentine at its widest span. Less lucky, as late as 1867, was the hasty Lord Hastings, who wagered Lord Chaplin that his horse Marksman would show Chaplin's Hermit a clean pair of heels in the Derby at Epsom. In the event Hermit won, losing the impetuous Hastings around £120,000, then a considerable sum. He died, ruined and ridiculed, a short time after. Perhaps the most macabre wagers ever, however, were those staked among the spectators gathered at Temple Bar as the executioner and his assistant brought the heads of the Jacobite Captain Towneley and one of his co-rebels of the Forty-five, still bloody and dripping from the scaffold on Kennington Common, to display there.

The crowd laid wagers as to which head was Towneley's, as hangman and helper sprinted up ladders to place the heads on their respective spikes. Their conduct seems to have disgusted even the hangman, for he refused to say.

Walpole's society particularly was one obsessed with trivialities, one with an outrageous sense of honour. Duels, illegal after 1666, were fought for the most extraordinary reasons by men always too willing to imagine their honour impugned and ultra-sensitive to the merest slight on their characters. The duel was the ultimate test of 'bottom', and saving face was *de rigueur*. In 1804 Lord Camelford, a gentle man of the arts, died from such a mistaken sense of duty, misguidedly taking on the best shot in England, one Captain Best, a professional duellist. When Lord Winchilsea in 1829 alleged treason and treachery against the Duke of Wellington, then Prime Minister, over the Protestant cause, the pair had no option but to repair to Battersea Park. Happily the encounter turned to fiasco: Winchilsea, for some unknown reason, failed to raise his arm when given the order to fire and the duke deliberately fired wide. Winchilsea then discharged his own pistol into the air and apologised profusely. Another touch of the extraordinary, but as tragedy not farce, occurred in the 1680s from the quite ordinary situation of two brothers in love with the same girl. They met in a meadow behind Gower Street while the object of their affections watched from a grassy knoll as each suitor stepped his twenty paces, turned – and fired. They killed each other instantly. The meadow would become forever known as the Field of Forty Footsteps; the grass, they say, slowly withered and grew no more.

Hyde Park was always a possible venue for those illegal and sinister appointments in the dawn mist, and it was here in 1772 that Captain Matthews, a thorough-going rake, met the playwright Richard Sheridan over the affections of the singer Elizabeth Linley. (Duelling for the third time over the lady at the Castle tavern in Henrietta Street, they hacked each other about so badly that thereafter pistols became the more acceptable weapon for such encounters.) Two years earlier Charles James Fox was only slightly hurt in his duel with William Adam, a duel (Walpole said) of 'so much good temper and good sense, propriety, easy good humour and natural good nature'. Much more savagely, the Park in 1712 was the field for one of society's most famous confrontations, that between Lord Mohun, one of the capital's most obnoxious characters, and the 4th Duke of Hamilton. Hatred and political rivalry flared between the men and festered over a lawsuit. Mohun was an aristocratic thug, earlier implicated in dark deeds, including the attempted kidnap of the actress Mrs Bracegirdle, on which charge he went free. On a bleak November morning the two contestants' mutual loathing exploded: 'They fought with so violent an animosity that neglecting the rules of art, they seemed to run on one another, as if they'd tried who should kill first, in which they were both so unhappily successful that Lord Mohun was killed outright and the Duke died in a few minutes.' The report is unattributed but is probably that of one of the seconds, who made a habit of reporting first-hand accounts of such encounters in the public news-prints. Green Park was also conveniently placed for the settling of scores and was the choice of Count Alfieri when he fought the husband of his mistress, Lord Ligonier, and returned with a sword wound to sit through the last act at the Haymarket theatre; as he famously explained: 'Ligonier did not kill me because he did not want to, and I did not kill him because I did not know how.' Among the capital's other venues for deadly redress were Knightsbridge village, Primrose Hill, Putney Heath and Dulwich Common.

In that glittering era of gaming at brag, lanterloo, basset, picquet, ombre and whisk [whist], when dinner could last from four to five hours and chamberpots were kept in the sideboard so that the gentlemen could relieve themselves immediately the ladies withdrew without interrupting the flow of their conversation, and not forgetting that tendency to take easy offence, manners and etiquette were fierce. It took courage just to enter a room full of fashionable people. Bows and saluting had to be observed in correct order. A gentleman's deportment, if it were pleasing, helped his cause (or his suit). There were lessons available on how to take off one's hat and how to put it on again. The wrong vowels could condemn one to the outer fringes. Boswell, unhappy at his own country ways and lack of sophistication, was deeply aware that London was the place where men and manners might be studied to the best advantage: 'The liberty and the whim that reigns there occasions a variety of perfect and curious characters.' Then there were the crowds and all the rush and bustle of the city's business and diversions; its innumerable venues of entertainment, the 'noble' churches and the splendid buildings. All these things elevated the mind. Invited to a rout at Northumberland House (on the evening of 7 December 1762) he was all but overwhelmed; it was a 'magnificent' occasion – three large rooms and the large gallery, packed with the best company, 'between three and four hundred of them'. He was in his element. To cut a better figure he bought a violet-coloured frock-suit for his tireless social round, detailed in his *London Journal*; he was constantly taking dishes of afternoon tea with influential ladies while being careful to avoid the gambling craze that accompanied all such invitations.

Appearance was all. Coat colours, as Boswell's purchase suggests, were exotic: dove-coloured, salmon-coloured or the softest pastel shades, and their wearer usually slept in a flowered satin nightgown with a silk sash – and welcomed late or early callers in a dressing-gown, slippers and cap to match. An enormous amount of time was dedicated to the dandy's appearance. He probably sent to Holland for his shirts (they were expensive) – and if vanity demanded he could buy false calves to give him an attractive leg in his breeches, which he wore with silk stockings and buckled shoes. To facilitate running repairs the fashionable, ornamented snuff-box he carried would have a mirror inside the lid so that he could check his rouge under the pretence of taking a pinch. That superior dandy Lord Petersham, who gave his name to a type of overcoat and a style of silk ribbon, had a snuff-box for each day of the year and would have *died* had he been caught using his light-blue Sèvres summer box in December.

George (Beau) Brummell became recognised as the arbiter of seemly male fashion. He went to Eton and was (until he got a little above himself) a protégé of the Prince of Wales. His edicts honed down the showiness of Regency dress to a spare elegance that spoke taste in every line. He bathed each morning in milk and eau de cologne with some added water, his morning *toilette* usually taking five hours. He endured agonies just tying his cravat. Among those who admired his maxims was the courtesan Harriette Wilson, who perceptively said that 'many . . . wished to be well with him through fear, for all knew him to be cold, heartless and satirical'. He had his boots polished in the froth of champagne but died penniless in exile and in debt.

Ladies responded to the male challenge, and appeared in public heavily scented – to minimise personal odours. They painted and powdered their complexions and wore black fashion patches. They dressed unashamedly to attract male attention in fashions that included near-transparent muslin gowns, and clearly indicated an interest in amorous dalliance. Stays were laced tight and the bosom daringly exposed. Lace and silk stockings were worn and the person enhanced by combs and every kind of decorative brooch and dazzling adornment.

Georgian society particularly was one of aggression and passion, and of violent expression. That life itself was a gamble only sharpened the appetite for pleasure. Beneath the veneer of manners, the exaggerated concern for honour and station, ran a strong grain of coarseness. There was serious nepotism; men, as we have

A late eighteenth-century dandy preens at his dressing table. (Billie Love Historical Collection)

seen, bought favour with their wives' services: John Nash, the architect and the Prince Regent's favourite, profited, it is said, by his wife's kindness. Although the lash was liberally applied – one might say brutally – thus moulding men but perpetuating the same harshness through society, it was permissible for Englishmen to cry. Those who duelled and drank and gamed and whored blubbered unabashed when moved, at the theatre, for instance, or when dismissing a mistress. Hangmen wept emotionally while fitting the noose in place – and even highwaymen, according to the knowledgeable Walpole, shed a tear as they took your valuable possessions. The drinking was indeed prodigious, leading collectively and individually in the fashionable hierarchy to acts of madness as well as the kind of bravado that could only end on the duelling field. Mad John Mytton, a six-bottle-a-day man, once introduced a live bear to enliven a dinner party; when he had hiccups he set fire to his nightshirt to cure them – and burned to death.

Hostesses of variable and questionable virtue vied with one another to bring the smart and famous to their door, concurrently or consecutively. At Carlisle House, a luxuriously appointed marble-floored mansion in Soho Square, built for the Earls of Carlisle and formerly the residence of the Neapolitan ambassador, Mrs Theresa Cornelys, who had arrived in the capital in 1759, succeeded brilliantly, gathering into her set such figures as the visiting Casanova (a former lover and the father of her daughter). The Viennese singer with a colourful past rented the house but made it a capital landmark ('by far the most magnificent place of public entertainment in Europe', according to a contemporary account). In the 1760s the most important members of the aristocracy were flocking to Mrs Cornelys's in costume and out, and scandalously (adding grist to the gossip-mill) with little on at all. Fanny Burney the writer, who may not (at just eighteen) have known all that was going on there, was stunned by it all: 'the magnificence of the rooms, splendour of the illuminations and embellishments, and the brilliant appearance of the company exceeded anything I ever before saw.' Mrs Cornelys's, undoubtedly, was the hottest ticket in town. When the Duke of Brunswick married George II's sister Princess Augusta the wedding ball was held there – and Casanova attended.

Mrs Cornelys's entertainments and masked balls raised questions of morality even in that free and easy time. She staged twelve balls and suppers yearly for the nobility; another twelve (at two guineas a head) for the middle classes, and once a year an extravagant fancy-dress ball. Among other attractions the inventor of the

Supper at Vauxhall Gardens as the band on the balcony plays on. (Billie Love Historical Collection)

roller-skate, Joseph Merlin, was invited to demonstrate the craze and turned out to be less the master of his art than one would have supposed, smashing some of the valuable mirrors. One regular attender there, to cast his eye over younger and firmer flesh, was 'Old Q', the Marquess of Queensberry, a noted voluptuary inordinately fond of women and the pleasure he found with them, who kept up his sexual appetite by eating hot buttered muffins as he took his bath in almond-scented asses' milk – for good measure also inhaling the breath of dairy-maids. Another was the extrovert Duchess of Kingston, who appeared there in the guise of several characters, including, diaphanously draped, that of Iphigenia, a role that enabled bold ladies to exhibit their charms to admirers almost without concealment. The Duchess of Bolton, not to be outdone, came as Diana, accompanied by a young Adam, identity unknown (perhaps a young footman), in fig-leaf apron with flesh-coloured tights. So far as we know, the only thing Mrs Cornelys ever banned was men wearing boots.

From about 1762, for an entire decade and more, her establishment reigned supreme as the rendezvous of the famous and notorious. Her Sunday-night promenades were unmissable: there was to be seen there, according to Hickey, 'the whole beauty of the metropolis; from the Duchess of Devonshire down to the little milliner's apprentice from Cranbourn Alley'. Sometimes as many as eight hundred of the quality would be there; even princes and kings came. Then, inevitably, the golden Mecca began its slow slide into decline, challenged among others by Almack's Assembly Rooms. Mrs Cornelys's extravagance had been her undoing. An American visitor in 1780 observed laconically that the 'ladies were rigged out in gaudy attire, attended by bucks, bloods and macaronis, though it is also resorted to by persons of irreproachable character'. An inference may be drawn. By 1773 in fact, the splendid furnishings of the house were coming under the hammer, though Mrs Cornelys continued defiant in the face of turning fortune. But finally the Circe of Soho had to relinquish her role. She ended a crowded life selling asses' milk (perhaps to 'Old Q') in Knightsbridge and died in the Fleet prison.

Towards the end of the eighteenth century, at Montagu House in Portman Square, Mrs Elizabeth Montagu dispensed the favour of her acquaintance as one of the most interesting and influential hostesses of her time, 'brilliant in diamonds, solid in judgement' as they said of her. Hers was a more select circle. She was the founder of the Blue Stocking Society (from the colour of her hosiery), the name given to her literary gatherings. Her rooms, ahead of her time,

The beau monde enjoying a summer ball in Regent's Park. (By courtesy of the Guildhall Library, Corporation of London)

were painted in bright colours, with cupids, roses and jasmine abounding. Every May Day she entertained an entirely different company when she gave a dinner of roast beef and plum pudding to the capital's chimney sweeps.

Holland House too would become the focus for a potent mix of intellects, literary and political, and entertained among many of the era's luminaries the great orator and later prime minister George Canning, the French diplomat Talleyrand, the duelling playwright Sheridan, Scott and Wordsworth. Sydney Smith, wit and Anglican divine, opined to its hostess Lady Holland, ex-mistress and now wife of the 3rd Baron Holland, that he did not believe 'all Europe can produce as much knowledge, wit and worth as passes in and out of your door'. At Gore House in the nineteenth century the Countess of Blessington, an Irish beauty, and her friend the dandy Count d'Orsay (who happened to be her step-daughter's husband) would carry on that tradition of lavish parties that drew the cream of the capital's society to their famous salon, including Byron, a close friend of the couple. Wellington and Disraeli were frequently to be seen there, as was the young Dickens. Their salon was one of the most celebrated of the period – until their extravagance led to the inevitable and they were forced to flee to Paris.

Almack's Assembly Rooms, off St James's Square, built in 1765 for William Almack, a former valet to the Duke of Hamilton, like Mrs Cornelys's, ran exclusive subscription balls and suppers during the London season. The magnificent ballroom could hold 1,700. Only those of the most unimpeachable pedigree were invited to attend, and parvenus were strenuously shown the door. The Rooms even barred that great gadabout the Duke of Wellington when he arrived wearing trousers; the guest list was controlled by seven high-ranking ladies, and it was a rule of the house that men must wear knee breeches and white cravats. The acme of social acceptance was a ticket to the Wednesday ball:

> All on that magic list depends;
> Fame, fortune, fashion, lovers, friends.

It was the entrance to a 'dancing and gossiping world'. Gronow in his memoirs stresses: 'One can hardly conceive the importance which was attached to getting admission to Almack's, the seventh heaven of the fashionable world.' It was, he says, the 'exclusive temple of the beau monde; the gates of which were guarded by lady patronesses, whose smiles or frowns consigned men and women to happiness or despair'. Refreshments were confined to tea or lemonade with bread and butter and unexciting cake. The Rooms came finally to the zenith of their fame in the early nineteenth century, and it was here in 1815 that Lady Jersey, mistress to George IV, introduced the quadrille to the capital's fashionable society. It was followed a year later by the voluptuous waltz, shocking in its body contact, the friction of thigh on thigh, when Madame de Lieven, the promiscuous young wife of the Russian ambassador, took the floor on the arm of the equally promiscuous Lord (Cupid) Palmerston and finally did for the former diet of unruly Scottish reels and clumsy rustic dances. But Almack's too in time lost its appeal; the victim of a fickle society, it closed in 1850.

In Little Argyll Street, a fashionable address in the Regency period, the Argyll Rooms, aping the earlier exemplars, were opened in 1806 by Henry Francis Greville and instantly became a place to be seen. It was a casino, but also much more. The dance hall was at ground level (entrance: one shilling); in the gallery (for an extra charge), with its cosy alcoves and soft banquettes, one could mingle

Regency style for a stroll through Kensington Gardens. (By courtesy of the Guildhall Library, Corporation of London)

with ladies of the town – or study the newspapers. It was superbly run. In the 1850s a visitor reported the ladies 'pretty and quietly though expensively dressed'. The proprieties were at all times observed, a nod of understanding perhaps or a discreet exchange in which the lady might consult her pocket-book and graciously suggest that the inquirer, should he wish, might call at a stated time some days hence for a twenty-minute visit, for which favour she would accept a fee of £25. The Rooms' main rival was the Holborn Casino, with its magnificent octagonal ballroom. For masked balls the usual 2s 6d entrance charge was increased to 7s 6d for gentlemen, 5s for ladies. As at the Argyll Rooms, professional ladies were discreetly admitted.

There were other places for the determined social climber to be seen. Charles II had taken Hyde Park into royal hands and enclosed it, and there the world of fashion congregated every afternoon at five, the men mounted on superb horseflesh, the beauties of the *bon ton* in their carriages, attended by their liveried footmen, their coachmen bewigged with three-cornered hats and wearing French gloves. Pepys himself went there on May Day 1663, no doubt hoping for a royal glance; he bought new clothes for the occasion, including 'painted gloves'. His hired horse, however, a wilful beast, threatened to unseat him, and rather than suffer that indignity before the royal gaze, the diarist retired and went home, honour intact. The Mall, however, itself dating from the Restoration, became *the* promenade – and would remain so. Swift in 1711 ingenuously expressed his surprise at the number of ladies walking there. Not a few were discreetly plying for hire, an example of the relaxed code of the time. The freedoms then allowed the Londoner astonished the visiting Baron von Pöllnitz in 1733:

> The grand walk they call the Mall is full of people every hour of the day, especially in the morning and evening and their Majesties often walk in it, with the Royal Family, who are attended by only half a dozen Yeomen of the Guard and permit all persons without distinction of rank and character to walk there at the same time with them . . . The ladies always appear in rich dresses . . . now embroidered and bedaubed as much as the French.

A decade later another guest in the capital would echo that wonder: 'it is in this walk that we always meet some of our friends and here we see the ministers, the courtiers, the *petits maîtres* and the coquettes; here we learn the news of the day . . .'

The fashionable people on afternoon parade in Hyde Park. (By courtesy of the Guildhall Library, Corporation of London)

The proliferation of spas, where gambling by both sexes was endemic, gave the lesser gentry an excuse to mingle with the smart set, and Hampstead lost much of its rural innocence in the early eighteenth century when it became a popular resort, with its Well Walk and Great Room, in which were several assembly rooms (for concerts and dancing) and also the Pump Room, where one took the waters. The craze for gambling, however, brought it the wrong people and gave it a bad character for a time until its revival as a spa where people like Garrick and Johnson, not to mention the fastidious Fanny Burney, were happy to disport themselves until it finally lost its lustre. Royals, naturally, went to the wells at Tunbridge.

Less exclusive but more fun was Lambeth Wells, opened in 1697; there was music and dancing through the night for threepence (until they lost their licence in 1755 because of brawling and rowdy behaviour), and the same admission charge took you into Pancras Wells, whose waters the local tavern owner (who was selling them) extolled as 'a powerful antidote against rising of the vapours', claiming also that they 'cleansed the body and sweetened the blood'. More to the point was the dancing and dinner with 'neat wine'. Richmond Wells opened a year earlier and continued successfully, with wells and dancing, until its rowdy revellers became a too-frequent problem.

Islington spa, opposite Sadler's Wells, drew the fashionable set in droves to its arbours, its walks, its coffee room and dancing, among them Lady Mary Wortley Montagu and the Princesses Caroline and Amelia, the king's daughters. Up to 1,600 people took the waters daily at its peak around 1730; paeans of praise were heaped on it by poets and writers. Inevitably it was discovered by the bourgeoisie and slid into decline. Streatham's spa enjoyed much the same cachet, and at night, during the height of its fame at the beginning of the eighteenth century, one could rub shoulders with the absolute *crème*. The adjoining High Street, along with the common, became the promenade for its visitors. Samples of the waters (good for worms and the eyes) were sent daily to vendors in the city at St Paul's, the Royal Exchange and Temple Bar. The recommended dosage was three cups – allegedly three times as effective as the equivalent of Epsom's waters. The spa lasted out the century without compromising its reputation.

Bagnigge Wells at King's Cross had honeysuckled tea arbours, a bowling green, a skittle alley, fishponds, fountains and a grotto – and, it was rumoured, Nell Gwynne sometimes entertained the king there for small concerts and breakfast. It cost threepence to taste the waters, while half a guinea bought a season ticket. Entertainments, including cards and dancing, were held in the pump room. Certainly that sociable highwayman Sixteen-string Jack found its slightly downmarket ambience to his liking before his career was cut short at Tyburn. So, apparently, did others of his ilk. For the latter part of the eighteenth century the wells were still fashionable, while simultaneously the haunt of Jack's fellow-highwaymen, prostitutes and pickpockets. People went to spas, Defoe conjectured, more 'for the diversion of the season, for the mirth and the company, for gaming and intriguing, and the like'. Perhaps especially for the like.

CHAPTER III
Life in the Fast Set

In February 1685 the Merry Monarch died as he had lived. His collapse came suddenly on a Sabbath evening amid all the scandalous frivolity of his Court – while he was enjoying a pleasurable Whitehall evening toying (Macaulay's word) with the 'three women whose charms were the boast and whose vices were the disgrace of three nations. Barbara Palmer, Duchess of Cleveland, was there, no longer young, but still retaining some traces of that superb and voluptuous loveliness which twenty years before overcame the hearts of all men. There too was the Duchess of Portsmouth, whose soft and infantine features were lighted up with the vivacity of France. Hortensia Mancini, Duchess of Mazarin, the niece of the great Cardinal, completed the group.' Around him as he flirted with his 'three sultanas', despite the holy day, were revellers and gamblers intent on their play. Evelyn, recollecting events, would write: 'I am never to forget the inexpressible luxury and profaneness, gaming, and all dissoluteness and, as it were, total forgetfulness of God (it being Sunday evening), which . . . I was witness of; the King sitting and toying with his concubines, Portsmouth, Cleveland and Mazarine . . . a French boy singing love-songs in that glorious gallery; whilst about twenty of the great courtiers and other dissolute persons were at basset round a large table, a bank of at least £2,000 in gold before them . . . Six days after, was all in the dust.' In a last flicker of humour, the king, with something of his father's flair for a soundbite for the momentous moment, apologised for his delay in dying. (Thirteen years later, in 1698, as though ending a chapter, Whitehall would burn down and the royal focus would shift to the Palace of St James, making it the new hub of fashion and intrigue.)

Gone then from the stage on which his had been the principal part, in Macaulay's sweeping opinion, was a heartless voluptuary who had found 'neither truth in man nor fidelity in woman'. Half the flirting of the capital had taken place under his roof. It may be a harsh verdict. None the less, his reign had set in train a passion for pleasure that would continue unabated. The Hanoverian dynasty, after a brief interregnum, would set no better example. George I's pleasures, wrote one of his circle, were 'lowly sensual', almost animal, it is said, in their gratification: he liked women and he liked them pneumatic, like his chief mistress, the buxom Duchess of Kendal, who was considered to be not bright. He went out on the town incognito to gamble at the houses of trusted friends. George II, while adoring his queen Caroline, a woman with a strong sexual drive, took mistresses and had piles, badly. He went nightly at nine (precisely) to the apartments of his favourite, Mrs Henrietta Howard. George III, that mad but moral king, capitulated to similar appetites by producing offspring with a conveyor-belt regularity with Charlotte, his dull, snuff-taking queen, while George IV's was a rake's progress of comical yet tragic stupidity. As the Prince Regent, and likened by Charles Burney to Charles II, he committed serial infidelity at an alarming rate, his one particular favourite being Maria Fitzherbert, whom he inveigled into a mock marriage. When he feared he might lose her he attempted suicide, which made her relent to their secret bonding. She was twenty-eight when they first met, and, inconveniently, a Roman Catholic, twice widowed. Their association lasted for some twenty years, incommoded of course from time to time by the prince's wife, Princess Caroline of Brunswick. A drunken sot, often getting involved in club brawls and once thrown out of Ranelagh pleasure gardens by the stewards, the prince was an obsessive lover who also preferred his ladies plump and mature, and later threw himself at Lady Bessborough, who had been several times around the block and recognised that it was not flattering lust that propelled his advances but a strong sense of insecurity. A somewhat inert pudding of a man, the athleticism of ardent passion was now beyond him and he had to settle instead for Lady Hertford, who may have been a confidante rather than an eager bed companion.

In such hands the baton passed down. Ladies would continue to be gracious with their favours in and out of the connubial bed; indeed one suspects mostly out of it. Our invaluable commentator Horace Walpole may have been a byblow of his mother's alleged affair with Lord Hervey; he certainly had none of his Prime Minister father Robert Walpole's coarse features or gross bucolic build (a man, they said, who, had the PM's part not cropped up, might have done well as a cattle dealer), though he was amiably acknowledged by Walpole as his fourth son. Little Horry's entrance into any salon, in contrast, was 'in that style of affected delicacy, which fashion had made almost natural, *chapeau bras* between his hands as if he wished to compress it, or under his arm; knees bent, and feet on tip-toe, as if afraid of a wet floor. His summer dress of ceremony was usually a lavender suit, the waistcoat embroidered with a little silver, or of white silk worked in the tambour, partridge silk stockings, gold buckles, ruffles and lace frill. In winter he wore powder . . . He generally dined at four . . . His dinner when at home was chicken, pheasant, or any light food, of which he ate sparingly.' He wrote, among other things, that first thriller in the English language, but it is to his letters we now turn for diversion, for their amusing portrayal of events and the marked cynicism of his age. He spent his days gambling moderately with distinguished or otherwise well-connected ladies, notably at hazard or loo, a compulsive correspondent and a conduit for all the gossip of the day. He was eighty when he died, gout-ridden and having succeeded to the title of the 4th Earl of Orford – and having lived close to the action through dramatic times.

The Herveys were dandies, eccentric and unpredictable, themselves a constant source of gossip and intrigue. One married and bigamously passed on the celebrated (and often scantily clad) Miss Chudleigh to the Duke of Kingston, provoking on the duke's death the 'most notorious matrimonial scandal' of the century in 1776, when she was tried in the Lords before six thousand spectators. Yet another member of the family went on to tie his father to a bear, and rather unsportingly wore padded waistcoats to fight duels; he ended on the gibbet. Miss Chudleigh, as a woman of her time, had entertained a string of lovers, including in sequence the Earl of Bath, the Duke of Hamilton (whom she *almost* married), and the king himself, George II. She was allowed to slip away to Russia, where she continued her career as a comforter of noblemen. But she was only one of the age's remarkable women, who led lives as free and wilful as those of the men they married.

Such scandals were commonplace, some scarcely causing a ripple in society, others of such piquancy and intrigue that they threw the capital into a froth of speculation. A former milliner, plucked from her Covent Garden workbench, was the elegant hostess at the Admiralty dinner table of the First Lord, the Earl of Sandwich, a well-thought-of statesman in Lord North's government. Her name was Martha Ray, her beauty exceptional. The earl paid for 'finishing' her education and then, at twice her age, made her his mistress, introducing her openly at his family seat in Huntingdon. There her looks beguiled the heart of an Army captain, James Hackman. He proposed honourable marriage and was rebuffed, with the comment that the lady had no wish to carry a knapsack for the rest of her life. Hackman took the hint; he espoused holy orders and became the vicar of a Norfolk parish.

The earl, apparently now mistrusting his mistress's devotion, had meanwhile hired a *duenna* – a chaperone – for her, and it was she who accompanied Ray to Covent Garden one April evening in 1779. Ray was being handed into her carriage after the performance when Hackman rushed from the coffee-house opposite, drew a pistol and shot her through the head. Before the crowd could stop him he drew another weapon, intending to spatter his own brains with hers . . . He missed badly – and set about trying to bludgeon them out with the butt of the pistol until he was foiled by the arrival of the Bow Street runners, leaving Walpole, not for the first time, to fill out the details of the whole sorry affair:

> Miss Ray, it appears, has been out of order, and abroad but twice all winter. She went to the play on Wednesday night, for the second time with Galli the singer. During the play the desperate lover was at the Bedford coffee-house and behaved with great calmness, and drank a glass of capillaire. Towards the conclusion he sallied into the Piazza, waiting till he saw the victim handed to her carriage . . . Hackman came behind her, pulled her by the gown, and, on her turning round, clapped the pistol to her forehead and shot her through the head. With another pistol he then attempted to shoot himself . . .

There is a macabre footnote. Walpole's friend, the sinister gambler and wit George Augustus Selwyn, who so loved executions, donned a long black cloak and as a mourner sat the night long with the corpse, which had been taken into the Shakespeare's Head tavern.

What the fate of the delectable actress Mrs Bracegirdle might have been had the plan by another demented admirer been successful we can but speculate – but it too ended in murder and involved the black-hearted Lord Mohun. Mrs Bracegirdle's beauty, like Ray's, was beyond words; she was 'of a lovely height with dark brown hair and eyebrows, black sparkling eyes, and a fresh blushing complexion'. Every man in the audience lusted after her, yet her virtue was seemingly beyond reproach. Congreve was among those who wrote plays for her; she lived next door in the same street and, it was suspected, was secretly his mistress until the younger Duchess of Marlborough enchanted him. Macaulay would put forward a rather different view of the actress, describing her as a 'cold, vain, interested coquette, who perfectly understood how much the influence of her own charms was increased by the flame of severity which cost her nothing, and who could venture to flirt with a succession of admirers in the just confidence

Hogarth's bleak Morning *in Covent Garden, after the dissipation of the night before.* (By courtesy of the Guildhall Library, Corporation of London)

that the flame she might kindle in them would not thaw her own ice'. Was Mrs Bracegirdle a tease? It may well have been so. Certainly in 1692 she had succeeded in exciting the ardour of Captain Richard Hill, who was particularly jealous of her co-star William Mountford, who, he persuaded himself, must be the reason for his own rejection. Hill sought Mohun's help in the actress's abduction, but first he lay in wait outside Mountford's house in Howard Street, striking him as he came out, and then running him through before the bewildered actor could speak. Hill then fled, leaving Mohun to be acquitted of murder and to die, as we have seen, another day.

In such an openly licentious age, when the capital's fashionable procuresses were known and accepted into the outer fringes of society, even men of quality and position might darken the doors of the smartest bordellos without censure. Such establishments had multiplied at a tremendous rate since the Restoration. Indeed it was considered a necessity for a man to visit a brothel at least once a week, or better still to keep a lady. As Chancellor (and later premier), Lord North, a clean-living lawyer and model of probity, came under deep suspicion and was advised to keep a whore to improve his image with the country and at Court. Members of the Commons were regularly hauled out of the bawdy houses to vote legislation through Parliament. In the new climate, the bagnios too were enjoying a renaissance; within a week of his arrival in London, Casanova had visited one and found himself convivial company where the 'rich go to sup, sleep and bathe themselves with a high-class prostitute, a creature not rare in London. It is a magnificent debauch and costs only six guineas. One may economise and reduce the expense to a hundred francs but an economy which detracts from pleasure is not for me.' Well, we might have guessed as much.

His adviser in such matters was the man they called the English Casanova – Sir John Augustus Hervey, later the Earl of Bristol and the man who married the notorious Miss Chudleigh before passing her on to the Duke of Kingston. He and Casanova met at the salon of Lady Harrington, one of the capital's leading hostesses, famous for her gallantry and herself living down a scandalous past. Casanova also made a friend of Henry Herbert, 10th Earl of Pembroke, at twenty-nine a celebrated rake (and appropriately an ex-lord of the bedchamber), who knew a great many 'ladies of the town'. He was of instant help to Casanova and pointed him towards the Shakespeare's Head in Covent Garden. There, Pembroke advised, he would find the prettiest girls in London. Visiting the tavern, the great lover was assured that such indeed was the case; calling a waiter,

Maudlin Midnight *in St John's coffee-house near Temple Bar, again by Hogarth.* (By courtesy of the Guildhall Library, Corporation of London)

the landlord ordered him to send for a girl – in the same casual tone that he might have used to command a bottle of wine for a certain table. A dozen girls were summoned in succession before the for-once-diffident Casanova, for which he was asked only to pay a shilling each for the porters of their sedan chairs. At several of the city's taverns and bagnios this was the usual custom, the girls receiving nothing unless their services were enlisted.

As night fell over the capital the focus of pleasure moved into the discreet alleys and the heavily curtained houses that lined them. Ladies hurried to their lovers and the committed rakes headed for subtler venues; perhaps to *The Folly*, a vessel moored by Cuper's Stairs, down off the Strand. For the amorously inclined the nether deck had curtained compartments and boxes. Pepys visited it (reconnoitring, no doubt). It finally lost favour with discriminating lovers to become blatantly a place of 'folly, madness and debauchery'. A German visitor to the capital in 1710 reported himself disgusted by the drove of harlots he found there and by the 'prodigious' prices (but whether of the whores or of the refreshments we do not know).

The fast set would find their pleasures elsewhere, probably at the White House in Sutton Street, a rendezvous so exclusive that only the seriously rich or the impeccably titled could gain admission. Here again Old Q was a fervent attender, as was the then Prince of Wales, from which may be concluded the nature of its entertainments. Entrance through its portals was said to have brought ruin and shame to innumerable young women. It had Gold, Silver and Bronze rooms, all with walls incorporating large mirrored panels. Other rooms had such evocative names as the Coal-hole, the Grotto, the Skeleton Room and even the Commons, all intended to give a perverse pleasure to the appointments kept in them. The White House would long continue its attraction for the jaded voluptuary, its naughty history, alas, unrecorded.

Eighteenth-century Covent Garden was less exclusive. In what had once been the residences of the aristocracy, there now clustered houses of ill-fame. There was infinite variety in Drury Lane. Gin shops and ladies of the town occupied every corner, and it was here that Hogarth set Plate 3 of *A Harlot's Progress*. The Rose tavern in Russell Street stood cheek by jowl with Drury Lane theatre and Pepys himself had been no stranger there, stepping in before a performance or maybe for supper afterwards, or even during the play (getting a boy to keep his theatre seat). It was the haunt of drunken actors low in self-esteem, loudly toasting their mistresses, whether present or absent. It had, however, become one of the most dangerous after-dark places in town, the resort of debauchees, with 'murderous assaults' a common occurrence. Men ventured into its precincts at their physical as well as moral peril. Thus John Gay in his *Trivia*:

> O may thy virtue guard thee through the roads
> Of Drury's mazy courts and dark abodes!

In the hundred of Drury Lane there were at one time no fewer than 107 pleasure houses, according to the usually well-informed *London Spy*. Here, according to Pepys, in her days of earlier fame Nell Gwynne could be glimpsed 'standing at her lodgings door . . . in her smock sleeves and bodice . . . a mighty pretty creature'. Fielding, living there close to his magistrate's work, thought all the prostitutes of the capital had gathered there. He was wrong, as he probably knew.

Exclusively and absolutely, Almack's Assembly Rooms were for the capital's elite. (By courtesy of the Guildhall Library, Corporation of London)

And with the drift of fashionable flesh westward pleasure would come powdered and pampered in the society of high-class procuresses and selective courtesans. Young swells, at a loose end after the theatre and tired of attacking the watch, went in search of more amusing decadence at the Cider Cellars or its great rival the Coal Hole, certain of their ill-repute.

Boswell's entry into this brittle yet dazzling world of the English capital – 'the circles of the great, the gay and the ingenuous' – came first in the spring of 1760 and was engineered by the Earl of Eglinton, whose housekeeper shared his bed. Given his mentor, a well-known rake and devotee of the seedier pleasures of Vauxhall Gardens, his entry was at the deep, licentious end. His *London Journal* is thus a slanting light on the capital's beau monde. In St James's Park and in the Mall he would walk and mingle with the ladies of the town; after dark (few streets were lit) the park became a pullulating hive of sexual activity. The young Boswell would be always on the lookout for an opportunity for gallantry, and his pursuit of it through the capital's society (and indeed through its more sordid fringe)

Ranelagh Gardens en fête, *'a place for courtships of every kind' according to Gibbon.* (Museum of London)

mirrors the life of the young blade of the time. His approach, as we shall see, was remarkably Pepysian. His *Journal* has an engaging frankness, concealing nothing of his own nature or of the activities he engaged in. In passing, it reveals the deplorable mores of the demi-monde. His Scottish friend, 'a spirited young dog', has struck up acquaintance with a Miss Temple, an exceedingly pretty young lady kept by 'a man of £4,000 a year'. She is 'very amorous', and willing to give comfort to those who find favour with her without any consideration of self-interest. We may conclude that not all the capital's ruined housemaids threw themselves from the top of the Monument.

This then was the society that had earlier corrupted the puritan Pepys. He was shocked at first by the behaviour he found at Court. In his naval post as Clerk of the Acts he was conscientious and hard-working, and enjoyed a high-profile respectability. So close to the centre of affairs, he watched the king run through a stable of mistresses, and came finally to ape his betters. He was much smitten with Barbara Villiers (whom Evelyn castigated as 'a lady of Pleasure & curse of our nation') and with the ever-popular Nell Gwynne. Villiers was a great beauty –

blue-eyed, with deep auburn hair and a willowy figure – who turned many other heads besides that of Pepys, who contrived at the theatre, the Court or its pageants to find a position from which he could gaze on her beauty. In the Privy Garden where the washing was pegged out each day he would stop to gaze upon the lady's underpinnings. It lifted his spirits, he said, though in his heart he knew she was just a pretty whore. Taken backstage to meet Nell, Pepys found her a 'most pretty woman' whom he kissed with great pleasure; on another visit he encountered her *en déshabillé* and ecstatically confirmed that opinion.

Up at Cambridge he had shown an inclination for bawdy company but it had gone no further than that. He was a late starter in the quest for carnal pleasure, clearly not getting enough in his marriage. He acted circumspectly. Not for the diarist an affair with one his equal in society. He could not play the bold lover, and preferred the company of doxies and drabs and a furtive assignation in some out-of-the-way tavern room. Only his now invaluable *Diary* knew of his love-life. Like Boswell's *Journal* a century later, it is a dialogue between a man and his conscience. As a charmer Pepys's assets were not obvious; his appearance was passable but not handsome. Westminster Hall, which he visited almost daily, was a rowdy place with trade stalls and booths round the inside walls, rather like an enclosed market. It was a popular place of resort, and a poorly paid seamstress might often be lured away to augment her pittance of an income. It was here that the diarist finally entered the lists of pleasure. His priapic progress, once begun, however, would continue unabated. He could not keep his hands off his wife's maids or anyone else's, and when his wife died he promptly seduced the current one, who settled quietly into his bed. Such amicable arrangements were by no means uncommon in a society that set no parameters on love – or lust.

CHAPTER IV
Gardens of Dalliance and Delight

The capital's pleasure gardens were the fashionable retreats of the mid-seventeenth and eighteenth centuries. They were a source of wonder and delight, initially drawing all classes of a pleasure-seeking society, but falling eventually into disrepute as the resort of the amorously inclined and as a rendezvous for ladies of the twilight. The raffish aftermath of the Restoration hardly hindered their appeal; in summer the young blades left the city's pavements for the boskier glades of the gardens, where there were lights, dancing and light-hearted girls, heading downriver to Rosherville (near Gravesend) or upstream to Vauxhall or Ranelagh or, later, Cremorne gardens. Downstream too lay St Helena's Gardens with their romantic suppers lantern-lit under the stars and the kind of musical *oeuvre* that would draw the Prince Regent, connoisseur and stern critic; while in Southwark, Island House Gardens brought weary city-dwellers to a country idyll of millstreams and simple solitude. Some were loved and rightly famous; others gained their celebrity for all the wrong reasons. The Temple of Flora in Lambeth, for instance, with all the fastidious embellishments of the great gardens, including a hothouse, was an invitation to see all the beguiling charms of the natural world; in fact its natural activities resulted in the owner being sent to prison for six months in 1796 – for keeping a disorderly house.

The love of gardens lay deep in the English heart, a wonder to all those who visited our shores or travelled through the countryside. As Fynes Moryson observed in his *Itinerary* of 1617: 'There is no country wherein the gentlemen and lords have so many and large parks only reserved for the pleasures of hunting, or where all sorts of men allot so much ground about their houses for pleasure of gardens and orchards.'

In the pleasure gardens' sylvan surroundings, canopied by trees and frequently graced by classical statuary, and all for a modest admission, the aspiring genteel could ape their betters and even rub shoulders with them. In a lusty and licentious age, as a lure for libertines of both sexes, they also reached across the chasms of class to offer just a frisson of heady temptation to the respectable and God-fearing. There was a striving for elegance, an enchantment; people came to enter a world of make-believe. In their fairy-lit avenues late on a balmy summer evening their patrons, rich or poor, could forget the brutal cares of the day and let fantasy soften their lives.

But whatever their individual appeal, the pleasure gardens spread through and around the capital like a contagion, continuing their popularity into Victoria's reign. Their spread would be aided and abetted by the parallel rise of another fashionable craze, the passion for tea-drinking, rapidly gaining ground with the increasing importation from the plantations into the Isle of Dogs' developing docks; there the blending of the tea, still an inexact science, was done on the warehouse floors from the different heaps – by men with wooden shovels. Gardens such as Vauxhall would become the glamorous playgrounds; the prints of the period show a parade of the fashionable people – promenaders with pretensions to a more gracious lifestyle. An exaggerated and flirtatious degree of gallantry is evident in the encounters depicted; what was taking place in the shady arbours was often entirely different. For those whose days were lived in the full glare of the crowded alleyways and cramped tenements of the capital these secret bowers offered undreamed-of privacy.

The gardens' other diversions were considerable and wholly laudable; they became the focus for much of the capital's entertainment, much that was culturally good and inspiring, including splendid orchestral performances. Many incorporated on their bills an element of circus, with magicians, clowns, acrobats, jugglers, stuntmen, high-wire walkers, trapeze artistes, freakshows and even more outlandish acts, besides being mainly the cradle where balloonists could show off their daring before an admiring audience – all this, of course, with the staples of dancing and drinking and dining. Fireworks became an exciting and thrilling part of the capital's amusements in the later eighteenth century, and the pleasure gardens provided the perfect venues for the pyrotechnical spectaculars.

The crowds flocked to them. Writers of the day seized on them, as on the old-time fairs, as an exciting setting in which to plunge their characters into crises – Fielding, Congreve, Dickens and Smollett among them. The last vividly portrays their astonishing social mix: 'The different departments of life are jumbled together – the hodcarrier, the low mechanic, the tapster, the publican, the shopkeeper, the pettifogger, the citizen, the courtier all tread upon the kibes [heels] of one another: actuated by demons of profligacy and licentiousness, they

Ranelagh Gardens, which in Horace Walpole's view 'totally beat Vauxhall'. (By courtesy of the Guildhall Library, Corporation of London)

are seen everywhere rambling, riding, rolling, rushing, justling, mixing, bouncing, cracking and crashing in one vile ferment of stupidity and corruption.'

Fanny Burney, on the other hand, clearly loved them and obviously knew them well, setting a seedy scene of *Evelina*, published in 1778, the heyday of the pleasure garden, in one of them. Evelina, lost and in a panic in Marylebone Gardens, is accosted by two gallants who have misunderstood the reason for her presence there. It is her first acquaintance with the raw and reckless netherworld of the gardens and their rough sexual licence, which co-existed with their more innocent amusements and tone of high culture.

The capital's most celebrated gardens were undoubtedly those at Vauxhall, Ranelagh, Marylebone and Cremorne, though mention should also be made of the enticements of Highbury Barn and the Eagle tavern and some others which found their attractions in tune with their time – and their patrons. The idea was launched on an unsuspecting city by the Earl of Arundel's retired gardener Abraham Cuper, who opened his south bank riverside retreat of ultimately ten acres in about 1640. The leafy walks of Cuper's Gardens (soon, significantly, to be called Cupid's Gardens) were furnished with statuary borrowed from the earl's garden, just across the river. Entrance cost one shilling, and in a shrewd move a tavern, The Feathers, was associated with the venture. A watchman was hired to protect the pockets of patrons, who included not only the aristocracy but, in that freer age, even royalty. Alas, Cuper's story would turn out to be a prophetic one; the gardens were eventually closed by the authorities in 1760 when they became a hotbed of pickpockets.

Cuper's inspiration may have been the earlier Paris Gardens, a stretch of the riverside in Southwark, which geared its amusements to a coarser audience, providing a somewhat different bill of fare. It suffered a setback in 1583 when a balcony collapsed as patrons watched (and betted on) the bull-baiting, crushing to death many of those trapped below it. But the mould for those which followed was set by the earl's gardener, whose ideas would be seized on and upgraded to incorporate new elements and stay abreast of the times and the demands of a feckless and insatiable society.

The most popular were the gardens at Vauxhall, opened (as the New Spring Gardens) with free admission in 1660, the year of the Restoration, and after a later make-over continuing into Queen Victoria's time. Pepys loved them, remarking in 1667 that it 'is very pleasant and cheap going thither, for a man may go to spend what he will, or nothing – all is one, but to hear the nightingale and other birds, and here fiddles, and there a harp, and here a jews trump, and here laughing, and there fine people walking, is mighty divertising'. So, later, did the young Dickens (but with qualified praise) and that great luminary Addison, who could not stay away despite his complaint in 1712 about the presence – even then – of so many strumpets.

Their first serious rival was Ranelagh's, though their eclipse would come at the hands of the later and more sophisticated Cremorne Gardens in Chelsea. Vauxhall's opened daily, except Sundays, from May to September. Boswell was an immediate addict, as one might expect, rather waspishly describing them as being very much in tune with the taste of the English, 'there being a mixture of curious shew, – gay exhibition, musick vocal and instrumental, not too refined for the general ear'. By then the admission fee was one shilling.

The gardens covered twelve acres; their enticements included pavilions, temples and grottoes. Scattered amid this 'paradise' with its grand river-gate from the Thames were concert halls and secluded supper boxes. The famous Grand Walk was bordered with elms; at the end of it, appropriately, stood a gilded

Marylebone Gardens staged savage sports and were the familiar haunt of highwaymen. (By courtesy of the Guildhall Library, Corporation of London)

statue of Aurora, the goddess of the dawn. Paths criss-crossed the Grand Walk or ran parallel, and were graced with triumphal arches. Down its walkways each evening, lit by romantic lanterns, strolled the capital's elite. (Each evening the hundreds of lights were lit simultaneously, or almost so, though some of the walks were deliberately left dark.) The beckoning centrepiece, however, was the large rotunda, where the orchestra played classical works from opera; on smaller platforms, hidden amid the greenery, small bands serenaded the evening strollers. Remodelled by a new owner, Jonathan Tyers, in the mid-1700s (when Francis Hayman painted the supper boxes), the gardens were frequently the venue – as indeed were others – for some landmark event.

Tyers would add ruins, arches, statues, a cascade, a music room and Gothic orchestra [the platform] to seat fifty musicians. By no means philistine, the gardens showed the work of Hogarth and of Roubiliac (Louis François, 1705–62), the French sculptor who had come to England in 1732. For the gardens' entrance he created a statue of Handel, a rehearsal of whose *Music for the Royal Fireworks* by a hundred musicians took place in 1749 before an audience of twelve thousand. Their carriages caused gridlock.

In celebrating fifty years of public support with a ball and concert (tickets: half a guinea), the gardens asked guests to come in the guise of dominoes. Again it was a huge affair, with thousands of chickens slaughtered to feed the multitude. They came, from dukes down to mechanics, though fashionable ladies deemed it prudent to shun the celebration, fearing loss of reputation in such a *risqué* environment. They may have been right to do so. Men from the Inns of Court were there, it is reported, throwing probity to the wind, along with rising bucks in the City. All behaved badly. Also present were a number of 'half-reluctant pampered nymphs of boarding school education' loitering with goodness knows what intent in the 'love-exciting shady groves'. When the gardens were host to a masked ball in 1792 some three thousand tickets were sold at a guinea a time. It was the heyday of the masquerade and the masked ball, and mingling incognito with the patrons was the pleasure-loving Prince Regent. People came as link-boys and watermen and chimney sweeps and Punches and Pantaloons and Harlequins, in costumes hired from masquerade warehouses such as Richman's or Goodacres's who provided changing rooms close by. In the gardens' splendid supper room there was feasting on raised pies, ribs of lamb, fowls and crayfish and prawns – all accompanied by the finest wines – through to breakfast time. The dance floor was so tightly jammed that a warm intimacy was guaranteed. That year the entrance fee would be raised to two shillings.

The vital battles of British history were routinely refought there, including the victory at the battle of Vittoria (with the Prince Regent present) and that of Waterloo (with a cast of a thousand foot and horse soldiers). The Duke of Wellington, by then a national hero, came often, perhaps to revisit his past glories, and earlier fervid patrons had included Walpole, Goldsmith and Dr Johnson. Boswell, who on his own account regarded the gardens as 'delicious', would have been less astonished than Pepys to fall in with a company of young courtiers and be privy to their 'mad, bawdy talk'. The group, calling themselves the Ballers, usually ended their pleasure forays with a visit to Lady Bennet's, where they lived up to their name by dancing naked with the young ladies there and engaging in 'all the rogueish things in the world'. The group and others of their ilk, in a drunken state, would trawl the avenues, forcing their attentions on the young women there, flirting mainly but sometimes with a boorish menace. Pepys, fond of spending an evening in one or other of the capital's pleasure

Tea-garden pleasures as patrons promenade, eat, drink and listen to music. (By courtesy of the Guildhall Library, Corporation of London)

spots, was dismayed by what he saw, and by the dangers run by women without escorts: 'How rude some of the young gallants of the town are become, to go into people's arbours where there are not men, and almost force the women – which troubled me, to see the confidence of the vice of the age.'

Although there had initially been no admittance charge, in the time-honoured way of managements Vauxhall's compensated for that by over-pricing the refreshments. The food, it was generally agreed, was a disgrace, with a meat platter costing one shilling. It seems never to have improved: even as they neared the end of their reign the young Dickens would take the gardens to task over their stingy food policy with a savage satire in *Sketches by Boz*: 'It was rumoured . . . that Vauxhall Gardens by day were the scene of secret and hidden experiments; that there, carvers were exercised in the mystic art of cutting a moderate-sized ham into slices thin enough to pave the whole of the grounds; that beneath the shade of the tall trees, studious men were constantly engaged in chemical experiments, with a view to discovering how much water a bowl of negus [port or sherry with hot water, spiced and sweetened] could possibly bear . . .'

The hoi polloi may have been less critical of the menu as, increasingly, they became the gardens' stalwart patrons. In the words of the ballad:

> Each profession, ev'ry trade
> Here enjoy refreshing shade,
> Empty is the cobbler's stall,
> He's gone with tinker to Vauxhall,
> Here they drink, and there they cram
> Chicken, pasty, beef and ham.
> Women squeak and men drunk fall
> Sweet enjoyment of Vauxhall.

In 1825 – and an indication perhaps of the decline beginning to set in – the magistrates ordered the darkened walks to be lit. In 1836, in an attempt to stave off the now flagging fortunes, the gardens even opened in the afternoons. It was not the answer.

Proud Vauxhall's last years were a sorry tale of repeated closures, bankruptcy and outright muddle. No fewer than seven farewells were staged, but from the one of mid-1859 there would be no rising from the ashes. In true showman tradition, however, the gardens went out in style, striving for one last night that would recapture a little of the old magic, the atmosphere that had once made it the place to be seen, and what its patrons had always expected of it, with a concert, fireworks and an equestrian display – and of course, music and dance. It gave grand masked balls to the end. Its last night was a manager's benefit, and deservedly so, for Mr G. Stevens, who had been in charge since 1824. For the previous two decades he had striven to rekindle the old glory. The masquerades, alas, had become only more of a scandal and the gardens' unruly crowds had become a local nuisance. Now even Mr Stevens' long-standing customers were deserting him in droves for Cremorne, and Vauxhall had become steadily poorer value for half a crown (at the gate), with the addition of a further half-crown for special events (such as balloonist Charles Green's exhibitions). The bid to entice afternoon customers had proved a tragic mistake. Vauxhall's excitement, after all, was always by night when it was lit by thousands of lamps. The entrance fee for Mr Stevens' last night was just a shilling; one hopes he took a

PEDESTRIANISM

GRAND TREAT AT THE

FLORA CARDENS, BAYSWATER.

On Monday, July 16, 1849,

A HANDICAP

WALKING MATCH,

Seven Miles, for a

Very Handsome Chased Silver Snuff Box

Weighing five ounces.   Open to all England.   Entries free.   Already entered—

SMITH and WESTHALL, of Ipswich, WRIGHT, of Bermondsey, and

GEORGE BRADSHAW.

To be followed by a

Race for 100 Yards

And to leap over 5 Hurdles, run in heats, the heats to be arranged according to the number of entries, for a handsome

SILVER SNUFF BOX.

Several other Matches will come off on the same day.

The Silver Snuff Boxes to be given by Fred. Chandler, of the Prince and Princess. Gravel Lane Southwark, where the Entries are to be made.

A Grand Stand will be erected for the accommodation of the visitors; and a Band of Music will be in attendance to enliven the Sports of the day.

The Flora Gardens is half-a-mile from Oxford Street.   Omnibuses pass to and fro every 5 minutes.

SKITTLES, BOWLS, QUOITS, AND LAWN BILLIARDS.

Portman Press--G. Nurton, Printer, 48, Church Street, Portman Market.

The sporting attractions of Flora Gardens were sometimes of a more illicit kind. (By courtesy of the Guildhall Library, Corporation of London)

little profit from the deal. He may, one feels, have been glad to be at the end of the road.

On the north bank of the Thames, Chelsea's Ranelagh Gardens, opened in 1742 in Lord Ranelagh's house grounds, had an elegant *covered* rotunda that allowed concerts in comfort whatever the weather, and stretched down to the river's edge. In Walpole's opinion Ranelagh was best, though he loved both. He said: 'Every night . . . I go to Ranelagh, which has totally beat Vauxhall. Nobody goes anywhere else – everybody goes there. My Lord Chesterfield is so fond of it that . . . he has ordered all his letters to be directed there.' According to Hickey 'people went there well-dressed, the men always in swords'. Smollett in *Humphrey Clinker* praised the gardens as an 'enchanted palace of a genius'. They were, he wrote, 'adorned with the most exquisite performances of painting, carving, and gilding, enlightened with a thousand golden lamps, that emulate the noon-day sun; crowded with the great, the rich, the gay, the happy, and the fair; glittering with cloth of gold and silver, lace, embroidery, and precious stones'. It is a touch of writer's over-hype, but we get the extravagant picture. And certainly Ranelagh was for the elite, initially at least. It had a reputation for elegance (as Smollett implies) and staged masquerades as well as prestigious concerts (Mozart once played there) and promenades – though the masquerades, as elsewhere, would at times descend into occasions of intrigue. It had, besides its famous rotunda, a lake, a canal and a Chinese pavilion. Fanny Burney's heroine, Evelina, thought Ranelagh 'a charming place' and, outdoing Smollett, 'the brilliancy of the lights, on my first entrance, made me almost think I was in some enchanted castle or fairy palace'.

Ranelagh's large rococo rotunda for 'eating, drinking, staring or crowding' was reputedly 200 feet in diameter – a large promenade with glittering chandeliers – with a huge fireplace at its centre. It was acknowledged as one of the capital's wonders. Round the walls were two tiers of booths for wine- and tea-drinkers. The fashionable set paraded round and round in slow circles, or as Walpole put it, 'like asses in an olive mill'. But that after all was what the pleasure gardens – and Restoration and Regency society – were all about: why people went. They went for fun, waltzing sedately and polka-ing extravagantly in their top hats and overcoats and bonnets and Paisley shawls while the Thames became yet again the scene of England's great naval victories.

Unquestionably, Ranelagh drew the 'flash'. Walpole complained: 'You can't set your foot [down] without treading on a Prince or Duke of Cumberland.' Edward

Gibbon, a devotee when he was not dealing with the downfall of the Romans, considered it a place for 'courtships of every kind'. The entrance fee was two shillings and sixpence with tea and bread and butter inclusive. For the spectaculars or fireworks nights the fee was doubled. Typical of Ranelagh's panache was the celebration by royal command to mark the end of the 1740–8 War of the Austrian Succession. For Walpole 'nothing in a fairy tale ever surpassed it . . . When you entered, you found the whole garden filled with masks and spread with tents . . . In one quarter was a Maypole dressed with garlands, and people dancing round it to a tabor and pipe and rustic music, all masked as were the various bands of musicians that were dispersed in different parts of the garden . . . On the canal was a sort of gondola, adorned with flags and streamers . . . There were booths for tea and wine, gaming tables and dancing, and about two thousand persons.'

Surprisingly, having damaged the monopoly of Vauxhall, the gardens and the famous rotunda barely lasted out the century and were demolished in 1805. Besides royalty Ranelagh had attracted other celebrated guests. It spelt mixed fortunes for the great lover Casanova during his 1763 sojourn in the capital. Lady Harrington, offering him a late lift home from the gardens in her carriage, allowed him to seduce her in the gently swaying vehicle as they trotted through the darkened streets – but cut him dead when they later met socially. A more bitter memory involved the woman he truly loved, a prostitute named Marianne Charpillon, who consistently spurned him – a humiliation for any great seducer. Hearing that she was dying, Casanova was on his way, with a suitable weighting of lead, to throw himself into the Thames, when he met a friend in whom he confided. The friend persuaded him instead to go with him on an evening's debauch and took him later to Ranelagh – where he found Charpillon dancing a graceful minuet!

The conquest was not revived, but Casanova became a dedicated patron of the capital's pleasure gardens. Visiting Marylebone he encountered a past mistress but here too found that the once-ardent flame had died. Marylebone's gardens were opened in 1650, offering patrons a thoroughly blood-soaked evening of cock-fights, dogfights, bull- and bear-baiting and boxing matches, the usual fare of the time. But they became more selective with an upmarket move in 1738, with assembly rooms for balls and concerts being added a year later. Pepys thought the gardens 'pretty' but like all of their kind they acquired a reputation for notoriety: in *The Beggar's Opera* John Gay lets his highwayman Macheath loose amid the gardens' wealthy gamblers, sharpers and general riff-raff. Turpin, on at least one occasion, put in an appearance, and to mark his visit kissed a VIP's wife with the remark that she would henceforth be famous and able to dine out on the episode (or words to that effect). Marylebone was enlarged as the gardens phenomenon approached its heyday; the intention was to make the gardens more exclusive, and an entrance fee of sixpence was made (season ticket: half a guinea). A determined attempt was made to exclude the unsavoury crowd. Marylebone had a good walk and latticed alcoves; in its assembly rooms an orchestra played throughout the evening, and it had food that tempted the gourmet palate. People listened to good music, heard fine singers, and witnessed (Dr Johnson among them) fireworks spectaculars conducted by the pyrotechnics wizard Morel Torre.

Fashionable Cremorne gardens, the late-comer, running along the riverside, predictably maintained the preference for masked balls and all the excitement and intrigue they engendered – perhaps bowing to what patrons had come to expect, an opportunity for dalliance. Even so, the mood of society was changing and the gardens would enjoy but a brief span of fame (or infamy) before becoming the somewhat sullied resort of glamorous young ladies (or, in other words, high-class whores). Cremorne, according to the *Saturday Review* in 1861, was 'a point of attraction not only to all London but to all England. The provincial farmer who comes to the capital on business and seasons his business with pleasure, would scarcely think he had his full measure of enjoyment if he did not visit the famous Chelsea gardens. In the country, he is perhaps a strict Puritan . . . but he feels that when in Rome he must do as Romans do.'

Cremorne's grand entrance was from the river. Daringly, considering Vauxhall's experience, it was an afternoon as well as an evening place. Thousands came to relax in what was the last fashionable gardens worth being seen in. Their attractions were well hyped, as a typical handbill demonstrates: 'Three Grand Bands/The Original Tyrolese Singers/Grand Fairy Ballets/Vocal and Instrumental Concerts/Bono Core, the Salamander or Fire King [he entered a blazing furnace]/Grand Cirque Oriental/Antonio Poletti (the Roman Wizard)/Cooke's Educated Dogs and Monkeys/Talented Company of Concert Singers/The Stereorama (the Most Splendid Exhibition in England)/ Cosmoramic Pictures/The Savannah Minstrels/Elegant Acrobatic Displays/ Balloon Ascents/Splendid Pyrotechnic Displays/Dancing on the Crystal Platform/Romantic Grotto and Fernery.' And on one memorable night, in 1861,

Madame Genevieve crossed the Thames on the high wire. Those who dared could go aloft in an anchored balloon for ten shillings; one lady who did so went up astride a cow in the basket. An excellent supper cost half-a-crown and observant diners might spot the sauntering artist Dante Gabriel Rossetti, who often found his models there.

But the *Saturday Review* also spoke of the transformation that took place in the gardens in the late evening. Its contributor, a Dr Acton, lurches into lyricism on the change of ambience: 'On a pleasant July evening . . . as calico and merry respectability tailed off eastward by penny steamers, the setting sun brought westward hansoms freighted with demure immorality in silk and fine linen. By about ten o'clock age and innocence had seemingly all retired . . . leaving the massive elms, the grass-plots and the geranium beds, the kiosks, temples, "monster platforms" and "crystal circles" of Cremorne to flicker in the thousand gaslights . . . On and around that platform waltzed, strolled and fed some thousand souls – perhaps 700 of them men of the upper and middle class, the remainder prostitutes more or less *prononces*.' More specifically, and again shedding an interesting light on the class of its male patrons, yet another observer reports: 'All the men are well or properly dressed; the women are harlots, but of a higher class than those of the Strand; they wear bright shawls, white stuffs or gauze or tulle, red cloaks, new bonnets; there is a dress which has cost £12, but the faces are rather faded, and sometimes, in the crowd, they raise terrible cries – the cries of a screeching owl. What is most comical, and proves their state of excitement, is their notion of pinching people, particularly foreigners.'

Cremorne was opened in 1832 by Baron de Beaufain (one of his many aliases) shortly after a spell in the King's Bench prison, where he had been lodged after a stock market irregularity. Cremorne House itself had a rather finer pedigree, having formerly belonged to Viscount Cremorne and earlier to the Earl of Huntingdon. Essentially at first a sports stadium, it broadened its scope – and its takings – by staging pony races, dancing and balloon feats. The gardens, of about twelve acres, had an American-style bowling saloon, grottoes, a banqueting hall, a theatre and, of course, 'lavender bowers' for 1,500 patrons. It had a circus and sideshows, and like its rivals (or those that were left) it was fond of enactments of some of the great historic moments, such as the siege of Sebastopol – when the stage collapsed under the combined weight (and feet) of five hundred bayonet-wielding soldiers.

Cremorne flourished as its rivals faded and closed their gates. On gala nights three hundred cabs clustered round its King's Road entrance, bringing three thousand to see that night's spectacle. Then in 1871, the start of a decade that saw a savage clampdown on fairs and such popular events, the gardens lost their licence for dancing and music. They regained it in 1874 and managed to struggle on in the face of Victorian displeasure, to close, finally, in 1877 after one local pastor had lambasted them as a 'nursery for every kind of vice'.

It was the end of an era. A year earlier, another of the capital's well-known pleasure haunts, Highbury Barn, had fallen foul of authority and been forced to close. It had risen on the tide from a cakes-and-ale shop in 1700 to a full-blown amusements retreat with a dining room that could seat a thousand people, and while it covered only four acres it had a very large (4,000 square feet) lamp-lit, open-air dancing platform, added about 1856. It was said to be among the best in Europe. The Barn opened at four (sensibly compromising) and dancing continued from seven. Its then proprietor, having paid £3,000 for the lease, felt an understandable need to advertise, and with a mind to the quality who might be persuaded to forsake even Cremorne, chose *The Times*. The Barn's attractions were indeed comprehensive: 'Ball rooms, club rooms, banqueting halls, cosy private rooms, panorama of Constantinople, swings and tittle-cum-totters, battledore and shuttlecock, trap-ball, foot ball and other rural sports.' How could anyone resist? It was, he felt the need to add, a 'renowned place of harmless pleasure unequalled by any other'.

With admission at sixpence a time, its Sunday evenings were popular with Londoners. When taken over in 1861 by the clown Edward Giovanelli, the Barn underwent a further transmutation into something approaching theatre, with comedy turns and pantomimes (starring the proprietor and his wife), Blondin, the high-wire performer, music-hall acts and freakshows. But its rowdiness and a riot undid Giovanelli. Its 'harmless pleasures' proved too much for the local magistrates, and the Barn too would fade from the scene.

The Eagle, however, located in the City Road and once dubbed 'the most disreputable place', set out to please a more genteel, lower- and middle-class patron, and must largely have done so. It escaped the Puritan pogroms of the 1870s and Dickens loved it. With its pleasure gardens, the famous tavern could attract up to six thousand customers nightly. It had sideshows, a rotunda, dancing (in a Grecian saloon) and much else, and it sent the young Dickens, in *Sketches by Boz*, into raptures. Let him conjure up the scene for us:

Balloonists and balloon flights were among the delights at Vauxhall's famous gardens. (Museum of London)

There were the walks beautifully gravelled and painted, and the refreshment-boxes painted and ornamented like so many snuff boxes, and the variegated lamps shedding their rich light upon the company's heads, and the place for dancing ready chalked for the company's feet, and a Moorish band playing at one end, and an opposition military band away at the other. Then the waiters were rushing to and fro with glasses of negus, and glasses of brandy-and-water, and bottles of ale, and bottles of stout, and ginger beer was going off in one place and practical jokes going on in another.

The Eagle at least would survive into the twentieth century, to be demolished in 1901 and rebuilt as a pub. It would have survived anyway, in the lines of the popular song:

Up and down the City Road
In and out the Eagle,
That's the way the money goes.
Pop goes the weasel.

'Popping' something was to pawn it; a 'weasel' was a tailor's iron. And tailors, as everyone knows, had prodigious thirsts.

The pleasure-gardens craze had seemed unstoppable; they blossomed, some to gather fame and a fond clientele, others to fail spectacularly. It is difficult now to escape the conclusion that they acted like the capital's boisterous old fairs, as a safety valve for a society that teetered constantly on the brink of revolt. Not a few did in fact take their cue from the fair, as did Clerkenwell's New Wells, when the eighteenth-century spa jumped on the bandwagon and extended its evening entertainment with clown acts and acrobats and pantomime. A Madame Kerman danced on the high wire – on stilts; the Youthful Giant (7 feet 4 inches) made an appearance, as did the Saxon Lady Giantess (at 7 feet) and a 'wonderful little Polander' aged sixty (at 30 inches). A Mr Dominique stopped hearts with his flying jump over the points of twenty-four swords held upwards by twenty-four men. Further thrills were provided by flying squirrels and a young crocodile. Beulah Spa diversified in 1831 to encompass a grand octagonal reading room, an archery area and a camera obscura. Dancers tripped to the music of a military band and coaches ran daily from Charing Cross, sometimes bringing Mrs Fitzherbert, the Prince of Wales's golden-tressed mistress. It was left to Strombolo Gardens in Chelsea to close a gap in the market; they opened in 1762 to offer just peace and the gentle tinkle of their fountain. They must surely have been welcome.

The paradox of the pleasure gardens is that they were at their hedonistic peak as the country's administration muddled its way through a time of acute tensions in society, war crises and threatened insurrection at home. Walpole for once was disparaging – and deadly serious. Surveying the scene he saw about him in 1773, he castigated his fellow-countrymen as 'a gaming, robbing, wrangling, railing nation without principles, genius, character, or allies . . .'. Perhaps what his contemporaries sought so desperately was an escape from the harsher realities and the hazardous state of their country. In the pleasure gardens they may have found it: the gardens had a mystery, a magic that took their patrons out of the rut of their ordinary lives and into a gentler world of music and enchantment, and of gallantry perhaps by no means unwelcome under the fairy lights, or in the soft, warm glow of the supper boxes. Dickens, aware of that magic as their era came to a close, again in *Sketches by Boz* confesses: 'We loved to wander among those illuminated groves . . . The temples and saloons and cosmoramas and fountains glittered and sparkled before our eyes; the beauty of the lady singers and the elegant deportment of the gentlemen, captivated our hearts; a few hundred thousand of additional lamps dazzled our senses; a bowl or two of reeking punch bewildered our brains; and we were happy.'

He was speaking of Vauxhall before, folly of follies, the great gardens did the unthinkable and opened in the afternoon, to let the harsh light of day into their mystery. Nothing, after all, was as it seemed. All was exposed. Writing in the *Morning Chronicle*, the disillusioned young reporter would lament: 'Our favourite views were mere patches of paint; the fountain that had sparkled so showily by lamp-light presented very much the appearance of a water pipe that had burst.' Indeed the whole bubble was about to burst. The ball was over. The gardens' stories were ultimately depressingly familiar: a start in the grandiose style and then, imperceptibly, the fickle drift of the smart set to pastures new, and a slow and agonising decline into the dependence and tolerance of a seamier stratum of society whose behaviour would eventually shock the genteel and provoke the magistrates to action. By then the elements and culture that had sustained the pleasure gardens would have taken root in other citadels: the theatre, the circus, the concert hall and especially the music hall. Dancing would move into its own separate and dedicated temples, where its romance and its sexual frisson could be sustained. In the meantime the minds of men had expanded into the milieu of an undreamed of and increasingly scientific age. The capital would have fresh and exciting avenues to explore.

CHAPTER V
Citadels of Wit and Wisdom

History may have been unfair to the capital's taverns: their important role in Restoration society and in the years that followed has gone seriously unrecognised. Nor could the place of the coffee-house in the city's affairs be exaggerated. Both drew the society of their time away from drinking as a singular act and into an emerging and more civilising world of new and diverting interests. In both there occurred a meeting of intellects to consider matters above the mundane, to trade philosophies and argue in spirited contention till the rafters rang. Social enclaves, often with good fare, honest ale and fine wines, they crossed the cultural divide in the affairs of men and loomed significantly as the proving ground of politics – as well as the convivial hub of pleasure. As Dr Johnson so profoundly confessed, as soon as he entered the door of a tavern he experienced 'an oblivion of care, and a freedom from solicitude; when I am seated . . . wine there exhilarates my spirits and prompts me to free conversation . . . I dogmatise and am contradicted; and in this conflict of opinions and sentiments I find delight.' That sentiment is unchanging, as true now as it was two and a half centuries ago.

The return of the Stuarts to the throne, for good or ill, threw open the door to a different society, giving the nation a fresh cohesion. From about 1650 flying stagecoaches swept out from the capital to reach, eventually, all compass points of the country: they left from the inns and taverns, giving their rogue porters and ostlers a chance to tip off the neighbourhood highwaymen to a rider or coach worthy of their attention. Yet still the English gentleman of means (and sometimes not) rose late after a night of dissipation, about ten or eleven, breakfasted (with tea), and perambulated around town till about four or five (his dinner-time). At nine he would make his way to the tavern to drink and gamble with friends. On wet mornings his stroll would be curtailed – to the inviting new intimacy of the coffee-house.

With the arrival of the Merry Monarch the latter had found its niche alongside the tavern. The precise details of the coffee berry's arrival are contentious; suffice it to say that there is a general acceptance that its first appearance was in the City's St Michael's Alley, and that it was originally sold by a man from a tent. The man came from Smyrna. He got here just marginally ahead of the country's new ruler – and stirred a much greater controversy. The 'fashionable' drink, it was feared, would put Englishmen under the spell of Islam, or make them abandon religion entirely. Not of least concern in that free-wheeling, pleasure-loving society was how the new drink affected the libido; whether it was repressed or stimulated. One petition in the Restoration capital, in 1674, supposedly on behalf of city wives, drew attention to their plight from the 'Excessive Drinking of that Drying, and Enfeebling LIQUOR' that made husbands incapable. There came a swift and strong rebuttal from other quarters, pointing out that coffee was the general drink throughout Turkey 'and those Eastern Regions, and yet no part of the world can boast more able or eager performers than those circumcised gentlemen'. The defending pamphlet, with admirable candour, continued: 'Coffee Collects and settles the Spirits, makes the erection more Vigorous, the Ejaculation more full, adds a spiritual escency to the Sperme, and renders it more firm and suitable to the Gusto of the womb, and proportionate to the ardours and expectations too, of the female Paramour.'

The coffee-houses would proliferate, the good, the bad and the dingy. In 1739 (according to Maitland's *History of London*) there would be around 550 of them, each with its own distinctive clientele. Most were chokingly smoke-filled and rather less than clean. Gossip and good fellowship rather than any hope of prowess from the coffee berry was the engine that drove them – that and the ready access to the capital's intelligence and the current news-prints. They were, increasingly, where the idle, pleasure-seeking set met. Thus John Macky, traveller and Scottish observer of the beau monde:

> About twelve . . . [it] assembles in the several Chocolate and Coffee Houses: The best of which are the *Cocoa Tree*, and *White*'s Chocolate Houses, *St James's*, the *Smyrna*, and the *British* Coffee Houses; and all these are so near one another, that in less than an Hour you see the Company of them all . . . If it be fine Weather, we take a Turn in the *Park* till two, when we go to Dinner; and if it be dirty, you are entertain'd at *Picket* or *Basset* at *White*'s, or you may talk *Politicks* at the *Smyrna* and *St James's*.

Ale, then universally drunk, even by children, was being challenged simultaneously by tea. It was sold, expensively, from Garraway's coffee-house in

Exchange Alley. Thomas Garraway was the first man in the country to sell the new commodity – still £10 a lb in the 1670s – as a 'cure for all disorders'. But those with discerning palates also beat a path to his door to drink his fine cherry wine, his sherry, pale ale and punch. The Greek who kept the Grecian would go one better; by 1664 he was advertising his 'Turkey coffee-berry, chocolate, sherbet and tea, good and cheap', along with the promise to instruct his customers on how to make the 'liquors'.

Twining's tea warehouse was established confrontationally close to the Grecian coffee-house, and the capital's fashionable ladies rode out in their carriages to the few established outlets to drink from small china cups at a shilling a time. (The shop price by then was twenty to thirty shillings a lb.) Dr Johnson drank it in prodigious quantities, astonishing Boswell: 'I suppose no person ever enjoyed with more relish the infusion of that fragrant leaf . . . The quantities which he drank of it at all hours were so great, that his nerves must have been uncommonly strong, not to have been extremely relaxed by such an intemperate use of it.' Boswell himself liked to have green tea when he was down, finding relief from it and claiming: 'I am so fond of tea that I could write a whole dissertation on its virtues.' He also pointed out that it gave comfort and solace without the risks encountered by drinking spirits.

By the start of the reign of the unfortunate George III (1760) tea was well on the way to becoming the national drink – to the disgust of the aristocracy who, though they sipped it themselves, thought the habit must surely sap the strong sinews of soldier and yeoman alike. Everyone was drinking tea at home, despite the heavy duty on it – a tax that made smuggling rife. In 1784 Pitt's estimate of the country's tea consumption was thirteen million lb, at least half of it entering the country on the smuggler's ketch. (Even Parson Woodforde got his supplies on the contraband market: in 1777 he was paying ten shillings and sixpence a lb to the local smuggler.)

The tavern, the coffee-house and the ordinary of the seventeenth and eighteenth centuries blurred the boundaries of their individual functions. With a shrewd entrepreneurial flair the tavern could become a coffee-house when it suited it to do so, while the coffee-shop, as its period passed, would convert (or reconvert) to a tavern, or establish itself as a hotel. Even the ordinary seemed unsure of its role, and would aspire to slightly higher status. The ordinary was an establishment serving dinner (also called an 'ordinary') at a fixed time, which in Pepys's day was often at noon, gentlemen retiring to their midday meal with a little gaming to follow. They would have the choice of several dishes and, usually, all ate at one large table.

One of the capital's most popular was Locket's, where the meals were punctiliously timed. The gentry came, giving it an envied cachet, and it was as well patronised for pre-theatre dinners. Another was opened in Covent Garden in 1754 by the celebrated actor Charles Macklin in an attempted career-switch and was aimed determinedly upmarket. It opened at four o'clock and its 'ordinary' cost three shillings, with the claret, port or whatever other liquor the diner chose included. The ritual of this somewhat extraordinary ordinary is retold in *London Recollected (Vol III)*: 'When the clock struck, a large bell . . . was rung for five minutes, and the dinner was ordered to be served. In ten minutes more it was put upon the table; the door was then closed, and no other guest was admitted. Macklin himself always brought in the first dish, in a full dress suit and with a napkin on his left arm; and when he had set it down he made a low bow and retired to a sideboard, surrounded by a bevy of waiters.' There he would stay. Not until the dinner had ended would he walk among the company inquiring if they had enjoyed their meal. Then, with another low bow, he would retire.

The diners at Chatelain's had more fun; it was a French ordinary, a merry place where the capital's wits congregated to trade barbs in the later seventeenth century. Pepys, though, was once less than happy there at having to pay out eight shillings and sixpence a head for a dinner that had pleased neither him nor his guests. The less salubrious ordinaries charged between a sixpence and a shilling per head (two courses perhaps for your shilling); some had private rooms where even the aristocracy might come to dine – and behave abominably.

The ordinary, except in the matter of timing, was barely distinguishable from the chop-house or the steak-house; all were places where one could dine relatively cheaply. To the young Boswell, on a budget, they were a godsend and numerous. As a newcomer to the capital scene he spent much of his time at first in the various chop-houses and coffee-houses, just listening to the conversations going on around him. He liked to dine for a shilling, or one shilling and sixpence at most. Sometimes, however, carousing with Dr Johnson, whose famous *Life* he would write, the bill would cut savagely into his allowance. Dining the great man at The Club, in 1785, the tavern dinner cost him twenty-four shillings, an extravagance that went, one supposes, mostly on wine.

The interior of Dolly's steak-house, beside St Paul's, so popular with Boswell. (By courtesy of the Guildhall Library, Corporation of London)

The chop-house was the 'fast-food eatery' of its day, where the dishes were cheap but adequate, the tavern a long-stop option where one could linger – eat in a private room with female company perhaps, a serious paramour or a wench already known to the waiters. Dining alone, Boswell might favour Dolly's steak-house in Paternoster Row, where he would wolf down a 'large fat beefsteak'. He describes in his *Journal* the more relaxed atmosphere and the reason for his choice: the beefsteak-house was a warm, comfortable place. One entered and joined those seated at the large table, taking whatever place was empty. One called for the required dish, 'which you get well and cleverly dressed'. One could chat to fellow-diners or not, just as one wished. His dinner, of beef, bread and beer, at only a shilling included the waiter's one penny tip. All the same, he admitted: 'The mode of dining, or rather being fed, at such houses in London, is well known to many to be particularly unsocial.'

But he rang the changes; dining at Chapman's Eating-house in Oxford Road, he promised himself he would try several of the capital's eating-houses. And he did. He went on to sample Harris's Eating-house in Covent Garden; Clifton's Chop-house ('a very good chop-house') in Butcher Row, close to the Temple; St Clement's Chop-house and New Church Chop-house, returning to his particular favourites. He prospected the coffee-houses, praising the breakfast at the Somerset; breakfasting also at Slaughter's; visiting Tom's coffee-house; drinking negus at the Piazza; and taking tea and coffee at the Turk's Head coffee-house in the Strand, where the woman owner was a friend of Johnson. There cannot have been a more assiduous gourmet of his time. He especially loved to breakfast and read the papers and eavesdrop avidly to the talk at Child's in St Paul's Churchyard – once the favourite haunt of those literary lions Addison and Steele – and visited it without fail on Saturday mornings. Going or coming he would drop in at the Temple Exchange coffee-house in Fleet Street to buy Wilkes's *North Briton*, an acrimonious journal of dissent.

There was in the coffee-house a remarkable degree of democracy: rank was abandoned; the nobility might be seen seated elbow to elbow with trade. A penny paid at the bar entitled one to a seat by the fire and the perusal of the news-journals, hence its sobriquet 'the penny university'. It was a kind of poorer man's club: Johnson thought it the place to be (like the tavern) for good company, and for a few hours of its entertainment a man need spend as little as threepence. Like the chop-house, it was warmed by a good fire, alive with the buzz of conversation, and with men in small groups arguing earnestly or intently studying the day's news.

Boswell was a clubbable man, gregarious and desperate to impress, and the capital he found himself in afforded every opportunity. Delight of delights, he was soon taken to the famous Beefsteak Club, then meeting in a luxurious room above the Covent Garden theatre. Its president sat under a canopy, above which were emblazoned, in golden letters, the words *Beef and Liberty*. On Boswell's visit the chair was taken by Lord Sandwich, 'a jolly, hearty, lively man'. The company was a mixed one, and included Lord Eglinton, who had introduced Boswell, Mr

Inside one of the capital's early coffee-houses, the atmosphere is peacefully sedate. (Billie Love Historical Collection)

Beard, manager of the theatre, Colonel West of the Guards, Charles Churchill the poet, John Wilkes the controversial editor of the *North Briton*, and many more. The young Scot was in his element: 'We had nothing to eat but beefsteaks, and had wine and punch in plenty.'

Had he but known it – and perhaps he did – Boswell was travelling in fast company: their 'jolly' chairman Lord Sandwich was also a devotee, like his fellow-members Wilkes and the profligate Churchill, of the scandalous orgies of the Monks of Medmenham Abbey. The rebellious Wilkes, whose inky riposte to Bute's government's newspaper would land him in such hot water, was then in his mid-thirties; he was cross-eyed and in other respects equally ill-favoured, and Boswell no doubt found it hard to credit his success with women. Boswell thought him a 'lively facetious fellow' – he was a man fond of the limelight – but, though their paths crossed occasionally, Boswell was careful not to cultivate too close an acquaintance. The son of a merchant, Wilkes lacked the gift of good birth and had never risen above his resentment, bearing a grudge against his betters that he seemed compelled to satisfy.

The Sublime Society of Beefsteaks was a club for movers and shakers, for men about town, with a limited membership. This 'society of roysterers' meeting to honour the beef of Old England was founded in 1735 and (like many such clubs) frequently moved location. While occupying a room at the Lyceum Theatre – a room suitably fitted out with oak – it met on Saturdays from November to the end of June. Then, and no doubt earlier, pickles were banned until the third helping. With the beef came baked potatoes, onions and beetroot and toasted cheese, all washed down with whisky toddy, porter or punch.

Culturally they were exciting times, particularly for the middle-classes who would shortly be able to devour the works of Walter Scott, Maria Edgeworth and Fanny Burney, and tune in to the quintessentially English consciousness of Jane Austen; from the end of the eighteenth century subscription libraries would find themselves struggling to satisfy an ever-widening demand for novels for the genteel reader. Journals, pamphlets and magazines spewed from the presses on all imaginable matters, disseminating knowledge and providing subjects for earnest debate at the growing number of literary and philosophical societies – most of them meeting in the new citadels of enlightenment, the capital's coffee-houses or its celebrated taverns. Each had its coterie and its commitment to the advance of the arts, science and general understanding of the world and man's place in it.

It was becoming apparent, too, that the coffee-house was much more than simply a convivial retreat for the stressed-out merchant or daring entrepreneur. It was the centre of his universe, where he networked with others of his kind, exchanging ideas and keeping his finger on the pulse of trade. Brokers of all shades and interests met in its smoky atmosphere to sell anything from silks to ships and salvaged cargo; insurers met to weigh the risks of almost every known activity; and adventurers came to hire vessels where there gathered the men who could command them. It was, apart from the waitresses in their decorative caps, mainly a male-only preserve, though some, as we shall see, were quietly brothels beneath their façade.

Criminal activity was plotted there: swindlers used it in their plans to dupe innocent country farmers, working a scam when they came to town; slaves were sold – every commodity, from every continent, ship, shop or tract of land in some distant colony, might be auctioned under the ritual of the candle; letters could be sent from or collected at it under the capital's primitive postal system; most acted as reward houses in the recovery of items lost or stolen ('and no questions asked').

A number were 'hotels' (offering 'good food, good beds, the best wine') and men coming to town would base themselves there to conduct interviews, having earlier announced their intention of doing so, along with their hours of attendance, in the news-journals. Local merchants blatantly used it as their business address and made sure they could be contacted there. News-hawks, even then reviled, ingratiated themselves on to the fringe of any important group to pick up titbits; quacks congregated with their cures and elixirs, and round the city's main coffee-houses on a daily timetable came Thomas Smith, the self-styled 'first Master Corn-Cutter for England'. Surgeons dispensed an instant diagnosis for patients, without shifting from their chairs, from the symptoms related to them by another. Ball tickets could be bought, and, occasionally, the costume hired for your next masquerade. In some, passage might be booked for distant landfalls.

The coffee-house acted, also, as an early servant registry. And on a similar, unromantic basis one could select a suitable bride. It could also be of use in discarding a mistress who had become an embarrassment: this from the *Morning Post* in 1779:

A GENTLEMAN of Fortune, whom Family reasons oblige to drop a connection which has for some time subsisted between him and an agreeable young lady, will give a considerable sum of Money with her to any Gentleman, or person in genteel Business, who has good sense and resolution to despise the censures of the World, and will enter with her into the Holy state of Matrimony. Letters addressed to Mr G.H. at the Cecil Street Coffee-house, will be paid due attention to.

Other notices, despite the delicacy of language, were quite transparent about what was being offered to applicants who might have been slightly beyond the bloom of youth: this again from the *Morning Post*, a few years earlier:

A Young Gentleman of the most liberal education and a genteel address, would be happy in having an opportunity of devoting his services to a lady of real fashion and fortune, who may wish to have some particular deficiencies thoroughly supplied, without subjecting herself to any disagreeable restraint. Any lady to whom such an offer may be suitable, will receive the fullest Explanation, in answer to a letter addressed to A.X., Turk's Head Coffee House, Strand.

The British coffee-house in Cockspur Street, a suitable venue for a convention. (By courtesy of the Guildhall Library, Corporation of London)

Increasingly the coffee-house would play a significant role in the nation's economy. When the Royal Exchange, the epicentre of the business world, became impossibly overcrowded, money-market dealers moved in 1697 into Jonathan's coffee-house in Change Alley – and the Stock Exchange was born. It was a lure for speculators and would become the focus of the ill-fated South Sea Bubble, which rocked the country's financial structure. Some time later the Baltic Exchange would flower from the Virginia and Baltick coffee-house in Threadneedle Street. Lawyers unsurprisingly claimed the Grecian (near the Temple); the clergy clung to Child's (at St Paul's); shippers and marine insurers famously commandeered Lloyd's (in Lombard Street), scene of illicit gambling, ship auctions and once of three thousand loads of manure lying on the banks of the Thames; and some stock-jobbers favoured Man's (near

Charing Cross). Catastrophically, on 10 January 1838, both Lloyd's and the Royal Exchange would fall victim to fire, ironically with the Exchange's carillon bells ringing out the Scottish air *There's nae luck aboot the hoose* even as they melted down.

As one might predict, the best rum in the capital was that at the Jamaica coffee-house (Cornhill), which occupied itself with the Jamaica trade. The Jerusalem coffee-house (also in Cornhill) by 1776 had become the hub of the East India trade, enjoying a reputation approaching that of Lloyd's. Batson's (Cornhill) was a clearing house for dealers transacting business with Russia and Turkey; in Garraway's (Exchange Alley), started in connection with the sale of the Hudson's Bay Company's furs in 1669, and again a place of outrageous wagers, ships and even whole plantations were auctioned by the candle, as were commodities such as spices, indigo, coffee (of course), timber and textiles and much more.

Politically the coffee-house was volatile, frequently a place of intrigue whose patrons were subject to discreet surveillance by government spies. As early as 1663 an Act of Parliament had brought their cautionary licensing by magistrates, and Charles II, for all his tolerance, in 1675 found a need to close them briefly as 'places where the disaffected met, and spread scandalous reports concerning the conduct of His Majesty and his Ministers'. The Smyrna, in Pall Mall, was one such enclave, a Whig hangout and Jacobite stronghold where the porters and chairmen, it was said, picked up an education just by eavesdropping on the conversations of members like Swift and Steele. Somerset coffee-house in the Strand, where Boswell sometimes took breakfast, was the focus of speculation in the years from 1769 to 1772; it was here that the letters of the mysterious commentator Junius – most probably Sir Philip Francis, a Whig politician carrying a torch for the young Duchess of Devonshire – were secretly delivered into the hands of the waiters en route to the columns of the *Public Advertiser*. The letters, taking sides with the Whig opposition, attacked the king's circle.

St James's hosted a cluster of chocolate- and coffee-houses: Ozinda's chocolate-house, started in 1694, was a Tory enclave where the main activities were 'drinking chocolate, betting and reading the newspapers'; no decent-thinking Tory, however, would darken the door of St James's coffee-house, opened a decade later, and a Whig house, though Garrick, Goldsmith, Swift and Reynolds had no qualms about retreating there to chat and scour through the news-prints. The essayist Joseph Addison, along with Richard Steele, reformers both, found it a congenial 'office' from which to pen their work for the *Tatler*, and beyond doubt it was convenient for gathering gossip and taking the temperature of affairs of state.

In Bellamy's, adjacent to the Commons, Members of Parliament took time out from the more boring debates while still within hearing of the division bell. The coffee-house, one observer claimed, had 'some of the best wine that can be drank in London, and some of the best chops and steaks that were ever sought to be cooked . . . The steaks were so hot and so tender and so accurately dressed.' The famous last words on William Pitt's lips as he died in 1806 were, allegedly, 'I think I could eat one of Bellamy's veal pies.'

The club owed its origin largely to the tavern and the coffee-house. In the Crown in Drury Lane there took place nightly a charade that aped the atmosphere of Bellamy's, in the meeting of the Flash Coves' Parliament, a gathering of men-about-town, lawyers and ambitious men of trade who took on for the evening the names and characteristics of the current ministers and Members of Parliament and acted with corresponding irresponsibility. There were formed clubs that would shine their beam down the years: in 1753 the Society of Arts, dedicated to the furtherance of the arts in manufacture, was formed in Rawthmell's coffee-house in Covent Garden. The Society of Gardeners was inaugurated, appropriately one might feel, in Chelsea's Newhall's coffee-house in the early eighteenth century, and immediately advocated the integration of flowers into the dusty city landscape. In the Stratford coffee-house, off Oxford Street, in 1804 the Royal Water Colour Society came into being.

Truly there was a meeting of minds as never before. If that intellectual life of the mid-eighteenth-century capital had a dominating figure it was the lumbering bulk of Dr Johnson, whose own melancholic life would touch that of so many of the important and influential talents of his time. The Great Debater and author of the first English Dictionary, prepared to slang-it-out with any Thames bargee, was an unprepossessing hulk. Boswell, his biographer, was in no doubt of that: 'Mr Johnson [*sic*] is a man of most dreadful appearance. He is a very big man, is troubled with sore eyes, the palsy, and the king's evil [scrofula]. He is very slovenly in his dress and speaks with a most uncouth voice. Yet his great knowledge and strength of expression command vast respect and render him very excellent company.' We need not take his word for it;

Johnson's omnipresence in so many of the capital's coffee-houses is testimony enough.

Sometimes the two would have a room at the Turk's Head coffee-house; it was a livelier place than the Mitre tavern in Fleet Street, where they often supped. Johnson said: 'I love the young dogs of this age: they have more wit and humour and knowledge of life than we had.' At the Strand coffee-house he even had his own chair.

Deprived of domestic bliss, it was here that he felt most at home. But he was a regular too at Tom's coffee-house in Covent Garden in the 1760s, a favourite after-theatre call for courtiers and commoners alike, along with Garrick and Reynolds, the daring Admiral Rodney and a whole raft of dukes, earls and lords. Tom's in the latter half of the eighteenth century had a clientele of some seven hundred 'of the nobility, foreign ministers, gentry and geniuses of the age'. There, or at Will's adjoining, it was claimed, 'there was playing at picquet, and the best conversation until midnight'. Tom's was a favourite with wordsmiths, however, and having dined there, the young Boswell would probably wander through the darkened alleys of its precincts for some female companion with whom to round off the evening.

The equally famous Will's came into being on the heels of the Restoration, and quickly became known as the Wits' coffee-house. It too had a strong literary connection with, at one time, John Dryden in the warmest chair by the fire (which would be pulled out onto the balcony on sunny summer days). Pepys paid his respects, as did the playwright Wycherley. The coffee-house was kept by Will Urwin, and entry to his circle was by no means easy; Will was almost as choosy about his clientele as Almack's. His was possibly the most celebrated haunt of all. Macaulay said of it: 'Under no roof was a greater variety of figures to be seen.' The wit and high conversation, alas, would wither and give way to gambling and finally closure in the mid-eighteenth century. The *Tatler* lamented: 'Where you used to see songs, epigrams and satires in the hands of every man you met, you have now only a pack of cards.'

Long before that the literary giants had fled to Button's, also in Covent Garden and established in the early eighteenth century by a former servant of the Countess of Warwick, and sponsored by her husband, the essayist Addison, who found it a convenient bolthole from his vexatious spouse. Among its patrons was Sir Godfrey Kneller, who painted the portraits of his distinguished fellow-members. Here, it is said, the bold but gentlemanly highwayman James Maclean exposed himself to the greatest risk by dropping in regularly to flirt with the barmaid, the owner's daughter. Maclean died prematurely, on the Tyburn gallows, in 1750, a year or so before Button's closed. It had declined badly after Addison's death and the retirement of his close crony Steele, wit and fellow-essayist. Between them they had lifted the culture of the coffee-house and reflected its tone in the columns of the *Tatler* and later the *Spectator*.

Old Slaughter's in St Martin's Lane, 'a very respectable house', opened in 1692, blazoning the name of its owner, Thomas Slaughter. It was a gaming house of sorts with its patrons vying to outdo each other at chess, whist and games of pure chance. It attracted illustrators, engravers and artists, among them Hogarth, and was a rumbustious place full of would-be orators. There was silence, however, for the well-known surgeon John Hunter when he could be persuaded to tell how he had tried to resuscitate the unfortunate Reverend Dr Dodd, 'the dissolute divine', after his hanging at Tyburn – by plunging his corpse into a bath of hot water at the undertaker's. The coffee-house's most notable character was one its waiters, a rogue named Sock, who regularly supped the patrons' wine on the way to their tables – and then apologised profusely for having spilled it.

London coffee-house, established in Ludgate Hill about 1730, was highly reputable, drawing the clergy, academics and physicians – and the inquisitive Boswell – to its door. It had a clique that debated matters of philosophy and social issues. It also had the prestigious custom of Joseph Priestley, discoverer of oxygen, and Benjamin Franklin, who investigated the behaviour of electricity and helped to draft the American Declaration of Independence. One London guidebook found it 'the most elegant and extensive of any that come under the name of coffee-house in the three kingdoms'. Praise indeed. And it had a further distinction: it was where Old Bailey juries, unable to reach a verdict, were locked up overnight.

Nando's, down the hill and up Fleet Street, purveyed a fine coffee or punch and enticed members of the Bar, including one Lord Chancellor whose lengthy liaison with the barmaid and daughter of the house produced two children. Along the Strand at Charing Cross, Alexander Man, of Man's coffee-house, around from the 1660s, had the honour of being the 'coffee-man' to the king. Reflecting this, the house became, in 1676, the Royal coffee-house. Also at Charing Cross there was the Salopian, a tavern-cum-

Anarchy: the coffee-house became a hotbed of news, gossip and political plotting. (By courtesy of the Guildhall Library, Corporation of London)

coffee-house which Thomas Telford, the Scottish engineer, made his London headquarters for twenty years. It was his London 'home' and friends flocked to visit him there. Batson's, in Cornhill, had a somewhat similar arrangement with the noted surgeon Sir William Blizard, who could be found there for consultations. For those seeking a second opinion the house had the usual large quota of quacks.

Perhaps the greatest hub of enlightenment was Covent Garden's Bedford Head coffee-house. It enjoyed a huge patronage by the able and witty men of the time – and by high-class courtesans. It was a cauldron of critics, and drew in Garrick, Fielding, Pope and Smollett as well as such important commentators as Walpole and William Hickey. It had cliques and coteries from which the less famous were excluded and, according to the *Connoisseur* magazine, in 1754 afforded 'every variety of character. This coffee-house is crowded every night with men of parts. Almost everyone you meet is a polite scholar and a wit; jokes and *bon-mots* are echoed from box to box; every branch of literature is critically examined, and the merit of every production of the press, or performance at the theatres, weighed and determined.' With its good opinion, a man's reputation was made. It was here that the besotted clergyman James Hackman sipped his glass of capillaire while watching from its window for Lord Sandwich's mistress to leave the theatre across the street.

Some coffee-houses, it is true, did not fit into the familiar mould but had their own strange cliques. Hickey, in his fascinating *Memoirs*, facetiously throws light on the coffee society of the capital's young blades:

> . . . my chief place for eating was young Slaughter's in St Martin's Lane [as opposed to Old Slaughter's] where I supped every night with a set of extravagant young men of my own stamp. After some time we were displeased with the noise, and the promiscuous company that frequented the Coffee room, chiefly to read the newspapers, especially half a dozen respectable older men, whom we impertinently pronounced a set of stupid, formal ancient prigs, horrid perriwig bores, every way unfit to herd with such bloods as us. It was therefore resolved that we should have private rooms . . . where we established ourselves into a roaring club, supped at eleven, after which we usually adjourned to Bow Street, Covent Garden, in which street there were then three most notorious Bawdy houses, all of which we took in rotation . . .

Hickey in the 1760s was then aged eighteen or nineteen, a typically idle young blade of the time.

Tom King's in Covent Garden, another hangout for rakes and ne'er-do-wells, was formerly a nighthouse. Its patrons were mainly 'gentlemen to whom beds are unknown'. Kept by his widow, Moll, after his death, Tom King's was constantly in trouble for being a disorderly house, a reputation confirmed by Smollett in *Roderick Random* in 1748. He mentions a visit by his hero, who 'accompanied Bragwell to Moll King's Coffee-house, where, after he had kicked half a dozen hungry whores, we left him asleep on a bench'. Moll's establishment opened at midnight as the taverns closed and stayed open until dawn. It was said that 'noblemen and the first beaux of the Court would go to her place in full dress and swords and bags [bagwigs] and in rich brocaded coats and walked and conversed with persons of every description'. Hogarth's *Morning* conjures that scene. Moll's, alas, went from bad to even worse. In nearby Drury Lane Wetherby's, coffee-house-cum-bordello, attracted the after-theatre crowd with prize-fights between bare-breasted women. At Maltby's, another of Hickey's haunts, things were more civilised: any country squire coming to town in the late eighteenth century would have 'a bed and doxy ready prepared for him'.

There was indeed no end to the enticements of the coffee-house. In Chelsea's Don Saltero's, mentioned in Fanny Burney's *Evelina*, the owner (plain James Salter) was far from reticent about his services: besides serving a very fine punch, he pulled teeth, bled customers (literally), played the violin and ran, simultaneously, a barber shop. In his spare time he wrote verse.

Neither the coffee-house nor the tea-house hurt the tavern; the former at first were considered to be for the effete, while the tavern's manly image kept faith with the nation's past and was increasingly culturally buttressed by the addition of gardens, the hosting of concerts and other entertainment. Around the mid-1700s there were some 450 taverns (excluding inns and brandy-shops and the countless ale-houses, still the main haunts of the thirsty hoi polloi). Pepys reckoned he had visited over a hundred of them – on business of course, though one may question that. Those with private rooms were aware of what sometimes went on in them. It was to the King's Head on the south side of the river, with views over the Lambeth Marsh, that our diarist took Betty, his light-of-love haberdasher; but he sported with Sarah the young barmaid at the Swan in Westminster Palace Yard, and flirted too with the girl at the Harp and Ball beside Charing Cross, taking them separately on outings to Tothill Fields (greenfield country between Westminster and Chelsea) – and a tavern where he would not be recognised. Boswell, less circumspect or more urgently propelled, favoured the Shakespeare's Head in Covent Garden, which had 'handsome' rooms. It also had at one time the great cook John Twigg, whose cuisine drew clubs to its private rooms. Turtle soup was Twigg's speciality and the tavern bought fifty turtles at a time. Its head waiter was also famous: he was Jack (Pimp) Harris, who organised the Whores' Club (meeting on Sundays) and compiled the *List* of Covent Garden Cyprians, a sort of Michelin guide to the flesh.

The post-Restoration capital had plenty of taverns that managed to live up to Dr Johnson's expectation. Like the coffee-houses they often had their individual appeal. Some hosted clubs of equal prestige: in the Strand's well-known Bear tavern in 1707 there was born the august Society of Antiquaries of London; the Spitalfields Mathematical Society was created out of the mutual interest of minds at the Monmouth Head tavern; and a meeting of noblemen at the Thatched House tavern in 1822 would found the Royal Academy of Music with George IV as its patron. At the Turk's Head tavern in Soho, in 1764, the famous Club (later the Literary Club) was formed by Johnson and Reynolds, meeting one evening a week at seven for supper. The spirited talk and argument went on into the small hours. Members were elected by ballot and many were black-balled, including the roué Lord Palmerston. At first the Club was for authors only, though this proviso soon went by the board.

It was to the Mitre in Fleet Street that the young Boswell in 1763 took Johnson on their first *tête-à-tête* and sat imbibing the great man's words and doubtless thinking few his equal. They dined well and drank port and talked until one o'clock in the morning. It would be the first of many such evenings in that curious and affecting relationship. The Mitre was an orthodox tavern that had earlier been a coffee-house. Johnson was happy there, as he was at the Essex Head (later the Edgar Wallace) in Essex Street where, in 1782, he founded Sam's Club, not on his own behalf but to boost trade for Sam Grieves the owner; he pressed Reynolds, the painter, to join, promising that 'the terms are lax and the expenses light; we meet three times a week, and he who misses forfeits twopence'. He was at home too at the Crown and Anchor along the Strand; here he and Boswell would often be seen in deep conversation. As the old sage said:

You are sure you are welcome; the more noise you make, the more trouble you give, the more good things you call for, the more welcome you are. No servants will attend you with the alacrity with which waiters do, who are incited by the prospect of an immediate reward in proportion as they please. No Sir, there is nothing which has yet been contrived by man by which so much happiness is produced, as by a good tavern or inn.

Though it mattered little to the thirsty men who drank in them, some of the capital's taverns bathed still in the historical limelight; some in their time had accommodated strange guests: on 29 January 1661, in what must have been its most macabre visit ever, the corpses of Oliver Cromwell, John Bradshaw and Henry Ireton were booked in for an overnight stay at the Red Lion in Red Lion Square – on their way to the gallows at Tyburn. Some, like their neighbourhoods, were less than salubrious: the Rose tavern, in Russell Street, where Boswell would meet his friends before the play at Drury Lane, and which sometimes entertained royalty, increasingly became a haunt for the most debauched and allegedly held midnight orgies. That said, it offered excellent food and laid on fine suppers for the nobility. For theatre folk it was a home from home. Patrons at the nearby Fleece were in much more dangerous company. It was, John Aubrey said, 'very unfortunate for homicides'.

For all that, it would be unfair to discount the taverns' social influence. In a gross and sensual age they were places of pleasure but they were also outposts for change in attitudes and manners and thinking, and for the men who advocated them – men of the law, of letters, of science and the arts as well as dangerous free-thinkers. More than the coffee-house perhaps they gave everyday life a necessary cohesion; though they were, and remained, also the hideouts of footpads and highwaymen, the city's sharpers and cut-purses and general lowlife. Some were simply dens of thieves, owned by criminal godfathers.

In those around Fleet Street about the start of the eighteenth century you could even get married in them, entering into a clandestine union 'solemnised' by some in-debt clergyman taking time out from the Fleet prison. They were above all at the centre of local events, and the main venues of celebration (as they would continue to be). And while welcoming the wits and luminaries of society, most managed to keep a foot in the earthier past with ratting contests, cock-fights, dogfights, bull- and bear-baiting – and crowd-pulling prize-fights.

From the second half of the nineteenth century, however, as with so much in society, they would finally face change. The emergence of the restaurant would hit both the taverns and the coffee-houses. Eating would become fashionable and decorous rather than functional and fun. Some would cut their cloth accordingly and follow suit, but most would slowly accept a less important role, leaving only a determined rearguard, taverns like the Crown and Anchor, Johnson's Mitre, the Thatched House, fashionable from the start and host to so many prestigious clubs, and the London tavern in Bishopsgate, famous for its vast dining room and splendid dinners and the balls it staged for the genteel middle classes. The tavern's pleasures and the entertainments it had provided would be carried into the future across a broader spectrum. Transitionally, its role would not have been negligible.

CHAPTER VI
The Palaces of Despair

Drink fuelled the pleasures of the madcap capital: the raw and bloody spectacle of the bull- or bear-baiting, the frenzied excitement of the cock-fight and the brutal encounters of the shadowy world of the prize-fighters – and heightened, no doubt, the sensual delights of the boudoir. It sharpened the aristocratic mind to insult and assuaged the gambler's guilt as the cards or the dice fell relentlessly against him. Women were made careless or acquiescent against the better core of their natures, and in the lower classes came to ruin with or without their consent.

Both sexes drank to excess: Georgiana, the young Duchess of Devonshire, just home from her honeymoon in 1774, raised eyebrows with her flighty behaviour at the house parties of the *bon ton*, the fast set – though there was then no great stigma to being drunk in public. In the taverns of Pitt the Younger's administration heavy drinking was the norm – even by the men entrusted with the running of the country. The Duchess's close friend Charles James Fox, an astute politician, was a persistent toper, as was the Member and poet Sheridan and Pitt himself. Pepys needed a stiffener, his 'morning draught', to start the day well, and frequently chided himself about his wine consumption. A good binge was, like an active sex life, thought to be good for a man's health, and few with the wealth to indulge needed a second bidding. Lords slid nightly under their lavishly laid tables and had to have their cravats loosened and be carried to bed by servants who saw nothing odd in such conduct.

The Regency blade and his father binged themselves on food, wine and women, opera and theatre, either singly or simultaneously. Sherry, port, punch, hock, sack (a dry white wine from Spain) and much else poured down noble gullets to bring on a nightly stupefaction. A (quart) pot of porter (a special brew) quenched the market porter's thirst at the end of his shift and took its name from him. Waiting in his cab-rank, the hackney coachman supped half-and-half (mild ale and bitter beer or ale and porter) and in the shady arbours of Vauxhall or

Ranelagh the young swain with expectations would ply his sweetheart with negus (sherry or port diluted with hot water and sweetened and spiced).

Drinking was an obsession, a culture in itself from which, for many, all the other pleasures flowed; the newly married Duke of Devonshire, a rather dull young dog as it happened (already with a mistress and child), spent only a few evenings in his bride's company before rejoining his boon companions of the bottle at the gaming tables. Drink indeed was seen as a challenge. Men boasted of their capacity and were admired for it, proposing and drinking toasts to the point of absurdity (the Whigs in port, the Tories in claret or champagne). The drinking of healths became so preposterous as to make ludicrous the very thing or person they lauded. The call for a toast could beggar the recipient's digestion as he was forced yet again to rest his cutlery and stay solemnly silent to hear the toaster's declamation and his merits advanced, and let his chop go chill while he fulsomely responded. Again, in a riven society, toasts took on a quite subtle and insidious role, on which a man – and more importantly his loyalties – might be judged. The Jacobite, for instance, had to be exceedingly wary of showing his hand and would salve his conscience by drinking the king's health from a glass raised over the water-jug, thus toasting the 'king over the water', the Old or the Young Pretender. Mistresses were acclaimed for all reasons, and in this the overwrought custom took a turn to the macabre when it became the fashion for the toaster to cut himself and mingle a little of his blood with the wine in which he sang the lady's name.

Capacity marked out the man of character, and his peers broke their health trying to keep up with him. Bottom, that envied quality, was as much a factor in drinking as it was in gaming or in duelling. Men of rank (and occasionally of achievement) would sink five or six bottles of port each at a single sitting, and even Dr Johnson was known to boast of having once been a three-bottle man without being the worse for it. The feat though was beyond Boswell, who admitted: 'A bottle of thick English port is a very heavy and very inflammatory dose.' The morning after, it was still 'boiling in my veins'. That great social toper Hickey, who regularly had to be carried to bed, preferred to be under the influence of claret but also enjoyed port. Seriously in his cups he would stick to 'claret and madeira' or, on a bender, run the gamut of 'malt liquors, cider, port wine and punch'. The effects of such carousal could indeed be pitiable, sometimes fatal: the braggadocio of the previous night's imbibing might have to be answered in the cold reality of the dawn on the duelling ground; the wanton turn of a card at faro or fall of the hazard dice might turn starkly to ruin in the morning light.

For the swaggering blades there was a penalty to pay for their privileged, indulgent lifestyle. They had to take pills and quacks' elixirs in prodigious doses to cure their hangovers and continue in the mad, merry whirl; few, as we have seen, could function before noon, and some at least must have disappointed the ladies to whom they were bound in liaisons. Sooner or later it all caught up with them in a legacy of cirrhosis, gout, diseased kidneys and other disabling ailments. And there was an irony, an anomaly at the heart of it all: their brawling and bad conduct often took place in settings of gracious Georgian elegance. In their drunkenness they were violently sick over the most expensive and opulent carpets and exquisitely brocaded sofas. Restraint was not part of the Regency scene. Nor was the period that preceded it at all a decorous one. It might be wrong to suggest that the capital of the Restoration and later times existed in a state of high insobriety – but it must have come close. Right through society drink was the great sustainer. For the poor underclass it was a pleasure in itself but, importantly, it was also an escape from the pressures of debt, the agonies of hunger or general despair, the tranquilliser that made life's dreadful uncertainties bearable. In a time of plague and disease, it has been said, life itself was a gamble, so people *lived* like gamblers, tempting the odds, cocking a snook at Providence. It may well have been so.

As with so much else, the Restoration loosened the bonds of a Puritanism that had cast its long shadow over the recreations of the hoi polloi, frowning on (and at times banning outright) such things as wakes, masques, dancing (of course) and all Sunday sports. Bull- and bear-baitings, popular Sunday outings, were prohibited; the old mystery plays were banned and even church organs came under suspicion and were consigned to taverns, where they were better appreciated. It is scarcely surprising that the reaction to the lifting of the yoke on enjoyment and the recovery of freedom under the Merry Monarch was so dire – and such that the king himself soon felt the need for a proclamation against drunkenness which inveighed against 'a set of men . . . who spend their time in taverns and tippling houses and debauchees, giving no other evidence of affection for us but in drinking our health . . .'. Here the monarch may himself have been on shaky ground for there was complaint from time to time of his own lack of positive leadership for the nation – or as Pepys heard it, being too concerned in 'imploying his lips and prick about the Court'. His condemnation was of the world of swells and ne'er-do-wells.

In a capital of unsafe water the multitude supped ale without exception morning, noon and night until tea took a hold and became a viable alternative in the home. Bread and ale were the staples that had toned the sinews of the nation, with the alehouse, a place of primitive comfort, and the tavern, a community hub. If their *habitués* were sometimes given to regrettable excess there was the excuse that ale was nutritional and necessary to the hard lives of the coal-heavers and porters and dockside labourers – of all those in fact who sweated and toiled in the cause of the capital's commerce.

Ale was an old English drink, made from malted grain and water. There came, however, a blurring of beverages (as there had been of the places that sold them) as the city's brewers fought for what today would be called market share. The honest Pepys, for instance, under business stress, occasionally turned to mum, a brew finessed from both oat malt and wheat malt and found at the Fleece in the City and several other places. It was heavily spiced, as were many drinks at that time. No snob, our diarist was also willing to sup Lambeth ale or Margate ale, which were really beers, both of them variants of a brew in which the distinctions would become sharper as beer became based on hops, a Dutch influence. Ale was drunk, even by invalids, and Eton's boys had a daily allowance. And so it might have continued but for a change of king. In 1688 the Glorious Revolution brought William of Orange to the throne. With him came gin, the Dutchman's drink. England was about to enter the spirituous future of the Gin Age; for many its pleasures would be quick – and calamitous. They would be the casualties of a craze that would bring the capital almost to its knees.

Protestant William was no sooner ensconced than he enacted laws to assist the distillation of the spirit, in order to curb the brandy trade with France, a Roman Catholic country. It might also have been to diminish the livelihood of smugglers, who were doing nicely out of bringing brandy into discreet south-coast landfalls – and it would certainly have done so had the smugglers not been resourceful men. They began smuggling gin instead (the trade had become almost respectable). The duty avoidance and therefore the rewards, however, were lower.

Distilling was about to have a field day. Anybody could set up, giving only ten days' notice to the excise service. From about 1710 consumption began to soar, nearly tripling in the next twenty-five years, mostly in the capital. Beer would find itself embattled. Worse still, gin would change the city's drinking patterns for long years to come. The corner alehouse, admittedly, was spartan and sometimes sordid in the service it provided but it had a kind of bleak humanity.

The gin-shop or gin palace that would rise in its place – or at least alongside it – was something else, a citadel for the exploitation of human souls. It would take its adherents spiralling into the lower depths. The poor, alas, were not deterred.

Gin was cheap, an instant solace. It sold for a penny a quarter (quart-pint). As the famous saying went, you could get drunk for only a penny, dead drunk for tuppence. It was easy oblivion and it was available everywhere since, initially, it needed no licence (such was King William's perfidy). As well as in inns, it was reckoned, conservatively, to be obtainable in back rooms, dram-shops, barber-shops, tailors', haberdashers', shoemakers', off street barrows, in bordellos and even in prisons. In the courtyard 'village' of the King's Bench prison, thronging with life and including a community of tradesmen of every description, there were said to be thirty shops selling 120 gallons a week. (Essentially a debtors' jail, it was quite the best in the capital in which to be incarcerated. Those with rich friends dined in some extravagance and drank copiously; there was no pleasure that could not be bought.)

Taxes on beer inhibited competition from both strong and small beers (the latter made from the dregs and a weaker brew). The 1740s indeed would see beer eclipsed as the national drink. One powerful point in gin's favour was that, unlike wine, its supply was uninterrupted by the odd war here or there. Soon its consumption was an epidemic out of control. By 1739 London would have more than 8,500 spirits outlets compared with around 6,000 alehouses. Successive Gin Acts utterly failed to stem the tide. The authorities banned street sales, the sale by distillers to unlicensed premises, or direct sales by the distillers themselves, and increased licence fees, allied to contravention penalties of whipping, imprisonment and transportation – without effect. All that happened was that gin went underground, often dangerously adulterated as Ladies' Delight or Cuckold's Comfort, Madam Geneva, Strip-me-Naked or, with some piquancy, as King Theodore of Corsica (the 'brand' names, if not the drink, were exotic). A mid-eighteenth-century survey found that in the City one house in fifteen was a gin-shop; one house in eight in Westminster; and one house in five in Holborn.

An Act of 1736, recognising at last that drinking was making a large section of the population 'unfit for labour and business, debauching their morals and inciting them to perpetuate all manner of vices', and that the situation threatened the 'destruction of the Kingdom', increased the licensing fee (and the penalty for flouting it) – and led to riots. Again the product was doctored to escape the legislative net. It was spiced or mixed with wine. More new brand names were coined and so-called 'pharmacists' put the drink into coloured prescription bottles with the instruction that it should be taken so many times daily. Informers reporting infringements (at £5 a tip-off) were in danger and most, perhaps wisely, kept their mouths shut. Three were stoned to death and a further two were otherwise killed by the enraged mob. The magistrates they might have told failed to act for fear of their lives.

In Parliament Lord Lonsdale made an impassioned plea against the spirit: 'whoever shall pass along the streets will find wretchedness stretched along the pavement, insensible and motionless, and only removed by the charity of passengers from the danger of being crushed by carriages or trampled by horses, or strangled by filth in the common sewers . . .' (Actually, dyed-in-the-wool gin-shops did the decent thing and considerately supplied straw on which their paralytic customers could sleep it off. Men, women and children lay in insensible promiscuity till they recovered enough to go in search of funding for a further binge.) Lord Lonsdale continued with his dire warning: 'The use of distilled liquor impairs the fecundity of the human race . . . These women who riot in this poisonous debauchery are quickly disabled from bearing children . . .'

The shocking reality is depicted in Hogarth's *Gin Lane*, arguably his most disturbing print, almost over the top. At the time the taste for gin was at its height and it was drunk at the rate of two pints a week for every man, woman and child in the capital. It had led a sharp decline into the gutter of existence, encouraging robbery, vice and, to a disturbing degree, disorder in the streets. Hogarth, born in the unsavoury precincts of London's Smithfield, was well qualified for his task, though his work was then deeply undervalued and his pictures simply labelled as 'conversation pieces'. He was rebelling against the so-called history painting of his age, just as Gay rebelled from the diet of Italian high opera, with a brush that stroked his subjects with a savage humanity. Frequently and cruelly, he caught them in mid-spree, his rakes unbuttoned, his women undone.

He was not, it seems, an amiable man but he was clearly horrified – and fascinated – by human folly. His work, largely ignored by the privileged classes, as engravings reached a wider audience, sold as plain or coloured prints and displayed in inns, workplaces and sometimes in the home. He explained his aims: 'I . . . wished to compose pictures on canvas, similar to representations on the stage. I have endeavoured to treat my subject as a dramatic writer: my picture is my stage, and men and women my players who, by means of certain actions and gestures, are to exhibit a dumb show.' He gives us an astonishing series of social

Hogarth's famous Gin Lane *points up the horrific human cost of the Gin Age.* (Billie Love Historical Collection)

narratives about a society shamelessly capitulating to pleasure. His settings are real, his interiors *à la mode*, but his study is lowlife. His *Harlot's Progress* shows a pretty Drury Lane whore rising from a dishevelled bed about noon, *en déshabillé* after a night of pleasure bestowed on the bed's other occupant, now long gone.

Gin and sin were bedfellows. As Hogarth worked in 1751, consumption had reached a figure of 8,500,000 gallons. Henry Fielding in his *Enquiry into the Causes of the late Increase in Robbers* of the same year said of the pernicious spirit: 'I have great reason to think it is the principal sustenance (if it may be so called) of more than an hundred thousand people in this metropolis. Many of these wretches there are who swallow pints of this poison within twenty-four hours, the dreadful effects of which I have the misfortune every day to see, and smell too.' Fielding (1707–54) had just recently been appointed the magistrate for Middlesex and Westminster.

Change would come more quickly than he may have thought, when an Act of that year hit the gin barons where it hurt most – by breaking the credit cycle on which the distilling industry functioned, and making its debts no longer recoverable by law. By 1760 gin drinking had been dramatically reduced – to just over 2,000,000 gallons. Little though anyone suspected it then, it was to be only an interregnum. The Second Gin Age was yet to come. It would take the ethos of drinking into a new era.

By the 1830s gin had acquired a new image, a brassy confidence. According to Dickens, in *Sketches by Boz*, a kind of shop-front mania struck the capital's thoroughfares. In his view the gin-shops in and near Drury Lane, Holborn, St Giles, Covent Garden and Clare Market, none of them highly reputable districts, were 'the handsomest in London'. The gin palace was something new, unlike the inn, the tavern, or the coffee-house – sophisticated, and undoubtedly hi-tech. It was glitzy, a wonder of glass and brass. Brilliantly lit, it dazzled like the fair. All it lacked was humanity. 'Through the doors of these infernal dens of drunkenness and mischief,' observed the novelist, 'crowds of miserable wretches were pouring in that they might drink and die.' They boomed, paradoxically, these garish palaces in the parishes of the deprived, nirvanas for the crushed and defeated, with their customers now including the better-off.

The gin palace was a one-room, usually one-floor structure, utterly commercially functional. Its barmaids were 'showily-dressed damsels with large necklaces', dispensing the spirits and 'compounds'. Dickens again: 'Washerwomen wander in for their half-quartern of gin and peppermint. Ladies take their

Hogarth's Beer Street *is a potent argument in favour of the healthier home brew.* (Billie Love Historical Collection)

The disparate and despairing society of those who sought their solace in the gin palace. (Museum of London)

rum srub [lemon juice with sugar and a dash of rum, only mildly alcoholic]'. Dickens, then a young reporter on the *Morning Chronicle*, is understanding as he writes, in 1835:

> Gin drinking is a great vice in England, but poverty is a greater; and until you can cure it, or persuade a half-famished wretch not to seek relief in the temporary oblivion of his own misery, with the pittance which, divided among his family, would just furnish a morsel of bread for each, gin-shops will increase in number and splendour.

They did. For such wretches the brightly lit plate-glass window of the gin palace provided an overwhelming temptation, shining forth into the grimy street, a beacon in the night. Inside, all was wonder: 'A bar of French-polished mahogany, elegantly carved, extends the whole width of the place; and there are two side-aisles of great casks, painted green and gold, enclosed within a light brass rail . . . Beyond the bar is a lofty and spacious saloon, full of the same enticing vessels, with a gallery running round it, equally well furnished. On the counter, in addition to the usual spirit apparatus, are two or three little baskets of cakes and biscuits. . .' All was slick and uncaring; from its door the gin palace's customers had nowhere to stagger but the gutter, and the scandal of Sunday drinking was exacerbated by the habit of laying the seriously inebriated in the gutter (and into the path of the God-fearing church-goers) during the time of divine worship, when drinking was banned. The solution came in 1839 with an Act that shut the capital's drinking shops from Saturday midnight until noon on Sunday.

Yet the phenomenon of the gin palace, whatever its dubious pleasures, would leave something positive in its wake. It made the old alehouse or public bar look to its image. That legacy can still be seen. The humanity and good fellowship would return, in time. And who would not recognise in Dickens's 'showily-dressed damsels', bangled and bejangled and sometimes teasingly *décolletée*, the attractively coiffed barmaid of today's English pub. Pepys would have adored her.

CHAPTER VII

The Good, the Bad and the *Risqué*

Out of the tavern and alehouse came the music-hall. It was a boisterous infant; it fed from the same roistering roots as the tavern itself and the broad, often bawdy, humour of its folk-base. It was popular culture for the masses; it touched ordinary lives, those of the countless thousands who hummed its songs and fully understood its sometimes salacious humour. Its performers, almost without exception, were of the people and were widely loved by their audiences because of it. They were the great celebrities of their time, a gallery of famous names that still strike a chord in the mind: stars such as Marie Lloyd, Flossie Forde, Dan Leno, Little Tich (all of 4 feet 6 inches tall), the mighty panto dame Herbert Campbell (at 19 stone), Vesta Tilley, Harry Lauder and so many more. The unruly infant would eventually embrace a wide spectrum of entertainment – anything that would pull in the patrons: singers, dancers, highwire and trapeze acts like Leotard (who thrilled thousands and left us his name on an exercise garment), fire-eaters, jugglers, illusionists, *et al*. It was hugely patriotic, closer in war or crisis than any other medium to the hearts of the people.

It had many venues, many levels, places and palaces where performers nightly faced the bitter examination of their impolite audiences. Unlike play actors, they met their audiences head on; it was not the bear-pit, but it ran it close and only the tough survived. Unlike the theatre, the entertainer was only a part of the picture, competing for attention above the buzz of conversation, the clink of glasses and cutlery, and the all-pervasive sound of waiters as they scuffled between the tables. Its audience's attention was not stretched, nor were the demands on the intellect intense.

Its stars were hard-bitten but also hard-working, sweating over the songs they would introduce into their repertoire, and playing perhaps four halls in an evening, dashing by brougham, as Marie Lloyd regularly did, from say the Pavilion (in Piccadilly) to the Middlesex (Covent Garden), to the Tivoli (in the Strand) and then out to the Canterbury (in distant Lambeth) all in the space of two or three hours.

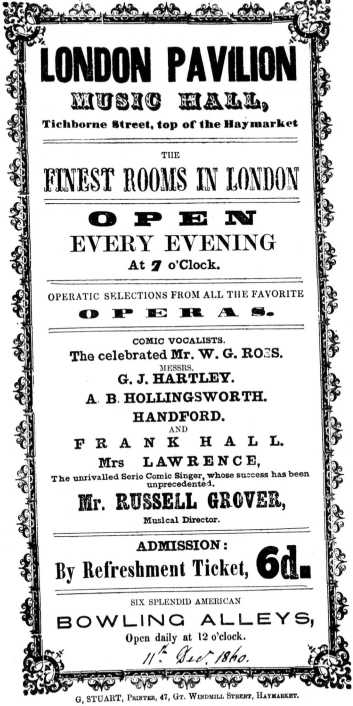

A typical bill of varieties, that of the old Pavilion music-hall in 1860. (Victoria & Albert Museum Picture Library)

With the years the venues they played had grown more showy and opulent, glitzy palaces that added colour and romance to their patrons' grey lives. Their names, as they say, were legion: the Palace, the Trocadero, Collins's, the Oxford and the Metropolitan, to name but a few, not forgetting the famous Empire and its great rival the grand Alhambra, which ran into a little difficulty when a dancer lifted her leg too far. Most were the result of the kind of social evolution typified by Covent Garden's Great Mogul tavern, which at first set aside a room for concerts, then built a hall (the Old Mo), which became the Middlesex music-hall and was finally rebuilt as the New Middlesex. The Canterbury had claimed the site of the Canterbury Arms, a country alehouse; the Tivoli took over the Tivoli Beer Gardens. Between them the halls robbed the circus, the fair and the pleasure gardens in the sacred name of entertainment. Polite and bland they were not, and their pedigree was far from unimpeachable, their social acceptability sometimes just this side of the brothel's.

Specifically they emerged from the alehouse parlour, the tavern supper room and the raffish nightspots of late-night London, such as the Cider Cellars in Maiden Lane, opened in 1730 especially for the sale of cider (thought to be less harmful than other intoxicants). It had tables and a platform and, as a haunt for 'frolic-loving men' of all classes, was essentially a music-hall ahead of its time. The free-and-easies of the pub's back room had always been rough, all-male occasions, gatherings ostensibly of singers – budding baritones, tentative tenors and men of good voice who forsook their respective daytime callings to shed a little of that respectability and assemble once or twice a week to entertain themselves with songs and verse, calling themselves the Harmonies of This or the Warblers of That. They needed a table and chairs and, importantly, pots of ale, for singing was a thirsty business. The chairman was appointed from their midst or the role might be assumed by the landlord himself, in his own best interests. Others were advised to join – by the publican. A piano might be provided if it was merited, even a small platform raised in a corner for performers, who might include 'room singers' and other entertainers, who did their evening itineraries like trams on a timetable.

Forward-looking pubs, sensing profit, built on concert rooms (the saloon), grandly got up, enabling them to raise the price of the drinks and perhaps charge a small fee for admission – catching the new tide as easily as they discarded the declining fashion for pleasure gardens. Luxury, or the appearance of it, was a prerequisite for any self-respecting tavern: the supper tables came marble-topped;

the chandelier that spangled its brilliance on the company was crystal. The songs, though, remained bawdy, not to say obscene, in content and as the evening went on they invariably took a turn for the worse. It was said of Hemmingway's infamous Mile End Saloon in 1840:

> On Tuesday evening at this house
> Is held what's termed a free and easy;
> The Chairman's like the fatted boy
> But much more dirty – far more greasy.
> In filthy songs and beastly toasts
> The snobby crew dispel their cares;
> And modest females creep by stealth
> To listen on the first-floor stairs.

Up in the City at the end of a business day the Londoner of rather more style and pretension would prefer to take himself (but not his wife) to the relative refinement and culture of glee-singing at Evans's Music and Supper Rooms; or perhaps to the crowded bonhomie of Wilton's. Evans's – later Evans's Late Joys – was a halfway house in the development of the halls. In the 1850s, after the conversion of its dining room, it was in the top list of the capital's song and supper rooms. Dickens, Thackeray and Landseer were among those who shuffled down the steep steps to its grill-room to join friends in a feast of chops and steaks, and to swig stout or ale. It was housed in a once-grand mansion in Covent Garden and patronised by the wealthy and bohemian. A journalist, obviously of the latter category, described the establishment:

> Ladies are not admitted, except on giving their names and addresses, and then only enjoy the privilege of watching the proceedings from behind a screen. The whole of the performances are sustained by the male sex, and an efficient choir of men and boys sing glees, ballads, madrigals, and selections from operas, the accompaniments being supplied on the piano and harmonium . . .

Our informant plugs it quite shamelessly, perhaps in the hope of free refreshment: 'The performances commence at eight o'clock; and we recommend Evans's to the notice of steady young men who admire a high class of music, see no harm in a good supper, but avoid theatres and the ordinary run of music-halls.'

Mr W.C. Evans's rooms seated eight hundred at table, and meals were served during the performances, which continued until two in the morning. Such segregation, however, was not the rule at the City Road's sometimes controversial Eagle tavern, with its splendidly appointed saloon. It was here, in 1885, round the corner from her home, and where her father was a part-time barman, that Marie Lloyd, just fifteen (and while still Matilda Wood) graced the professional boards for the first time.

The chairman's job was to keep the show on the road, whipping up the audience's enthusiasm and managing the turns of those whose stage until then might have been the street paving stones, or whose living was found travelling the fairs and church feasts of the city and surrounding countryside. His gavel ruled and, ostentatiously, he took to wearing evening dress, as did the professional singers. He drank copiously and smoked his cigar furiously as an example to others, since it all had to be paid for by the sale of the drinks – a condition that endured for as long as the old halls reigned.

Something else did not change: the colour of the songs. As the evening wore on and the liquor took hold, these would become increasingly blue. Early stars of the music-hall such as George Leybourne and the Great (Alfred) Vance, who both lived the good life of wine, women and song, were noted for the indelicacy of their material. And there was yet another factor that would not really alter: the mood, the atmosphere, the moral tone of the music-hall. It was defiantly irreverent, with comedy and laughter its abiding characteristics. It was entertainment tailored to the intellect of the thousands of audiences who crowded into it down the years and whose outlook on life was earthy and realistic, with a penchant for the *risqué*.

Its impresarios might try to elevate its appeal, to move it upmarket to draw in the genteel. There was latterly the love of ostentation, a preoccupation with pseudo-elegance and gilt, with swagging and expensive drapes and seductive comfort to widen the eye in wonder and enhance the experience. It was a struggle mainly in vain. Nothing could 'rescue' it from its roots. Even in the heyday of the halls in the later-1800s, its raw culture remained precariously on the cusp. What they did succeed in doing was moving the music-hall into the realm of mainstream entertainment. It became an institution, as was the theatre for the fashionable classes. Unlike the theatre, however, it had a social focus. People popped in for a drink at one of the bars (like their promenades, outside the auditorium), or stayed just long enough to hear an appealing song or a favourite performer.

The men who ran them, like the great halls themselves, were mostly larger than life, gregarious, big-hearted, flamboyant dressers – in hock frequently to the brewers – who moved easily in a world of plush luxury and bad taste amid the aroma of cigars and expensive women. Proprietors and managers had to be tuned in to their public's taste – or better still, be ahead of it, juggling the bill accordingly. Their special skill was in putting together their menu of variety; when the appeal of comic singers and serious balladeers slumped, they hastened for Blondin or Leotard or a strong man or other special acts to boost the box office. Again, at such times of crisis there was a tendency towards the louche, always an unfailing backstop; no music-hall manager ever went bankrupt by under-estimating his patrons' interests.

It is hardly coincidental that the scandalous can-can, the rage of Paris, was launched on the music-halls from the stage of the famous Alhambra in Leicester Square on the shapely legs of Finette, the painter Whistler's former Creole mistress. The writer Mark Twain had seen the dance in the French capital and concluded that the technique was to dance 'as wildly, as noisily, as furiously as you can; expose yourself as much as possible if you are a woman; and kick as high as you can'. It was first danced on stage in England on Boxing Day 1867. The setting was the Lyceum Theatre, the production *Harlequin, Cock Robin and Jenny Wren*, a panto by W.S. Gilbert (who had not yet met Sullivan). The then Prince of Wales adored it (which comes as no surprise) and so did *The Times* – although, in a splendid display of newspaper hypocrisy, it concernedly advised theatregoers to an 1869 production of *Orpheus* at St James's Theatre to leave before the can-can scene.

The dance led the Alhambra into trouble, however, a year later. Ballet, then a bit of a maverick, also found a home at this music-hall – as at several others. At the Alhambra they put it on with some style – more that of the Bluebell Girls than we would now expect. There the best can-can kicker of them all was Sarah Wright, *alias* High Kick Sarah or Wiry Sal, who lifted her leg too far while facing the audience – a feat she repeated several times, to repeated applause. Her kick cost the music-hall its licence and the threat of closure, a situation retrieved when the music-hall put itself under the Lord Chamberlain's authority to stage plays. At their tables the Alhambra's patrons could feast on oysters (a shilling a dozen with bread and butter), chops, stewed cheese and (of course) steaks. The drinks included such fearsome concoctions as the 'locomotive' and the 'mouth-tickler'.

An attempt to give the halls a better image had begun as early as 1858 when Charles Morton, the man they called 'the father of the halls', custom-built his Canterbury Hall in Lambeth. For the first time the architecture of the building

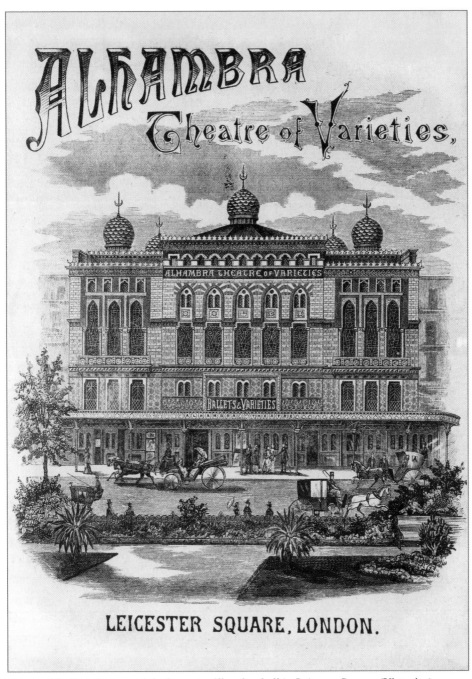

Scene of the high-kick scandal: the great Alhambra hall in Leicester Square. (Victoria & Albert Museum Picture Library)

Trapeze performers fly through the air over the heads of the Alhambra's audience. (Victoria & Albert Museum Picture Library)

was consciously considered in relation to the entertainment it would provide. Morton believed, perhaps mistakenly:

> The magnificent and brilliantly lighted hall in which the Concert is held exercises no little influence upon the minds of the audience. There is a

harmony between it and entertainment which produces a beauty of ensemble more easily felt than described.

Morton meant well. In trying to lift the tone he had given the Canterbury a supper room, 'a fine art gallery' and a billiards room. His music-hall would accommodate 1,500. Sixpence bought a table seat, ninepence entrance to the gallery. Three years later in 1861 he would take music-hall up to town, opening the Oxford in Oxford Street near its junction with Tottenham Court Road. It rose on the site of the Boar and Castle, an old galleried inn, and would be ravaged by fire on several occasions.

The music-hall had come a long way from the squalid back parlour room: the Oxford was vast and airy, a great, balconied room with buffet bars, large promenades – and access through its own grand portico. It was not quite virgin territory: Evans's had been up there since 1855; Weston's since 1857; the Pavilion (the first of the many) since 1859; and the Alhambra since earlier that year. Weston's music-hall, in what was formerly Holborn tavern (and rebuilt in 1887 to house 2,500) would see many of the great names strutting their stuff on its boards, among them Lottie Collins, Ada Reeve, Dan Leno of the piercing eyes and enormous mouth, and the coster comedian Albert Chevalier. It would become the Holborn Empire. The London Pavilion in Piccadilly Circus was the Black Horse Inn's song and supper room until it became a music-hall in 1859 (a new Pavilion would be built in 1885). In Leicester Square there would be joined the battle of the giants. The Empire would rise from the failed spectre of the Royal London Panorama, a theatre at first but later in 1887 making the transition to music-hall with the emphasis on ballet. Its longer-established rival the Alhambra, itself a conversion of the Royal Panopticon of Science and Art, inhabited a building in the Moorish style, which had opened in 1858 as a circus. A visit from Queen Victoria and her family gave it the push to become a full-blown music-hall. It kept faith with the past though, featuring Blondin (just back from walking across Niagara Falls on a tightrope) and also Leotard, the original 'daring young man on the trapeze' who did, as the song says, fly over the heads of the audience 'with the greatest of ease'.

The halls' antecedents were indeed varied and picaresque. The Trocadero Palace opened in 1882 as a music-hall after being closed down as the Argyle Rooms (not the original) because of their notoriety. The Tivoli, built in 1890 for £300,000, wooing patrons with its restaurant and private dining rooms, rose to

Canterbury Hall's attractions, revealed on a programme cover of 1888. (Victoria & Albert Museum Picture Library)

success under the immortal Morton before closing in 1914. But perhaps the most exotic of all the capital's haunts was the Surrey Gardens music-hall built in 1856 in the Surrey Zoological Gardens to the plans of Horace Jones, the man who designed the new Smithfield meat market. Like the latter, it was an architect's nightmare but riveting to the eye. It could seat ten thousand or more, but whether it ever did so is open to doubt.

Round the capital's central cluster there would coalesce a whole galaxy of halls, whose fringe locations did not necessarily mirror their standing: Collins's in Islington Green (where Sam Collins sang his Irish songs and died young), the Metropolitan in the Edgware Road, Crowder's in Greenwich, Wilton's in Stepney, the Winchester in Southwark, Gatti's in Westminster Bridge Road (where Harry Lauder made his London debut in 1900), McDonald's in Hoxton (in Marie Lloyd's home patch), the beloved Britannia, also in Hoxton, the Panorama in Shoreditch, which also had the London (known as the Sod's Opera, for such was the fickleness of its audience), the Cambridge in Bishopsgate – all of them perhaps more loyal to the tradition of the music-hall. The halls' charges reflected their status: in 1870 a seat at the Alhambra would cost from sixpence to five shillings, with the luxury of a box costing one to two guineas. Wilton's out in the East, a decade earlier, was charging from fourpence to eightpence for a seat, with a box at a shilling.

By 1870 London had around forty music-halls worth the name, three-quarters of them classified as large (i.e., with a capacity of up to two thousand). Most were marginally respectable and would strive, with occasional lapses, to remain so with little encouragement from their audiences. From their stages entertainers like Marie Lloyd ('A Little Bit of What You Fancy Does You Good'), Lottie Collins ('Ta-ra-ra-boom-de-ay'), Florrie Forde ('Old Bull and Bush') and Albert Chevalier ('My Old Dutch') would launch hundreds of songs and countless quips. But there were also 'low' music-halls where the patrons were shifty and the gags ran regularly to the bawdy.

By then hall design was again on the move. Like the gin palace, the variety palace would acquire a décor intended to dazzle the senses. There was, often with brewers' money, a trend towards even greater opulence, a florid extravagance; gilt and ornamentation were increased, the bars were mahogany and the controversial promenades made even more spacious and inviting. Footlights began to feature, and now the comedians dressed appropriately to play their characters. (Charles Whittle, who first took 'Let's All Go Down the Strand' on stage, appeared in top hat, morning coat, pinstripe trousers, patent leather shoes and spats, as the absolute toff.) But the traditional era was coming to a close as the halls began to think 'theatre'.

At first space-taking tables would be reduced in number and combined with ordinary seating. The London Pavilion in its rebuild of the mid-1880s would have cinema-type tip-up seats with (importantly) small shelves for patrons' drinks. The show was twice-nightly and the lights were lowered as the turns came on stage. Quietly and somewhere along the way the flamboyant, spittle-spraying chairman would be discarded. The proscenium arch and orderly rows of seats, generally eclipsing the tables (and waiters), would take the music-halls into the next century.

Yet the music-hall of that late nineteenth-century heyday still buried its tap-root in the culture of the lower classes. Comic singers, accused of lowering the tone, were only giving the patrons what they had come for. Its unquestioned star (of course) was Marie Lloyd, singer, comedienne and step-dancer. The American poet T.S. Eliot said of her that '[she] was the greatest music-hall artiste of her time in England, she was also the most popular . . . She was the queen of the halls.' It was, he said, 'her capacity for expressing the soul of the people' that made her unique. Sarah Bernhardt, the celebrated actress, regarded Marie as the 'greatest living comedienne', and C.B. Cochran, in tribute, perceptively said of her: 'The delicacy of her indelicacies was exquisite.' And the writer Arnold Bennett, after watching her at the Tivoli in the Strand, concluded: 'All her songs were varieties of the same theme of sexual naughtiness.' Others came close, singing from the same song-sheet.

And that, in essence, was the dilemma that dogged the music-hall. Its material was unsophisticated, its patter improper. (Those old-timers and rivals George Leybourne and Alfred Vance sang songs that would have been at home in the Coal Hole in the Strand or in the Cider Cellars, the once-fashionable late-night sanctuaries where the all-male company sang such pornographic numbers as 'He'll no more Grind Again' and 'The Bower that stands in Thigh Lane'.) The songs were often trite, inane, unfinished; some implied criticism of the upper crust. It mattered little really, since they were firstly vehicles to take the entertainer on stage. Everything depended on the artist's charisma. Delivery was vital – as it still is. Marie, it is said, could make the most innocent-sounding lyric suggestive with a flash of the eye, the twitch of her skirt – or the inflection in her voice. Her rapport with a knowing Cockney audience was complete – a telepathy

A performer strives to be heard over the buzz and clatter of the Old Mogul music-hall. (Billie Love Historical Collection)

of the naughty thought that could leave the punters ecstatic but sadly left Marie excluded from the first Royal Command performance for the music-hall. And most certainly it was that exclusivity of appeal that worried the London County Council's Theatres and Music-hall Committee when it took over the licensing of the halls from the courts in 1889.

The formidable Puritan campaigner Mrs Ormiston Chant was sniffily dismissive of music-hall audiences. The halls, she said, supplied a 'class of entertainment to suit people, who, out of sheer tiredness of the brain or want of a superior education, could hardly appreciate a play . . . The music-hall caters for people who have a small proportion of brains . . .'. It was an incautious comment, unfair to those whose lives were lived in the hard, grinding world of work; lives never allowed the chance to aspire to something better. The committee's John McDougall (a Methodist rapidly rechristened as Muckdougall) was more constructive:

It is possible for a music-hall entertainment to be conducted as to be harmless. There is no necessity to surround these amusements with great temptations to drink. The two things might be kept entirely separate. It is unfair that people should . . . have their moral sense stolen by the temptations by which they are surrounded when they get inside.

McDougall, who also wanted song censorship, was reported in the *Era*, the industry's trade paper, in 1890. What he wanted was indeed feasible – only it would no longer have been the music-hall. And it was only the sale of liquor, as we have seen, that made the whole thing viable. But he may have had a point about the songs. Those spicier verses added as the original became familiar and boring (to both artiste and patrons) ran head on into Victorian rectitude and were, to McDougall's mind, 'beyond description'.

The halls had another embarrassing problem, one that was grist to the Puritan mill. Predictably, the ladies of the night paraded their wares outside – and frequently inside – these cathedrals of the suggestive song and the nudge-nudge patter, notably at the central Alhambra and the Empire. In the 1880s, as the infamous old night hang-outs ceased to function under the new morality, the *Spectator*, ever sympathetic, commented:

These poor creatures are rigidly excluded from every place where they would naturally take shelter. The recognised and regular haunts of vice have been suppressed by energetic action . . . of parochial authorities, and as the demand for prostitution still exists . . . the women who supply that demand are driven to frequent these places of entertainment.

It was claimed that by 10 p.m. Leicester Square was 'crowded by fast young men and loose young women attracted by these music-halls'. A particularly popular haunt was the square's Empire. Behind the circle, in its lush lounge and promenade, with dimmed lighting and comfortable couches, allegedly there loitered ladies at the top end of their profession – women fastidious about who enjoyed their favours. It is all said to have been discreet, no more than a slight nod of the head, perhaps only a glance of understanding, and although the halls strenuously denied that soliciting took place, the Empire was finally compelled to face the dilemma: it could have its licence renewed only if its lounge could be 'neutralised'.

Its magnificent promenade was ordered to be screened off – a measure that so incensed the young bloods about town that they mounted an attack on the reopening night in 1894 and tore down the 'improvements', claiming that they were liberating and reuniting the temples of Venus and Bacchus. One of them was a precocious young rake by the name of Winston Churchill. Typically, he made a speech. The Oxford too got a magisterial slap on the wrist 'for women being admitted without men', the obvious conclusion being drawn. At the Alhambra, no doubt unfairly, spinster ladies found themselves denied tickets to the promenade and nobody could quite tell them why.

If the first subtle breakaway from the traditional music-hall began with the restyled London Pavilion in the 1880s, it reached its apogee with the opening of such theatres as the London Hippodrome (1900), which made history with its water shows, and the Coliseum (1904), with its grand Edwardian interior. The variety bill was finally made respectable. When the now far-famed London Palladium, after housing Hengler's circus, came on the scene in 1910 as the last word in luxury, its future lay in staging revue extravaganzas. It had been a long trajectory from pothouse to palace, but finally *The Times*, so solicitous in averting the gaze of its readers from the quivering thighs of the can-can, felt able to say that the crowds of the halls had vastly improved, with entire families in the audience where, in the days of the supper room, it would have been mainly men 'accompanied by the least creditable of their female acquaintances'.

CHAPTER VIII
The Playhouse and the People

Pepys's grand passion was the playhouse; he loved its atmosphere, its air of decadence, its nubile, saucy actresses, often neglecting both wife and naval duties to attend it. But it was not the theatre as we know it today; in the post-Restoration period it was more of a flesh market, a place for casual pick-ups. The opera house, it was claimed, had the most expensive ladies, but the playhouse ran it close. In the pit, wrote one guide, sat 'the Judges, Wits and Censurers . . . in common with these sat the Squires, Sharpers, Beaus, Bullies and Whores'. Pepys watched with more than passing interest the ladies parading for companions of the night: painted doxies in 'black satin and rouge'; the demi-monde, some of them stunning beauties, their favours already spoken for, though society rakes would visit their boxes anyway to pay their ardent addresses in the hope of some future assignation. At the Theatre Royal, the diarist, besotted, sat where he could observe the 'pretty Castlemaine'. The poet Dryden, who lived nearby in Long Acre, was explicit about the theatre's alternative function:

> The *Play-house Puncks*, who in a loose undress
> Each night receive some Cullie's soft address;
> Reduc'd perhaps to the last poor *half-crown*
> A tawdry *Gown* and *Petticoat* put on
> Go to the House where they demurely sit
> Angling for *Bubbles* in the noisy *Pit* . . .
> The *Play-house* is their place of *Traffick*, where
> Nightly they sit to sell their *Rotten-ware*:
> Though done in silence and without a *Cryer*
> Yet he that bids the most is still the Buyer:
> For while he nibbles at her *Am'rous Trap*
> She gets the *Mony* but he gets the *Clap*.

Gay's The Beggar's Opera *with its bawds and highwaymen changed theatrical taste.* (Billie Love Historical Collection)

Brothel-keepers routinely took their newest recruits (innocents) to the theatre so that their clients could look them over. In their finery, hired for the night, the young girls lined up in the lobby of Drury Lane with their procuresses, quite distressing Hazlitt, then turning a penny as a play critic.

The Merry Monarch too was keen on the theatre – and particularly on its actresses. But despite the new patronage of royalty the playhouse was not a decorous place. Nor were its productions morally uplifting, existing as they did alongside the rawer and cruder pleasures of the city. Evelyn, a deeply religious man, was not a fan: taken to a performance in 1668 of the *Evening Lover*, he found it 'very prophane so as it affected me to see how the stage was degenerated and poluted by the licentious times'. John Gay's musical play *The Beggar's Opera*, like most productions of the time, also reflected that licentiousness – and all its emptiness and cynicism. In that society, as we have seen, there was almost a conspiracy against decency and idealism: a decadence ran through the ranks of the ruling classes, masters, as a matter of course debauching their maids (or at least making the attempt); ladies, having dutifully given their lords a male heir, feeling free to take lovers for their pleasure – or to fill the ennui of their lives.

The English were not then a nation subservient to the queue. People got hurt in the mêlée just trying to get into the playhouse. Ladies sent their servants to face the crush and buy tickets – and occupy the seats until they themselves arrived. Plays were changed by the day and music was played between the opening of the doors at four or five and the start of the performance at six, presumably in the hope of keeping minds off the idea of vandalism. Pepys was charmed by the interlude turns and 'openers' who would eventually be more at home in the music-hall. The Scottish traveller-writer John Macky, between the acts, was more 'diverted by viewing the Beauties of the Audience'. Great comfort was not an option. Seats were backless. The rowdy pit was second dearest, the boxes, obviously, the most expensive. Those coming in to see the last act were admitted at a cut rate. The stage, jutting beyond the boxes, reminded the actors of their vulnerability. They were regularly intimidated, and for their protection a row of iron railings extended along the front of the stage, with bouncers in attendance at the sides to discourage unwelcome backstage invasion. Even so they were frequently jeered and threatened by the rude audiences of the time, a mix of the fashionable rich and (in the gallery) their attendant footmen and the capital's apprentices and general riff-raff.

Disapproval of a performance was at least pointed, and sometimes physical. Insults flew, along with orange peel and even rotten oranges. It was not a crime to show violent displeasure; such protest was not illegal. It was simply that the theatre was a rough, unsavoury place – so contentious in fact that Queen Anne in 1712 made an attempt to curb such unseemly behaviour, issuing a Proclamation against Vice, which encompassed the capital's playhouses and players, along with brothels and gaming houses. The measure had little success; it was indicative, however, of the actor's standing and of an attitude that would persist. Governments were constantly suspicious of plays and their motives and had reason to be, for some playhouses had a policy of deliberately taunting the administration – until Robert Walpole's parliament brought them to heel under the Lord Chamberlain's scrutiny in the Playhouse Act of 1737.

A touch of tiered splendour in the ornate interior of Covent Garden. (By courtesy of the Guildhall Library, Corporation of London)

Covent Garden by then was in social decline. According to the historian John Strype the area earlier inhabited by 'a mixture of nobility, gentry and wealthy tradesmen' was rapidly losing its upmarket cachet. As they drifted away, they left their gracious homes to become the tenements of vice. The strumpets of the Garden who had found their trade in the taverns were soon plying in the pit, taking advantage of the opportunities the theatre presented. And Orange Moll, who had the franchise for the sale of oranges, lemons and sweetmeats in the theatre and who drank with the actors in the Rose tavern close by, could usually arrange a later meeting with one of her more carefree orange-sellers.

Away from Shakespeare sexual comedy was the thing, with plays like Wycherley's *The Country Wife*, Congreve's less-lauded *The Way of the World*,

Goldsmith's *She Stoops to Conquer* and the brilliant Richard Brinsley Sheridan's *The School for Scandal*. The Wycherley play was first performed at the Lincoln's Inn Fields theatre (by the King's Company of players) in the early 1670s. It was, as they say, rapturously received. Unsurprisingly, the plot is broad and bawdy, but as Macaulay observed: 'Though one of the most profligate of human compositions, it is the elaborate performance of a mind ingenious, observant, quick to seize hints and patient of the toil of polishing.' Wycherley, it should be said, was a favourite at Charles II's court, particularly with his mistress the Duchess of Cleveland – none of which saved him from spending seven years in the Fleet prison, as Charles negligently left it to his brother James II to get him out, paying off his debts and granting him a pension.

The first staging of Congreve's work in 1700, also at Lincoln's Inn Fields, was a complete flop and led the playwright into early retirement to act the role of a gentleman. He had been a gallant in his time, enjoying the friendship (at least) of the delectable Mrs Bracegirdle, but he jilted her for the charms of Henrietta, Duchess of Marlborough. The Irish Goldsmith's play, first staged at Covent Garden in 1773, was rated a success (except by Walpole), assisted by a claque led by his friend Dr Johnson, while his countryman Sheridan triumphed unequivocally at Drury Lane in 1777 with what was acclaimed a brilliant work.

The plays in their progression over a century show also the slow refining of taste that would take place in the licensed theatre, made possible by the king's recognition of the playhouse as an institution. Players there had always been – they performed in bullrings and bearpits and cockpits, like the one in Drury Lane, and captured an audience and something of the future theatre's ambience in the galleried yards of the capital's coaching and carting taverns. But the City kept them at arm's length, wanting none of it, fearful of the theatre on its fringe. In the early seventeenth century all such gatherings were viewed with suspicion; many given time would not disappoint the expectation and erupted into riot. The theatre, as a later time would show, had a huge potential for subversion. The City remained adamant. For half a century the capital's playgoers would have to make shift and have themselves rowed over the river to Southwark to see the plays of Shakespeare or the works of Marlowe or Ben Jonson.

Yet the City had not always been so set against involvement. In the fourteenth century its parish clerks were playing at the Skinners' Well beside Smithfield in a performance, in Stow's words, 'which continued three days together, the king, queen and nobles of the realm being present'. Another marathon lasted for eight

Playhouse crowds could be unruly – and unchivalrous – in the scramble to the pit. (Victoria & Albert Museum Picture Library)

days in 1409. But from there it had been all downhill. The strolling players, by a statute of 1572, were categorised as vagabonds or wandering vagrants, in the dubious company of rufflers (begging ex-soldiers), fortune-tellers, minstrels, palliards (beggars in patched cloaks) and priggers of prancers (horse-stealers), along with dells (virgin female beggars), doxies and bawdy-baskets (female pedlars). They moved in their small, disparate troupes from village green to village green, or from fair to fair – with the fire-eaters, strong men, jugglers and tumblers – mounting a make-shift stage as the main business of the dealing day wound down and the fairground gave itself over to revelry or worse; or sometimes declaiming for the guests of some sporting lord in his castle yard.

The birth of the capital's theatre may have been inspirational but it was less than auspicious. Shoreditch, with its later penchant for music-halls and melodramas, seems now an unlikely cradle. But it was here, out in the sticks in the Liberty of Holywell, that the first custom-built playhouse in England since Roman times was slowly and painfully erected in 1576, raising the standard at the aptly named Theatre and later (1577) at the Curtain. Both, says Stow, were erected for 'the acting and shew of comedies, tragedies, interludes and histories for recreation'. The Theatre was built by the carpenter-cum-common-actor James Burbage, assisted by his brother-in-law. The name has a resonance still. Shakespeare served his apprenticeship here, outwith the Wall, safe from the capital's authority if not from its frown. Richard Burbage, son of James, would later bring to life the Bard's heroes.

But Shoreditch was not conscious of the honour being done to it; the players were driven out, hounded by disapproval south of the river as the century ended – and taking their timber-framed playhouse with them to be re-erected by Richard's brother as the famous Globe in Bankside. Here one of the south-side's great entrepreneurs, Edward Alleyn, was already in business, notably with the Rose theatre which was built in 1587 and, like its new rival, was open to the sky. Alleyn in fact was cultivating two worlds, mingling his play venues with a corresponding network of brothels, an empire he enlarged by marriage to the daughter of one of his competitors in the latter line of business. In the end he would redeem himself by endowing Dulwich College, but the association clearly did little for the theatre's early reputation. And there were times, as we shall see, when the theatre itself seemed to connive at strengthening the bond.

On Bankside, for sure, it was not the cultural feast we expect of today's productions; it was more an explosion of passions within a confined amphitheatre. Because of its mainly unroofed structure, the Globe could be used only in summer, the players retiring to the Blackfriars theatre in winter. Shakespeare the player and playwright was now a shareholder in both. It cost one penny for the pit, tuppence for the gallery and threepence for a seat. The privileged could sit upon the stage. The pioneering theatre, alas, went up in smoke in 1613 when a cannon fired during a performance of *Henry VIII* set some thatch alight. A man had his breeches singed. Quickly rebuilt, however, the Globe reopened the following year to continue in fierce competition with the Rose, the Swan (1594) and the Hope (1613), which was essentially a bear- and bull-baiting arena with a removable stage, the two entertainments alternating. It was here that Jonson's *Bartholomew Fair* had its first staging in 1614. The Hope, sadly, failed to live up to its name, reverting to its cruder – and more profitable – amusement.

There was deep distrust of the awkward child. Philip Stubbes in *The Anatomie of Abuses* in 1583 had asked:

Do they not maintain bawdry, insinuate, and renew the remembrance of heathen idolatry? Do they not induce whoredom and uncleanness? Nay, are they not rather plain devourers of maidenly virginity and chastity? For proof whereof but mark the flocking and running to Theatres [*sic*] and Curtains [*sic*], daily and hourly, night and day, time and tide, to see plays and interludes, where such wanton gestures, such bawdy speeches, such laughing and fleering, such kissing and bussing, such clipping and culling, such winking and glancing of wanton eyes, and the like is used, as is wonderful to behold. Then these goodly pageants being ended, every mate sorts to his mate, every one brings another homeward of their way very friendly, and in their secret conclaves (covertly) they play the sodomites or worse. And these be the fruits of plays and interludes, for the most part.

In an equally strong letter, in July 1597, from the Lord Mayor and Aldermen of London to the Privy Council, the City finally defined its resistance to playhouses:

as usually they are containing nothing but profane fables, lascivious matters, cozening devices, and scurrilous behaviour, which are so set forth as that they move wholly to imitation and not to the avoiding of those faults and vices which they represent . . . They are the ordinary places for vagrant persons, masterless men, thieves, horse-stealers, whoremongers, cozeners, coney-catchers, contrivers of treason . . .

Well, they may have been. Cromwell's Puritans a little later clearly thought so. The theatre had questionable plays, and questionable morals as displayed in the lives of its players, who corrupted their audiences. All actors were now designated 'rogues', bringing them under the Beggars' Acts, like their strolling colleagues. By an ordinance of the 1640s the theatres in London were closed by Parliament. They faced the question: 'will not a filthy play, with a blast of a trumpet, sooner call thither a thousand, than an hour's tolling of a bell bring to the sermon a hundred?' The players demurred. The measure was unnecessary, ill-judged, according to a roguish pamphlet, *The Actors' Remonstrance*, a year later. Protesting the profession's reform, it goes on:

> we have left off for our own parts, and so have commanded our servants, to forget that ancient custom which formerly rendered men of our quality infamous, namely the enveigling of young gentlemen, merchants' factors and prentices to spend their patrimonies and master's estates upon us and our harlots in taverns; we have clean and quite given over the borrowing of money at first sight of puny gallants or praising their swords, belts and beavers, so to invite them to bestow them upon us; and to our own praise may it be spoken, we were for the most part very well reformed, few of us keeping, or being rather kept by our mistresses, betook ourselves wholly to our wives, observing the matrimonial view of chastity.

There were instances of spirited defiance. The open-air Red Bull in Clerkenwell continued to give illicit performances during the Commonwealth, as did the Salisbury Court Theatre (in Salisbury Square) until it was wrecked by the soldiery in 1649. It was one of the first theatres to reopen after the Restoration. Pepys was there, in September 1661, 'where was acted for the first time *'Tis a pitty she's a Whore*, a simple play and ill-acted, only, it was my fortune to sit by a most pretty and most ingenious lady, which pleased me much'. This is Pepys at his most teasing, though given the diarist's propensities we may imagine the rest.

The Restoration would make the theatre fashionable, no longer a fugitive amid the arts and the cultural renaissance but by no means genteel. In Covent Garden the cheeky Cockpit theatre – it too had defied the Puritans until the wreckers came – would reign confidently until Tom Killigrew, dissolute and witty and a royal crony at Court, was allowed to build, under royal patent, a theatre nearby. The Theatre Royal, at Drury Lane's junction with Bow Street, was a wooden

Garrick's famous fiefdom, the Theatre Royal in Covent Garden. (Victoria & Albert Museum Picture Library)

structure with a touch of elegance, two tiers of boxes – and of course a royal box – with the stage protruding into the auditorium. It opened in May 1663, seating seven hundred. Its actors were acknowledged as being of the Royal Household; off-stage they wore the appropriate livery to mark this distinction and were even required to take an oath of allegiance to the monarch. It set them well apart from the strolling 'vagabond' actors. They were known as the King's Company. Their theatre was one of two established in the capital under the royal patent, the first being Lincoln's Inn Fields theatre, which opened in 1660 on what had been a tennis court. Its players were the Duke of York's Company. It was the first theatre in London to have a proscenium arch and movable scenery. Pepys was impressed. These theatres were the only two licensed to stage dramatic productions – though a private fringe theatre existed, keeping a low profile and disguising its real purpose behind a smokescreen of concerts and interludes, sandwiching the play in between. At Killigrew's new theatre the boxes cost from four shillings; the pit half-a-crown; the middle gallery one shilling and sixpence; and the upper gallery one shilling.

Courtiers and the aristocracy, and the gentry, flocked to this new and fashionable if *risqué* diversion. The plays were bawdy, at best highly suggestive. It was the custom at first for the ladies to wear masks, concealing their identities on an occasion of such wickedness. With the rowdy and the lesser ranks occupying the pit and gallery, the scene generally was one of loutish, ill-mannered assembly with the orange girls touting their wares alongside the prostitutes vying provocatively for customers to take back to some convenient tavern or tenement room. The demi-reps, more discreetly, would accept the attentions of the capital's rakes. The actresses, too, came under open and lascivious scrutiny and were sometimes considered ladies of a feather. Many were indeed gracious with their favours, finding their way into illustrious beds, while the orange-girls might aspire to the boards. One, the most famous of all, would do both: Nell Gywnne made her debut in Dryden's *Indian Queen* in 1665 and eventually, as one of the king's mistresses, gave the nation a new dukedom.

Drury Lane down the years would remain the embodiment of all that is understood by the term theatre; it harboured greatness (and controversy) in every stone; it reverberated with such stupendous talents as Garrick, the troubled but mesmerising Kean and Irving; it encapsulated the fastidious elegance of Sheridan. Here the strolling player Sarah Siddons was put on the famous boards after being head-hunted by Garrick. It was a place of spectacle encased in wonder. As its co-manager and star performer, Garrick would reign over the capital's theatrical scene for thirty years. The playhouse would be his fiefdom from 1747 to 1776. He was a genius: choosing plays, directing them, acting in them, writing his own prologues – and even complete plays. He was also vain and pernickety, and quarrelled with everybody in his striving for perfection. He broke the theatre from its unfashionable past and put the Bard firmly on the boards. But he was no respecter of scripts, cutting and twisting Shakespeare with all the flair of a tabloid sub-editor. Johnson said of him that he had his celebrity 'dashed in his face, sounded in his ears and went home every night with the plaudits of a thousand in his cranium'. Johnson also said: '. . . here is a man who has advanced the dignity of his profession. Garrick has made a player a higher character.' That by itself was an achievement.

His rise was not unresented. Walpole was snobbishly spiteful: 'All the run is now after Garrick, a wine-merchant who turned player.' The actor, back in his native Lichfield, had been enrolled as a boy with his brother at Johnson's private academy. Nothing at the time would have suggested the distinguished future of either. Later, in moments of ribaldry, Garrick, a superb mimic, would describe the late Mrs Johnson and confess that, with his fellow young rascals, he had listened at the door of the couple's bedchamber. He and Johnson had left Lichfield for the capital together, with one horse between them, which they rode in turn. When they arrived Garrick had threepence in his pocket. His success, however, was almost immediate, and there is a suggestion by Boswell that Johnson envied that, and admired his former pupil only 'as a poor player who frets and struts his hour upon the stage'.

The new theatres had footlights, drop curtains and painted scenery; but there was something else that made them wonderfully new and exciting: *women* now took the female roles, and were able to display not only something of their real characters and acting ability but their physical charms as well in the revealing costumes of their roles. The young bucks as well as the capital's old lechers flocked to ogle them; some, unable to wait for the final curtain, climbed on stage to fondle them during the performance. Many, in their permissive demi-monde world, played fast and loose with any gallant who might take their fancy. Others made themselves available for love – or maybe to advance their social standing. The Irish actress Dorothea Jordan became most notably the mistress of the Duke of Clarence (later William IV) and produced ten children for him in as many years. She was a lady of some wit, not to say spirit, and when her royal lover attempted to cut her allowance she replied by handing him the notice invariably attached to the playbills of the period, proclaiming: 'No money refunded after the raising of the curtain.'

Young actresses were taken into keeping by lords. Evelyn put it another way, railing against the women who 'inflaming several young noblemen and gallants, become their whores, and to some their wives'. Naming no names, he added: 'and another greater person than any of these . . . fell into their snares . . . [to] ruine of body and soule'. The stunning Spanish ballerina Maria Mercundotti was 'adopted' by the Earl of Fife, apparently without providing the usual comforts, till she eloped with a rich dandy. Many would in fact marry into the aristocracy, their craft having given them the poise and social ease to do so without strain. Covent Garden ladies who became just that, gaining titles and position, included Miss Farren (Countess of Derby), Miss Brunton (Countess of Craven), Miss Bolton, a celebrated Polly in *The Beggar's Opera* (Lady Thurlow), Miss Stephens (Countess of Essex) and Miss Foote (Countess of Harrington). Betsy Farren had been introduced into fashionable society by the politician Charles James Fox. She was tall, willowy and a beauty, and she married the 12th earl, acting the part as well as any role she had ever taken on stage. Others, as serial amorists, would end up in long-term liaisons. At Drury Lane, almost alone, the matchless Mrs Bracegirdle drove the fops of her time to distraction. So beautiful but so remote, she had a bevy of suitors but never fell. One source believed she was 'that Diana of the stage before whom Congreve and Lord Lovelace, at the head of a troop of bodkined fops, worshipped in vain'. These included the Dukes of Dorset and Devonshire, and the Earl of Halifax, all of whom, it should be said, found frequent and suitable understudies. Playwrights put their cases in the scripts they submitted to her. She delighted her audiences (even her unrequited lovers) 'in melting tenderness and mocking coquetry'.

The tall, graceful and highly intelligent Nancy Oldfield flowered to fame as a celebrated actress at Drury Lane after quitting her barmaid's career for the boards, and with a string of admirers courted notoriety in her relationship with General Charles Churchill, a cousin of the Duke of Marlborough; her triumph ended in a grave in Westminster Abbey. The Prince Regent's preference was for Mrs Mary (Perdita) Robinson: the future George IV fell in love with her on his first visit to the theatre in 1779. She was twenty and appearing in *A Winter's Tale*. The prince, who had hitherto found his bed companions in the ranks of the courtesans, was infatuated. Soon his three-feathers crest was on Perdita's carriage. Kitty Clive, an Irish actress and a platonic friend of Walpole (and it has never been rumoured otherwise), became the mistress of the Earl of Lincoln before returning to stay with the diarist at Strawberry Hill.

Hannah Norsa was twenty and Jewish and became an instant celebrity when she made her début at Covent Garden in 1732. Four years later she met Sir Robert Walpole, brother of the famous Horace, and was soon his mistress. Eleanor Ambrose was also Jewish; after her début at the rival Drury Lane playhouse she became a demi-rep, sharing her favours with the admirals Lords Howe and Rodney, the Earl of Harrington – and Horace's rake-hell brother Sir Robert. Another of the great 'toasts', the actress Sophia Baddeley, similarly supplemented her income, solacing the current Duke of Cumberland and the Earl of Cornwallis. When she was refused entrance to the Pantheon in Oxford Street her companion of that evening, Sir William Hanger, got his sword out of its scabbard in a fury at the snub, since so many other well-known courtesans were already there.

Nancy Dawson was a singer and dancer at Drury Lane, dancing 'the jiggs to smutty songs'. Born in the Garden in 1730, she set up in a garret there and did rather well (or, if you will, rather ill) by it. She appears to have been less discriminating than some:

> Now Nan was a Free Port of Trade
> For every Vessel to unlade
> And whoever came to her
> French, Dutch, Italians, pimps or piece
> 'twas Si Signor, 'twas Ja Mynheer,
> 'was S'il vous Plait, Monsieur.

Jiggs, which she sang and danced also at Covent Garden, were ballads scripted for two or more performers cross-singing the dialogue while dancing suggestively. These came at the end of a play to amuse the lingering audience and were very popular. Nancy also danced occasionally at Sadler's Wells – performing the hornpipe in John Gay's ever-popular *Beggar's Opera*. Her provocative, and probably natural, performance brought her immediate fame, and while she was dancing at Drury Lane in 1760 visitors to her garret included the Duke of Cumberland, a vulgar little man famous for his lechery. Nancy made sure such patrons paid well, while allowing her name to remain on the Harris *List* of ladies. Isabella Wilkinson, the celebrated high-wire dancer at Sadler's Wells and Covent Garden in the 1770s, had a taste too for the social heights, and found time between acts to accommodate the Venetian ambassador, Count Giovanni-Battiste Pizzoni, whose name lent itself to a rude sobriquet. When she broke her leg Isabella took to visiting the local bagnios to ease the boredom, and later moved up west, discreetly entertaining members of the nation's diplomatic staff – until her leg mended. The list becomes embarrassing and it would be nice to be able to counter a long (almost unending) litany with the suggestion that the theatre paid poorly. Alas, the truth seems to be that its ladies had a taste for the reckless *amour* of their times and were ever ready to enter the lists of love. Following the evening's performances in the mid-1700s the players would meet in the Bedford Head coffee-house, still in their colourful and (in the actresses' case) revealing stage costumes. Assignations could be arranged for later. Even the young and soon-to-be-celebrated Peg Woffington was said to sacrifice herself on the altar of Venus at a high-class house nearby. She was beautiful, generous and promiscuous, and after ending a two-year fling with Garrick vowed never to speak to him again.

A riotous scene at the Covent Garden Theatre as patrons protest over prices in 1763. (Victoria & Albert Museum Picture Library)

She would be consoled by several of the period's best-known gallants. The profession's louche reputation, it seems, may not have been undeserved.

Garrick's playhouse had a formidable rival in John Rich's Covent Garden Theatre (the Royal Opera House), built on the wild success of Gay's *Beggar's Opera* at Rich's former theatre in Lincoln's Inn Fields in 1728. Gay's work was an exciting and revolutionary development: essentially the birth of the musical. It made Gay's reputation – and that of its impresario. Gay's musical was daring in that its characters, Macheath and Polly, portrayed the capital underworld of the highwayman and the whore. Its staging brought enraged protest and there were attempts to ban it on the basis that it glamorised crime and would encourage it. It ran for sixty-two nights, a record, was cheered by the nobility and upper-crust patrons, and made both Rich and Gay wealthy. At last Rich was ready in 1732 to challenge the Theatre Royal with the most luxurious playhouse of its day. Handel would write its operas and oratorios; it was here in 1741 that he launched the *Messiah*, but to a disappointing response.

At the Royal Cockpit, the betting, like the sport, was ferocious. (By courtesy of the Guildhall Library, Corporation of London)

Interior of a London eating house, where patrons sat down at a set time to a set menu. (By courtesy of the Guildhall Library, Corporation of London)

Highlife: a masquerade, with its heightened mystery and intrigue, at the Argyll Rooms. (By courtesy of the Guildhall Library, Corporation of London)

Lowlife: the roistering atmosphere of a Wapping alehouse as seamen come ashore. (National Maritime Museum)

Deals being done in Lloyd's coffee-house, 1798. (Billie Love Historical Collection)

Dealers undone, languishing in a debtors' prison, 1821. (By courtesy of the Guildhall Library, Corporation of London)

The daring aerialist Madame Saqui descends the rope amid a battery of fireworks. (By courtesy of the Guildhall Library, Corporation of London)

A feat of balance at the circus in Astley's famous amphitheatre. (Museum of London)

Naval men, after their battles at sea, on their way to further conquests. (National Maritime Museum)

Fair in Hyde Park. August 1814.

IG.

Celebrating the peace at the great Hyde Park Fair in August 1814. (By courtesy of the Guildhall Library, Corporation of London)

A couple of the capital's courtesans entice a drunken fat man to further pleasures. (By courtesy of the Guildhall Library, Corporation of London)

A couple of swells lingering at the entrance of the popular Oxford music-hall. (By courtesy of the Guildhall Library, Corporation of London)

Both theatres would have dramas not on the playbill. Neither was immune from the forces that kept capital society in turmoil. Riot was an everyday hazard. In a wrangle over prices in 1763, Rich's theatre had its interior ripped apart; in 1808 it was destroyed by fire. That night the Beefsteak Club lost its store of fine wines; Handel's organ was lost and, even more tragically, so were many of his manuscripts. The Prince Regent stepped in with financial aid. The theatre reopened with increased prices to recoup the building cost and was at once plunged into the Old Price riots in which the actors' voices were completely drowned out for sixty-one consecutive nights – until the management relented. Thereafter the theatre's fortunes sagged until it reopened as the Royal Italian Opera (by luring the entire operatic cast of the Haymarket theatre) in 1847. Seven years later it was again razed by fire. The fire took hold after a masked ball had ended at five in the morning; a few hours later the playhouse was heap of smouldering rubble. It found its feet again only in 1867, when the theatre that it had robbed of its performers itself burned down. Opera had come home.

Drury Lane suffered similar setbacks. When it was gutted by fire in 1672, Wren was called in to build a more substantial replacement (at a cost of £4,000). Failing fortune, however, forced a merger with the Lincoln's Inns Fields company in 1682. And the behaviour of the audiences did not improve. Brawls occurred almost nightly (caused as much by a loutish aristocracy as by the hoi polloi) and riot hovered in the wings. On the night of the start of the Gordon Riots (1780) King George III was in the house when the mob invaded – and he seemed mildly amused by it all. Later, in 1800, he would behave with courage when a would-be assassin shot at him as he entered the royal box. The audience, impressed by his bravery, insisted on singing the national anthem three times. Still the patrons (who now included a new elite of bankers, merchants, administrators and adventurers) came to be seen, to consolidate or enhance their standing, rather than to watch the production. With Garrick's retirement in 1776 Drury Lane was again renovated as he handed over the management to another brilliant mind, that of Richard Brinsley Sheridan, playwright and MP. Fire struck again in 1809. Sheridan, in the middle of a debate in the Commons, dashed over to watch the devouring flames with a drink in his hands. 'Surely,' he famously said, 'a man may take a glass of wine by his own fireside.'

So, from the turbulence of its beginnings and the location of its two famous playhouses, theatreland would claim its domain in a westward spread between Covent Garden and St James's, sandwiched between the unrelenting City and the

An extravagant production of Red Riding Hood, *probably at Bartholomew's fair.* (Billie Love Historical Collection)

royal palaces. With the Theatres Regulation Act of 1843 the playhouse would escape the stranglehold of the Lord Chamberlain, who could thereafter withhold his licence only for blatant irregularity. Those in-between houses of the fringe could at last end their painful masquerade. Some would prosper and rise to be important beacons along the way, part of that strange fascination, that world of make-believe where man would see himself and the issues of his times reflected; some would stay dark for long periods and finally fade into the oblivion of history, their names forgotten as they took on other identities and other functions.

In the suburbs (as in the provinces) the playhouse – like the music-hall – would become an established part of the local popular entertainment. With its repertoire of droll melodramas, chilling mysteries and tearful romances, its mix of pantomime and variety, it would bring pleasure to millions – until the cinema usurped its role. Only in the capital and important regional cities would the theatre become truly part of serious culture as an instrument of conscience and accountability in which the mores of society were questioned and analysed – and in which the human condition was rawly exposed. In that it can be said to survive as a somewhat different model from that of its birth – no longer the haunt of the amorous rake and the rowdy hoi polloi. The queues are mainly orderly, and nobody gets crushed in the rush to the ticket office.

CHAPTER IX
Raw in Tooth and Claw

In a society riven with corruption, vice and drunkenness, the hoi polloi, like the indolent aristocracy, took their pleasures brutally. It is an unpalatable truth that the English – women as well as men – liked their entertainment raw and the bloodier the better. They revelled in the savagery of the cockpit and the bearpit, ratting contests, horse- and badger-baiting, dog-and-duck encounters. Their love of such duels to the death – and the only fractionally less lethal conflicts of the bare-fist fighters – were all of a piece with an attitude that held existence cheaply, in peace as in war; that celebrated raucously even as a life ended grotesquely on the gallows. It has been argued that it was that very 'cheapness' – life's fragile, arbitrary nature – that fuelled society's frantic pursuit of pleasure as the other side of that doleful coin.

The capital had its abundant share of brutal amusement: the mauling of one, often tethered, animal by another or a host of others; the punishing humiliation of one human being by another. The remarkable adherence of the lower orders to their bruising heroes would ensure the clandestine continuance of the bare-knuckle contests long after they had been outlawed and the noble art brought within the confines of the professional arena (such as the later Blackfriars Ring) and the Marquess of Queensberry's rules. All such bloody encounters featured regularly on the bill at the capital's great entertainment venues. The Clerkenwell of Hogarth's childhood offered the pleasure-seeker not only bare-knuckle boxing but bear-baiting, cock-fighting and women's wrestling – even wrestling contests between a man and a dog.

The English, hardly surprisingly, were then regarded as the most barbarous race in Europe. The brutish example set by their rulers had not helped. Queen Elizabeth I had a taste for such spectacles, commanding for her amusement even as she neared her seventieth birthday 'the bears and the bull and the ape to be baited in the Tiltyard'. It was here, at Henry VIII's new Whitehall Palace, that bear-baiting was staged as a royal entertainment. He also had a cockpit built – and

Ratting was a popular sporting diversion that amused all classes of Regency society. (Museum of London)

a tennis court. James I, too, took it badly if he could not spend at least a couple of nights a week at the cockpit. As late as 1814 the then Lord Lonsdale felt it necessary to lay on an exhibition of this particularly English sport for the London gathering of the Allied Sovereigns, and the playboy prince who would be Edward VII felt no embarrassment in presiding at prize-fights, with a full knowledge of the rules (such as they were), and was equally at home at a 'ratting', in which one dog could kill five hundred rats in one hour.

At one time Londoners in their thousands on their days of leisure would sally forth over London Bridge for the bear gardens of Bankside. It seems singularly apt that in 1604 the then master of such South Bank 'entertainment' was the ubiquitous Edward Alleyn, who held the appointment of Master Overseer and Ruler of the Bears, Bulls and Mastiff Dogs. The venerable Stow in his *Survey* of the capital published a couple of years later reported: 'there are two bear-gardens, the old and the new places, wherein be kept bears, bulls and other beasts, to be baited; as also mastiffs in several kennels, nourished to bait them. These bears and other beasts are there baited in plots of ground, scaffolded about for the beholders to stand safe.' They were, said London's famous historian, 'much frequented'.

Bankside, certainly, was an appropriate venue. It had long been the resort of those with unbridled pleasure in mind. It had a raw deal from the start as the dumping ground for the city's noxious industries as well as its equally notorious entertainments. Fog-ridden, the mist oozing from its marshes, it had early gained a reputation for vice from its use as a garrison settlement for the Roman soldiery guarding the southern end of the capital's one and only bridge. Along the river's edge the bishops' palaces clustered, housing an ecclesiastical hierarchy from Durham to Canterbury. Its Winchester Palace was the residence in town (until 1626) of the wealthy and prestigious Bishops of Winchester, men with an important influence in the realm; it had been comprehensively sacked by the rebel Wat Tyler and his followers passing through from Blackheath in 1381. Jack Cade, another of the same ilk, and his mob seventy years later could not resist an encore when they based themselves at Southwark's White Hart Inn. Their heads both rolled in due course, or at least found an uncomfortable accommodation, as a warning to all, on the bridge they had crossed so boldly.

For long enough the bridge would be the capital's only dry link to its southern landscape, a wooden structure before the first stone-built bridge opened in 1209, its structure, fittingly, supervised by the clergyman Peter of Colechurch. He was never to see the work completed, though his remains would have their last resting place in its structure. His old London Bridge was 300 yards long, 13 yards wide, with houses lining either side until 1760. It endured for six hundred years, an open sesame to the city and the great gamut of its attractions. Westminster Bridge would only belatedly steal some of its thunder, in the process eventually losing the Archbishop of Canterbury the steady income he took from the tolls of the horse ferry beside his Lambeth Palace.

Southwark was never going to be salubrious; the stench of Bermondsey's thirty or so tanneries and its leather market wafted over it. But foreigners were responsible for the bear-baiting, introduced with bull-baiting by the Italians in the thirteenth-century reign of King John. These 'sports' were well established in Bankside by 1546, and both Henry VIII and his daughter Elizabeth were fond of taking visiting emissaries to see the barbaric spectacle, if not to enjoy it. But there would be a mushrooming of other venues, among them the bear gardens at Hockley-in-the-Hole; at Saffron Hill and at Tothill Fields; Copenhagen Fields

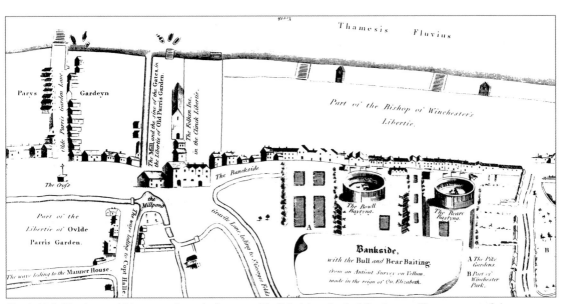

Bankside's bloody amphitheatres where the bear- and bull-baiting shocked foreigners. (By courtesy of the Guildhall Library, Corporation of London)

in Islington, like Tothill Fields and St George's Fields, was always a place of contention. The tea garden there did not hesitate to put a little live entertainment on the menu, adding bulldog fights to its bill of bear- and bull-baiting. Today the Café de Paris stands on the site of a Tudor bearpit, and Westminster Cathedral looks back to the past as a pleasure garden – and a bull-baiting ring. Tothill Fields would be used for bear-baiting up until 1793, for bull-baiting until 1820. In the rougher areas too, beyond the City's bounds, the capital's riff-raff congregated to witness such brutal sports, and when now-fashionable Belgravia was still a green and bosky open space every holiday drew the crowds to the bull-baiting and cock-fights staged there. Cruel and monstrous though such 'entertainment' seems to us now, a typical handbill for the notorious Hockley-in-the-Hole proclaims matter-of-factly: 'A green bull to be baited, which was never baited before, and a bull to be turned loose, with fireworks all over him; also a mad ass to be baited. With a variety of bull-baiting and bear-baiting, and a dog to be drawn up with fireworks.'

A German visitor to the capital, Paul Hentzner (1558–1623), author of *A Journey to England*, having been taken out on the town, witnessed the capital's popular pastime and reported impassively:

There is still another place, built in the form of a theatre, which serves for the baiting of bears and bulls. They are fastened behind, and then worried by those great English dogs and mastiffs, but not without great risk to the dogs from the teeth of the one and the horns of the other; and it sometimes happens they are killed on the spot. Fresh ones are immediately supplied in the places of those that are wounded or tired. To this entertainment there often follows that of whipping a blinded bear, which is performed by five or six men, standing in a circle with whips, which they exercise upon him without any mercy. Although he cannot escape from them because of his chain, he nevertheless defends himself, vigorously throwing down all who come within his reach and are not active enough to get out of it, and tearing the whips out of their hands and breaking them . . . In these theatres, fruits such as apples, pears and nuts, according to the season, are carried about to be sold, as well as wine and ale.

Another commentator, more horrified, suggested the bearpits' spectators were 'fitter for a wilderness than a city'. He was precise as to their character: 'Idle base persons (most commonly) that want employment, or else will not be otherwise employed, frequent this place . . . the swaggering roarer, the cunning cheater, the rotten bawd, the swearing drunkard and the bloody butcher have their rendezvous here, and are of chief place and respect. There are as many civil religious men here, as there are saints in hell.'

When the playhouses were closed by Cromwell's command, it seemed to the bold author of *The Actor's Remonstrance* that there was a massive injustice in that some entertainments were allowed to continue:

namely that nurse of barbarism and beastliness, the Bear Garden, where upon their usual days those demi-monsters are baited by bandogs; the gentlemen of stave and tail, namely boisterous butchers, cutting cobblers, hard-handed masons and the like rioting companions, resort thither with as much freedom as formerly, making with their sweat and crowding a far worse stink than the ill-formed beast they persecute with their dogs and whips; pick-pockets, which in an age not heard of in any of our [play]houses, repairing thither, and other disturbers of the public peace, which dare not be seen in our civil and well-governed theatres, where none used to come but the best of the nobility and gentry.

(To 'stave' was to beat back the animal; to 'tail' was to hold back the dog.)

In fact, Cromwell did try to curb the bloody sports but only partly succeeded.

In bull-baiting the unfortunate beast was usually tethered by the horns on a rope about 15 feet long and anchored to a stout pillar or stake. The challenging dogs, viciously trained for their task, were each held (by their ears) by their handlers just out of the circle of danger and were loosed to attack the bull one by one. The dog had to dodge the bull's defences – its hooves and its horns, the latter unfairly sheathed in wooden guards – to attack with its teeth. The sport was to see the tormented bull using its horns to toss the incautious dogs high into the air, breaking their necks or their spines as they landed – unless they were tossed into the crowd.

Pepys, ever venturous, took his wife (after one of their many quarrels) to Bankside and according to his *Diary* for that August day in 1666 'saw some good sport of the bulls tossing the dogs, one into the boxes'. All the same he considered it a 'very rude and nasty pleasure'. What Mrs Pepys thought is unrecorded. Evelyn, a little later, for once was of a mind with him: 'to the Bear Gardens where was cock-fighting, dog-fighting, bear- and bull-baiting'. To his delight, for he too hated the barbarity of what he called the 'butcherly sports', 'one of the bulls tossed a dog full into a lady's lap, as she sate in one of the boxes at a considerable height from the arena. Two poor dogs were killed, and so all ended with the ape on horseback.' The dogs usually got hurt, but the bull had the worst of it; regardless of the sport he provided, he was scheduled for slaughter as he left the arena. Bankside's bear gardens, however, would continue for only a short time longer, though others in and around the capital would persist and be well patronised until the bitter end in 1835, when bear-baiting was banned.

When such spectacles palled there was the diverting delight of duck-baiting – a solitary duck on a pond was put at the mercy of dogs, usually spaniels – and the thrill of placing wagers on the foregone outcome; Hogarth's Clerkenwell had one such pond (in Exmouth Street) and there was another of the many in fashionable Mayfair, where the patrons drank their winnings (where else) in The Dog and Duck. Equally bloody – indeed more so – was 'ratting', when live rats were brought into the arena by the squeaking, squirming bagful and tipped on to the floor. A dog was then released into their midst and the slaughter began. The German visitor Prince Puckler-Muskou, as late as 1826, watched one terrier kill a hundred rats in ten minutes. That was about the going rate. Held in some dirty old barn with a gallery and an upper gallery (for the upper crust and at three shillings a seat), these gory massacres inflamed the raw passions of the crowd, drawing shrieks of abuse or encouragement from spectators of both sexes.

Baron Zacharias von Uffenbach, yet another German visitor to our shores, in 1710 saw bull-baiting as an essentially English pleasure, one that the nation clearly loved though he himself was not enamoured. He was making a survey of English recreations and felt much the same about cock-fighting, which he thought 'very foolish'. Following a trip to the cockpit in Gray's Inn he reported that 'the people act like madmen and go on raising the odds to twenty guineas or more'. (Indeed, for a time more money was wagered on cock-fights than on horse-racing.) Among the cocks, he found, there were some with a strong sense of discretion or a desire for survival: 'When they are released, some attack, while others run away . . . and, impelled by terror, jump down among the people; they are then, however, driven back on the table with great yells and thrust at each other until they get angry. Then it is amazing to see how they peck at each other and especially how they hack with their spurs.'

It was a scene quite unparalleled anywhere else in Europe, with its spectators hysterically screaming the odds. Hogarth's famous 1759 depiction (laden, it is true, with satirical intent) shows the wild excitement of its amphitheatre with its central figure a blind gambler (reputedly Lord Albemarle Bertie); in the small arena two cocks are matched with deadly intent. They wear the customary steel spurs made for the sport. Only one bird will leave the combat alive.

Cock-fighting was a national addiction. Supposedly banned by Cromwell in 1654, it was enthusiastically revived with the Restoration. Perhaps the English psyche found in it a sublimation of its own warrior bloodlust. The cock-fight, like bear-baiting, had a long history in the land, and out in the country until well through the eighteenth century there were cock-fights in almost every parish as a regular rustic pastime – in the churchyard if not in somebody's barn or in a convenient inn-yard – in addition to the cruel amusement of cock-throwing and the ever-popular badger-baiting. Fitzstephen mentions cock-fighting in the reign of Henry II (1154–89), when it was the traditional sport of scholars on Shrove Tuesday. Its highpoint, however, was in the seventeenth and eighteenth centuries. In the capital the venues were numerous. Drury Lane's Cockpit theatre was built in 1609 specifically to cater for the 'sport', taking on its more acceptable role some years later.

Hogarth's painting is said to be of the Royal Cockpit in Dartmouth Street, demolished after its lease expired in 1810. Undeterred, the punters swiftly switched their allegiance to the pit in nearby Tufton Street. Yet another venue was in Shoe Lane. Pepys, near Christmas in 1663, shortly after it had opened, duly recorded in his famous *Diary*:

Hogarth depicts the blind gambler Lord Albemarle Bertie taking bets at the cock-fight. (By courtesy of the Guildhall Library, Corporation of London)

To Shoe Lane to a Cockefighting at a new pit there . . . But Lord, to see the strange variety of people, from Parliament-men, to the poorest prentices, bakers, brewers, butchers, dray men and what not; and all these fellows, one with another in swearing, cursing and betting . . . One thing more is strange to see, how people of this poor rank, that look as if they had not bread to put in their mouths, shall bet three or four pounds at one bet and lose it, and yet bet as much the next battell . . . so that one of them will lose £10 or £20 at a meeting.

Cockfighting, it is clear, had the same egalitarian appeal as many of the other sports of the period – and the same lure for society's losers.

As a spectacle it heightened the blood alarmingly, Boswell's as much as any man's. He once sat through five solid hours of contests, fascinated but, one suspects, also a little repelled by the spectacle. Of the capital's many venues, the most prestigious was the Royal Cockpit in St James's Park's Birdcage Walk. The pit advertised regularly, offering prizes of up to two hundred guineas for winning cocks. Boswell (by his own account) had set out to test a day lived in the manner of the 'true Englishman'. After a beefsteak dinner at Dolly's in Paternoster Row, he tells us, he went to the Royal Cockpit, 'a circular room in the middle of which the cocks fight'. Seating ranged upwards in rows round the small arena, all covered with mat. The cocks, 'nicely cut and dressed and armed with silver heels', were set down, and 'fought with amazing bitterness and resolution'. Some died quickly, though a contest could last up to forty-five minutes. 'The uproar and noise of the betting is prodigious', he observed. Money was changing hands at a furious rate and Boswell was plainly shocked by the behaviour of the crowd – and concerned at the cruelty to the cocks as they were 'mangled and torn'. Looking around he saw no sympathy or self-disgust on the faces about him.

Defoe in 1724, reporting on his famous journey round the country in *A Tour through the Whole Island of Great Britain*, was also amazed by the courage of the birds:

It is wonderful to see the courage of these little creatures, who always hold fighting on till one of them drops and dies on the spot. I was at several of these matches, and never saw a cock run away. However, I must own it to be a remnant of the barbarous customs of this island, and too cruel for my entertainment. There is always a continued noise among spectators in laying wagers upon every blow each cock gives, who . . . wear steel spurs (called gaffles) for their surer execution.

Tellingly, he adds: 'If an Italian, German, or a Frenchman should by chance come into these cockpits . . . he would certainly conclude the assembly to be mad.' Bets would be settled there and then – with those unable to meet their debts made to sit in a basket, which was then hoisted to the ceiling. There its humiliated occupant would be an object of ridicule and laughter. Cocks showing a lack of will to fight were tethered to a stake and used as living cock-shies.

Cock-fights were often staged as side-shows – at race meetings and other events, probably in a local inn-yard. At the Royal Cockpit the knock-out tournaments were for thirty-two cocks, which were eliminated one by one until only the champion remained. Many of them would have been bred for their bloody contests in Cock Lane, running east from Snow Hill. The spurs that girded them were mainly made in Cockspur Street, which linked the Englishman's sport with another he would embrace with an equal ardour.

It was off this street, in 1747, that John Broughton, the so-called 'father of pugilism' and for a time the English champion, set up his boxing academy in which gloves (mufflers) were first used, though not in the contests themselves. It was nevertheless a turning point in a sport that stopped short of the final *coup de grâce*, though only just. Prize-fighting had flourished since the Restoration, as part of the pleasure of the fair and as the kind of well-hyped event that could draw thousands to some remote location. Far from the city lights or the dazzling atmosphere of the pleasure gardens, these bare-fist contests were serious punch-ups on which huge amounts of money were wagered. They were fought on grass; four sticks stuck into the ground with a rope tied round them constituted a ring. The fashion for a raised ring would follow about 1820.

The nobility had a strong involvement, backing their favourites to an outrageous degree against arranged challengers in titled and untitled matches, sometimes held on their own estates. The fighters' stake was usually the amount they betted on themselves plus their share of the 'nobbins' – the money thrown into the collector's hat afterwards. On a fine December morning in 1821, in what would be one of the fights of the century, Bill Neat took on Tom Hickman (the Gaslight Champion) on Hungerford Downs near Newbury; carriages crammed the converging roads and the tension was all but overwhelming as an estimated 25,000 spectators crushed forward to the ringside, laying wagers totalling £200,000. Hickman, one of the greatest bare-knuckle challengers of his era, got his amusing sobriquet because the speed of his punches, it was rumoured, caused the lights to flicker out. On this occasion, though, he was defeated. He died tragically, aged twenty-seven, not in the dangerous ring in which he plied his trade but crushed to death by a carriage.

Such contests also took place within the capital's limits. They were regularly on the bill and traditionally associated with taverns: for instance, the Salisbury (once the Coach and Horses) in St Martin's Lane; the Lamb and Flag inn (rechristened the Bucket of Blood); the Plough in Carey Street; and with the tavern kept by the pugilist John Gully (1783–1863), who became the MP for Pontefract. At a low ebb, even Sadler's Wells stooped to put on bare-fist bouts.

The first prize-ring in the capital was in James Figg's Amphitheatre in Tottenham Court Road in the early eighteenth century. Figg, who called himself the English champion, features in Hogarth's *Southwark Fair* of 1733, where he entertained the fairgoers not only with boxing (taking on all-comers) but with cudgelling, foil-play and back-swording. In 1727 he had met Ned Sutton, the 'Pipemaker of Gravesend', in a contest involving the broadsword, the cudgel and the fists, winning all three categories. Figg, from Thame in Oxfordshire, had an 'academy' in Marylebone where he staged a wider band of amusements, including female boxing, cock- and bull-fights, bear- and even tiger-baiting. He died in 1734.

The poet Byron, a man avid for all experience, took lessons in pugilism from another of the best, Gentleman John Jackson, whose feats included signing his name with an 84lb weight tied to his little finger. It was at Coulsdon (then Smitham Bottom) in Surrey in 1788 that Jackson, then just nineteen, notched up his first win in the prize-ring, against a formidable challenger, William Fewterel. The Prince of Wales was there, handing the winner a money note as he left. The contestants fought bared to the waist, in white knee breeches and stockings. Jackson would reign as English heavyweight champion for eight years, and also fought celebrated engagements with George the Brewer and the Jewish fighter Daniel Mendoza, who also had his own boxing school. Against the Brewer in 1789 Jackson dislocated an ankle and broke a bone in his leg – but offered to continue the contest strapped to a chair. (Jackson and eighteen other prize-fighters, all of them dressed as pages, formed the bodyguard at the Prince's coronation.)

In their brutal encounters the old prize-fighters would batter each other for up to four hours; the damage inflicted was horrendous, sometimes tragic. When Broughton met George Stevenson, a coachman, in a challenge bout in 1741, Stevenson died; Broughton was deeply affected, and it inspired him in his campaign for stricter rules and codes of conduct. The nobility watched the slaughter, seemingly impervious as their men hammered each other senseless. When the legendary Tom Sayers met the American champion John Carmel Heenan at Farnborough, Hants, for the world title in 1860 it was before the Prince of Wales and the Prime Minister Lord Palmerston in what was billed as the 'battle of the century'. Early on Heenan broke a bone in Sayers's right arm

The legendary prize-fight, Sayers v. Heenan, that left both men bloody and battered. (Billie Love Historical Collection)

(something of a handicap) and Sayers was forced to concentrate on his opponent's eyes. The fight had gone to forty-two rounds (and over two hours and twenty minutes) before the police located the venue and stopped the contest – just as the American, his face a bloody mess, was trying to strangle Sayers on the ropes. The declared result was a draw and it was Sayers's last fight.

In an earlier marathon, the Game Chicken (Hen Pearce) in 1805 went sixty-four rounds with Gully before the latter conceded. In 1824, against the Irishman Jack Langham, Tom Spring had to battle through seventy-seven rounds before winning. The Irishman claimed he had been simultaneously roughed-up by the partisan crowd, and for the return match insisted on a raised ring, with a protective cordon of farm carts around it. At the end of their forty-nine rounds Langham was senseless and Spring's hands were lumps of raw meat.

In yet another historic but tragic contest in 1833, at St Albans, the Cockney James (Deaf) Burke and Simon Byrne traded punches for an astonishing ninety-nine rounds. Both, finally, were so exhausted that they were vomiting and had to be given reviving sips of brandy. Byrne died a few days later of a brain haemorrhage. He was thirty-two. In Paris fifty years later, in December 1883, the last English bare-knuckle champion Jem Smith fought a marathon of 109 rounds against the American Jack Kilrain in a fight staged on an inaccessible island in the Seine – from eleven minutes past two in the afternoon until seventeen minutes to five, when the time-keepers could no longer see their watches. It was marked an honourable draw. Primitive surgery had been needed on Smith's ear during the fight when it swelled to a tremendous size.

The rules of the prize-ring were elastic: gouging of the eyes and ears, tripping, head-holding and blows below the belt and so on were all allowed, and severe injury was commonplace. The Marquess of Queensberry was the referee in a fight in which Tom Oliver was taken from the ring after thirty-two rounds, alas 'in a state of stupor, and completely deprived of sight'. Crowds and backers could be unsympathetic. When Broughton fought his last match in 1749, he lost to his challenger, the bruising Jack Slack, a butcher to trade, when he was blinded by a blow between the eyes. The Duke of Cumberland, the Butcher of Highland history, had a £10,000 wager on him – and, badly miffed, never spoke to the boxer again. An amiable man, the darling of the crowds, Broughton retired to sell antiques in Lambeth. Slack's reign as champion continued for a decade, until 1760.

If King Charles's Restoration had spurred a revival in the bloodlust sports, the Regency gave full expression to them; all were allowed free rein in that frantic, hedonistic society. During the Regency, prize-fighting was *the* sport, more popular even than horse-racing. Men like Gully, the Chicken, the Gasman, Ned Turner, Tom Spring, Tom Cribb, Jem Belcher, brawny Bill Neat, Bendigo the Bold (William Thompson), Bill Caunt and the Tipton Slasher (William Perry) – all formidable fighters – hobnobbed with the racier members of the aristocracy and were seen publicly in their company; when Gully fought the Chicken, Byron took a party, including his mentor Jackson, down to Brickhill to see it. Jackson, if not quite a Beau Brummell figure about town, caroused with the likes of Byron in the capital's low dives in his scarlet jacket, breeches and silk stockings. The poet, like a love-struck teenager, had a picture of the boxer on his wall. By 1800 the prize-fighters would have their own Covent Garden clique meeting at Carpenter's coffee-house, the social hub of their fraternity, which included George the Brewer, Mendoza, Cribb, Belcher (who would give his name to a distinctive type of neckerchief, with white spots on dark blue), Dutch Sam and Big Ben Brain, to name but a colourful few.

By the mid-1800s, however, prize-fighting was losing its hold on the popular imagination. The riff-raff of the sporting fringe were becoming involved in scams, the fixing of fights and so on, and the nobility, whose involvement had kept the sport relatively honest and given a touch of glamour to its bloody engagements, were beginning to distance themselves from its unsavoury image, and indeed from the bloodier pursuits generally. Even by 1831 Surtees, who ran the *New Sporting Magazine*, was refusing to report sordid encounters that debased the whole sorry scene to the level of cock-fighting and bull-baiting. The noble art was becoming almost impossibly besmirched. Increasingly it would find its refuge in the fair booth, a natural home, as part of the rackety, colourful world of the showmen, where its practitioners would continue to be hailed as heroes – or sometimes villains – by the crowds. There, for a few coppers, they could witness an exhibition of sparring skills, or (more pleasurably) the drubbing of some local loudmouth who had foolishly allowed himself to be coerced into the ring.

Tom Sayers, one of the prize-ring's greatest champions, who dominated the scene for twelve years, fighting sixteen bouts in that time and losing only one, was about the last of the brave old breed, and his funeral at Highgate Cemetery in 1865 emphasised the esteem accorded to his kind. His coffin was followed by a hundred thousand mourning fans, many of them from the fashionable ranks of society. Most poignantly, the event would also point up the personal loneliness of the last years of the prize-fighter when he could no longer command the adulation of the crowd. His dog was chief mourner. Sayers was just thirty-nine.

His place in the sport's pantheon would be assumed by men like Jem Mace, a London-based prize- and glove-fighter – and an outstanding violinist – who had been fighting in inn-yards from the age of fourteen, and would appear regularly at events such as Lincoln's big fair to take on all-comers and dust the canvas with any serious regional opposition. Mace was a hero of the travelling boxing show with its exhibition bouts and the custom of inviting challengers from the crowd. He was a showman as well as a pugilist, from 1858 fighting many title encounters. More than anyone, perhaps, he gave the sport back its self-respect. One of his protégés, Harry (Kid) Furness, a welterweight, who himself became a showman, said of his famous tutor: 'He was one of the greatest fighters this country has ever produced – the man whose cleverness in boxing skill did most to change the tag of "prize-fighting" in the old bare-knuckle days to "the noble art of self-defence".' With the acceptance of the Marquess of Queensberry's rules in 1867, Mace 'retired' but kept on travelling, with the fair, with the circus – and to America in the 1870s, where he beat British-born Tom Allen for the title of champion of the world. When his fortunes crashed, as a result of his high living, in the early 1900s, he made a comeback in the circus and music-hall at the age of seventy-six as a lecturer, playing to packed houses and appearing on stage to the chant of:

> Good old Jemmy, Brave old James,
> Take a list and run all down the pugilistic names,
> Search through Fistiana and see if you can trace
> A man with such a record as old Jem Mace.

The memorable bloody encounters of the bravehearts of the prize-ring would live after them, crusted with legend. There were, however, other savage ways in which humans could inflict damage on each other for the amusement of their fellows: confrontations such as cudgelling, back-swording and single-stick fighting. These ancient sports were the normal Whit Monday entertainment at the Red House, a low dive in Battersea Fields, where such traditionally vicious activities were regularly on the programme – along with wrestling (old and more or less honourable) and fencing and gladiatorial broadsword contests between home-grown exponents and continental visitors. Single-stick veterans challenged all-comers. In the bear garden at Hockley-in-the-Hole there was sword-fighting by women, who battled without the benefit of stays and wearing only their shifts in what must have been the Regency equivalent of the wet T-shirt competition. The crowd shrieked its encouragement and then pelted the loser with rotten fruit or vegetables. There were bouts, also, between man and dog. The bloodlust was unbounded.

CHAPTER X
The Fun of the Hanging Fair

The capital's heroes and villains (often one and the same) made their last exits on the gallows or the axeman's scaffold in an atmosphere of near-carnival gaiety, the central players in that most macabre of entertainments, the hanging fair. Hanging days were like holidays, and executions were unashamedly staged as public spectacles. Bold men lost their heads on Tower Hill, or ended it all dangling grotesquely on a rope at Tyburn. There were gibbets on almost every heath and common around the capital – and it was not at all unusual for the culprit to be hanged at the scene of his crime – but it was mainly to Tyburn's tree that the city's hoi polloi came for a day of diversion in their drab lives – and to see the condemned die. Some, including the city's apprentices, were given time off to attend, in the hope that an important lesson would be driven home. There is, alas, not the slightest evidence that anyone took heed, and not a little that the reverse was the case.

Henry Fielding, Bow Street's second magistrate and arguably its most famous, who began the transformation of law enforcement in the capital with his chosen team of Bow Street Runners, believed that 'the executions of criminals . . . serve, I apprehend, a purpose diametrically opposite to that for which they are designed; and tend rather to inspire the vulgar with a contempt for the gallows rather than a fear of it'. He was also a novelist and found time to write, among other works, the comic masterpiece *Tom Jones*. More seriously, his *Enquiry into the Causes of the late Increase of Robbers* in 1751 confirmed his view. He wrote: 'The day appointed by law for the thief's shame is the day of glory in his own opinion. His procession to Tyburn and his last moments there are all triumphant; attended with the compassion of the weak and tender-hearted, and with the applause, admiration and envy of all the bold and hardened.' A visiting Scots minister was of a similar mind. He was taken aback at the scene before him:

Among the immense multitude of spectators, some at windows, some upon carts, thousands standing and jostling one another in the surrounding fields –

my conviction is that, in a moral view, a great number were made worse, instead of better, by the awful spectacle. Of the ragamuffin class a large proportion were gratified by the sight; and within my hearing many expressed their admiration of the fortitude, as they termed the harshness and stupidity, of one of the sufferers. 'Well done, little coiner', 'What a brave fellow he is!'

The only people who profited from the occasion were the inn-keepers, the orange-sellers and the broadsheet vendors – and those who rented out the grand-stand seats with a fine uninterrupted view of the gruesome spectacle. To the under-privileged the condemned were heroes who had dared to defy the rules of their oddly ambivalent society. Their lives might have been short but they had undeniably been sweet, with the consolation of wine and women. Not infrequently these popular heroes were young and handsome. Their imminent demise certainly awoke waves of sympathy in the underclass from which they had usually sprung. Not a few in the crowd would have known that it was the fate that might yet await themselves. The lifestyle that had brought them there was a familiar one, born in the deprivation and despair of the back-street slum. They had never had much to lose. The bold died usually as they had lived, with braggadocio, with a bravery that extended in equal, if not greater, measure to the aristocracy, whose end following their fall from grace could be even bloodier. Their crimes, however, were rarely motivated by avarice and were mainly political, their execution not infrequently an expediency that once put in train could not be countermanded. Those about to perish invariably exhibited the qualities expected of their class, however bungled their dispatch.

The day of the hanging fair had an awesome choreography. From daybreak the route to the gallows would be lined with rowdy, expectant revellers awaiting the fateful procession. Alehouses along the way did a roaring trade, as did those near the gallows tree. The condemned travelled like celebrities, some sombre and contrite, many in the charged atmosphere of the day revelling in their unaccustomed glory and swapping good-humoured banter with the crowd as the cart trundled them to their doom. The journey to Tyburn from their prisoner's cell in Newgate could take a couple of hours. Those bound for eternity were traditionally given the 'cup of charity' – 'a grate bowle of Ale to be their last refreshing in this lyfe' – at the door of the hospital chapel of St Giles-in-the-Fields, once a leper sanctuary, just beyond the City walls, but later stops might be made at other inns along the route. The custom of the 'last drink' (sometimes with the hangman) was long enshrined in the ritual, with the condemned man promising to pay for the round on his way back. Unless his courage had completely failed him the victim did his best to enter into the spirit of that hallowed tradition. It would have been considered bad form not to.

The journey resumed, up Oxford Street, known anciently as Tyburn Way, to the gallows at its western (Marble Arch) end. It is just possible that the wretches loaded on to the carts, manacled and with their coffins beside them, welcomed their ride in the sunlight after long incarceration in the grim tomb of the prison, and embraced the life to come (if they believed in it) as a better thing than the dark torment of Newgate itself. The prison stood, as it had done from the twelfth century and probably earlier, where that monument of the law, the Old Bailey, stands today, at the end of the street (of the same name) linking Ludgate with Holborn. It had been repeatedly restored and looked magnificently foreboding – on the outside. Inside, in its fetid stench, every disease festered and typhoid was a permanent hazard. In its confines the keeper amassed riches by selling supplies such as candles and seacoal and drink – and, scandalously, even food and water. A man could pay to have his leg-irons removed. The so-called Palace of Retribution was very far from being a model for the custodianship of society's feared and unwanted; it was just like all the others. One prisons inspector was astonished by what he found within its walls. Its prisoners were 'riotous and dirty'. There was no segregation of the sexes, who mingled without constraint. Many, of both sexes, were drunk and 'the prisoners play in the courtyard at skittles, mississippi, fives, tennis, etc.' Friends dropped in for a drink. It was a seething colony of malefactors whose crimes ranged from murder to basic, necessary thievery. Its occupants at one time or another would include religious martyrs, Daniel Defoe, the treacherous genius Jonathan Wild and Jack Sheppard, who made an incredible escape (for a time) after being manacled and chained to the floor. Defoe would return to the scene later, one of many who would publish Sheppard's remarkable story, shortly after his hanging. Rebuilt yet again after the Gordon riots, Newgate in the 1830s still managed to horrify the young Dickens. In *Sketches by Boz* his revulsion is plain.

The last days and hours of the condemned, however horrific their own crimes, were made gruesome by the rituals preceding their final punishment. In the prison's chapel they sat in the condemned pew, in the presence of their fellow prisoners, to hear their last sermon: 'a huge black pen, in which the wretched men who are singled out for death, are placed, on the Sunday preceding their

Condemned prisoners sit round a coffin in Newgate's chapel to hear their last sermon. (Museum of London)

execution, in the sight of their fellow-prisoners . . . to hear prayers for their own souls, to join in the responses of their own burial service . . .' Thus wrote Dickens in *A Visit to Newgate*, one of his most powerful pieces of writing. He continues: 'Imagine what have been the feelings of the man whom that fearful pew enclosed, and of whom, between the gallows and the knife, no mortal remnant may now remain . . .' At one time the condemned men's coffins were also placed in that pew, on the seat by their side, for the entire service.

Dickens, allowed entry to Newgate, poignantly portrays the last hours of vigil for the condemned man. His life ticks remorselessly away from him. The condemned cell is 'a stone dungeon, eight feet long by six feet wide, with a bench at the further end, under which were a common horse rug, a bible, and prayer-book. An iron candlestick was fixed into the wall at the side; and a small high window in the back admitted as much air and light as could struggle in between a double row of heavy, crossed iron bars.' Writing for *The Times* after the Mannings' hanging Dickens confided:

> I do not believe that any community can prosper where such a scene of horror as was enacted this morning . . . is permitted. The horrors of the gibbet and of the crime that brought the wretched murderers to it faded in my mind before the atrocious bearing, looks and language of the assembled spectators.

Society would take a little time to come round to the novelist's point of view.

Grimmer still, and more ghoulish in its vengeance, had been the custom once perpetuated at the Church of the Holy Sepulchre, just beyond the City walls at Newgate. A tunnel connected the church with the prison, and early in the seventeenth century this became for a time the instrument of a truly horrific ritual. The night before an execution the church's bellman would walk the tunnel's silent echoing length, chanting to the mournful toll of his bell the warning mantra:

> All you that in the condemned hold do lie,
> Prepare you for tomorrow you shall die.
> Watch out and pray the hour is drawing near
> That you before the Almighty must appear.
> Examine well yourselves. In time repent
> That you may not to the eternal flames be sent.
> And when St Sepulchre's bell tomorrow tolls
> The Lord have mercy on your souls.

In a grisly climax, the last couplet would be shouted through the keyhole of the condemned cells. Come the morning, in the church's tower the great bell would toll out as the prisoners were led out for their last journey. At the church's gate, as they passed, each would be given a nosegay. Mercifully, perhaps because its callousness offended even those case-hardened times, the bizarre tunnel ritual was ended in 1744.

The gallows – Tyburn Tree – stood at the fork of the Tyburn stream. It flowed past from its source in South Hampstead to serve City conduits or to empty into the Thames near today's Vauxhall Bridge. The condemned, traitors excepted, rode there by cart with, and occasionally sitting on, their coffins. Sometimes a chaplain travelled with them. The better class of condemned went by coach, stopping perhaps for a last brandy. When they reached Tyburn a homing pigeon would be released to fly back to Newgate, signalling their safe arrival.

Not all the condemned came from the criminal classes; even members of the clergy could come to an ignominious end. Yet mainly it was the lowlife of the capital's ghettos that graced the gallows tree, and for them there was a final irony: the hangman would be one recruited from their midst, one of their own. Their behaviour on the scaffold would be widely reported; and the date and venue of their demise (in the case of well-known villains at least) would have been well touted by the publication of pamphlets and chapbooks of their life stories. A typical hanging at Tyburn is depicted in Hogarth's *Industry and Idleness*, a vivid portrayal with all the elements of the thorough-going fair evident. Mingling with the crowd are orange- and ballad-sellers, pickpockets and prostitutes, gingerbread men and gin-sellers. The year was 1747, when the capital was at its most dangerous.

Crowds of up to a hundred thousand could be drawn to the closing drama of a famous manhunt that had captured the imagination of the capital, or to the last moments of some dashing figure like Jack Sheppard, or the highwaymen Claude Duval or James Maclean; the latter was the son of a Presbyterian minister and one of the social elite. Some estimates put the number at Sheppard's hanging at two hundred thousand, perhaps something of an exaggeration. The clergyman-forger Dr William Dodd, too, got a good attendance, though not for the same reason. People could be trampled to death in the mêlée; in one incident nearly a hundred people were killed or seriously hurt.

In a brutish and violent world the crowd took its pleasure, openly and unalloyed, without shame or guilt. As late 1864 *The Times* was reporting 'robbery and violence, loud laughing, oaths, fighting, obscene conduct and still more filthy language reigned round the gallows far and near'. Dickens, after watching the Mannings, man and wife, pay the penalty at Southwark's Horsemonger jail in 1849 for disposing of a friend under their kitchen floor, felt he was 'living in a city of devils'. Excitement was intense, riot always a probability. Said another observer: 'All the avenues to Tyburn appear like those to a wake or festival, where idleness, wantonness, drunkenness and every other species of debauchery are gratified.' From the huge stand, owned by a local cowkeeper and known as Mother Proctor's Pews, those who could pay could enjoy a panoramic view. High-

Street justice as Col. James Turner prepares to die at the Leadenhall scene of his crime.
(By courtesy of the Guildhall Library, Corporation of London)

born ladies booked their seats to see their idols off. From Lord Ferrer's execution in 1760 for killing his steward, Mother Proctor was rumoured to have made £500. Whores, almost certainly, did a fine trade. Ballads and broadsides, those opportunist chronicles of the victims' errant lives, were touted round the scaffold even as the noose was being placed round their necks. The day following there would appear the follow-ups, the tabloids of their time, with the 'full story': all the bloody and last-moment details. The atmosphere rose dangerously at times – to fever pitch. Last-minute reprieves, like that which freed Dr Hennesy, a fraudster, in 1758, were the last straw. Then the frustrated crowd took their revenge by wrecking the seating arrangements of the well-to-do spectators.

All journeys end. For the everyday miscreant there was little ceremony; and hardly time to say goodbye. It was usual up to the end of the seventeenth century and beyond it for prisoners to climb a ladder and then, with the noose in place, take a few moments to say farewell to friends, perhaps to sing a psalm or share a prayer – and then jump. As the moment of execution drew closer people would thrust forward, fighting their way to a vantage point, ears strained for the last utterance, necks craned painfully to witness the final seconds and the prisoner's bravery (or lack of it). The crowd expected the condemned to die with dignity and with a decent regard to time. Procrastination in their prayers would bring howls of anger and protest. It was then that the crowd judged whether the victim had 'bottom', then the vogue word for courage. The brave, having said their piece for posterity, in a fine last act of defiance that must have salved the hangman's conscience, 'turned themselves off'. Others would have to have the ladder kicked away from them. The sophistication of the cart and later the trapdoor drop would replace such crude improvisation.

With the cart's arrival, the hangman, stopping it under one of the gibbet's beams, fixed one end of the rope to the beam and fitted the noose round the unfortunate's neck. With this, the horse was given a lash with the whip, the cart was pulled perfunctorily from under the victim's feet, 'and there [in the case of a multiple hanging] swings my gentlemen, kicking in the air. The hangman does not give himself the trouble to put them out of their pain but some of their friends or relations do it for them. They pull the dying person by the legs and beat his breast to despatch him as soon as possible.'

Pepys recalls paying a shilling to stand on the wheel of a cart. The hanging was that of a Colonel Turner in 1664 and Pepys, as usual, viewed the execution with equanimity. Others were more squeamish, more ambiguous in their response.

Boswell, in his desire to sample all life to the full, was unable to stay away from such a spectacle. Early in May 1763 he attended the simultaneous executions at Tyburn of a city fraudster, a woman guilty of theft and a young Macheath, erstwhile gallant and highwayman. His entry in his *London Journal* for 4 May notes: 'My curiosity to see the melancholy spectacle of the executions was so strong that I could not resist it . . . I had a sort of horrid eagerness to be there.' Rather morbidly he wanted to see the 'last behaviour' of the handsome highwayman. He took a friend, and succeeded in getting a place on a scaffold very near the fatal tree, 'so that we could clearly see all the dismal scene'. The crowd, he reports, was 'prodigious' and the hangings shocked him badly, bringing on 'a very deep melancholy' – none of which stopped him rising early on another occasion and hurrying to Newgate to see fifteen men hanged simultaneously.

Disorder invariably followed the deed. Friends of a dangling man would indeed rush forward, to hang on his boots and shorten his last agony. Scuffles broke out as the superstitious surged forward to touch the still-warm corpse in the belief that it had medicinal properties; women bared their breasts before the gaze of the multitude, to have the hands of the dead man placed on them; chaos reigned as friends attempted to claim the body and surgeons, limited to ten bodies a year for dissection, fought them for possession of the precious cadaver. Afterwards people would pay to see the corpse lying at the undertaker's. By dashing to the body while it was hanging, friends might even hope to revive the victim before death ensued – as they did in the case of Half-hanged John Smith, cut down and saved in 1709. He had been on the rope for fifteen minutes before being cut down.

It was to curb such fracas and the street scenes of shocking profligacy, with the danger that riots posed to the capital, that the road to Tyburn ended; the gibbet was finally demolished in 1783. Important hangings thereafter would be outside Newgate on the first gallows to incorporate a trapdoor drop. Twenty could be hanged at a time and the landlord of the Magpie and Stump opposite did well by it – letting out his upstairs room as a superb viewing gallery. Given the nature of the day, he would also have turned a penny or two on the sale of strong spirits. For such upper rooms with a view of the hanging, the wealthy (or ghoulish) were happy to pay £50, breakfast inclusive. The prisoner's view was somewhat different. Emerging from his cell into the open air, what did he see? Dickens, obsessed with the sight and workings of Newgate, tells us in *Oliver Twist*:

A great multitude of people had already assembled; the windows were filled with people, smoking and playing cards to beguile the time; the crowd were pushing, quarrelling, and joking. Everything told of life and animation but one dark cluster of objects in the very centre of all – the black stage, the cross-beam, the rope, and all the hideous apparatus of death.

Such spectacles, after 1868, would be removed from the public gaze behind Newgate's grim walls. Only the black flag on the prison pole and the tolling of the prison bell would tell of the solemn event being enacted within.

A Tyburn execution would be overseen by the City sheriff, who hired the hangman, generically known as Jack Ketch, after the incompetent of that name who so dreadfully mishandled the demise of the Duke of Monmouth in 1685. He would have the further ironical title of the Lord of the Manor of Tyburn. Hangmen, one is happy to say, also sometimes came to a bad end, themselves gracing the gallows. But if the day went well, the job had its perks, including the right to the prisoners' clothes, and in the evening the hangman would probably be found in Fleet Street's Green Dragon or another of its famous taverns, dropping titbits in exchange for a drink or two and selling off pieces of the rope (or ropes) used at sixpence per six-inch length.

The capital's first permanent gallows site at Tyburn dated from 1571. Earlier, victims might have been dragged by the heels to the Elms of Smithfield beyond the City walls. This site had a long and sinister history in the four centuries before Tyburn took over: a grisly catalogue of burnings and boilings-alive, and as late as 1652 the diarist John Evelyn would witness the death by burning of a woman who had administered poison to the detriment of her husband's health. Triangular in form, the Tyburn gallows was some 18 feet high with cross-beams 9 feet in length. The condemned could be accommodated eight to a beam. But there were many other venues where justice was done, including Smithfield (still) and Tower Hill. At Execution Dock pirates (including the infamous Captain Kidd) met a more colourful end with the whiff of the river in their nostrils on a wharf where the River Neckinger (the word becoming a euphemism for the noose) ran into the Thames; the historian John Stow reports it as the 'usual place for the hanging of pirates and sea-rovers, at the low-water mark, and there to remain till three tides have overflowed them'. The offenders were then hung in chains in gibbets on the marshy margins of the river.

The outrageous and treasonable, with a savage logic, demanded justice on the spot. Thus the Gunpowder Plot conspirators had ended their abortive venture where it had begun – at St Paul's. When Lincoln's Inn Fields were still grazing pasture Anthony Babington and his unlucky thirteen henchmen used it for their conspiratorial plotting and made an unwelcome return one day in 1586 after their discovery – to be hanged, drawn and quartered. It gave the whole episode a satisfying symmetry. Babington was still conscious when his butchery began, and in view of this Queen Elizabeth, in her kindness, suggested that the others – six were disposed of one day, seven the next – should first be well and truly hanged. Later executions would disturb the far from Elysian calm of the famous Fields, including the beheading of William, Lord Russell, in 1683, for his alleged involvement in the Rye House Plot to kill the Restoration monarch.

Making an end, with two others, at Charing Cross, then a terminus of more sinister resort, the regicide Colonel Thomas Harrison was made to face the Banqueting House, where Charles I had died. Evelyn apparently missed the event, in October 1660, but Pepys was there. He tells us matter-of-factly:

I went out to Charing Cross to see Major-General Harrison hanged, drawn and quartered; which was done there, he looking as cheerful as any man could do in that condition. He was presently cut down, and his head and heart shown to the people, at which there was great shouts of joy . . .

For the diarist the occasion was doubly memorable. 'Thus it was my chance to see the king beheaded at Whitehall and to see the first blood shed in revenge for the blood of the king.' Harrison, a butcher's son, had been Cromwell's nominee to escort Charles I from Windsor for trial in Whitehall, where he also sat as one of the judges.

Pepys's description is a reminder of the callousness and barbarity of the then course of justice. After Harrison had been left hanging for a time, and his quartering commenced, his fellow-regicides Peters and Cook were brought forward; Peters, dragged to the front to witness the mutilation, was asked by the sweating, blood-soaked hangman what he thought about the thing that awaited him. 'I'm not terrified,' Peters said, 'do your worst.' Minutes later Peters's body, after strangulation, was quivering under the same bloody knife. Regicides too could die bravely.

One of the most macabre sights ever seen must surely have been the execution of three dead men, taken from the grave to face a belated punishment. Two years after the Restoration the body of the Lord Protector, laid to rest after his long illness, was exhumed, along with those of Bradshaw and Ireton, and all three were taken to pay the penalty for their earlier actions on the anniversary of Charles I's death. The three corpses were allowed to hang on Tyburn's gallows until sunset, and then taken down and beheaded. Their heads were displayed above Westminster Hall, while their bodies were buried under the gallows.

Down the years those whose lives ended at Tyburn – the capital's rogues and murderers and petty criminals – have largely been forgotten. Yet the names of a few ring still in the mind. To many of the capital's ladies of quality the highwayman Gentleman James Maclean was a man to swoon over. They mourned him deeply, visiting him in great numbers before his hanging in 1750. Visiting Newgate was then a popular Sunday outing, and on the Sabbath after he was sentenced three thousand people flocked to see him in his cell. His memoirs circulated widely. The highwayman Claude Duval was also considered to be a perfect gent – in one coach hold-up he danced with one of the lady passengers on Hounslow Heath. When he died, he too was accompanied inconsolably to the gallows by many ladies of high birth. Sympathy welled through Tyburn's mob as Sheppard died on the rope – with some difficulty. He was the subject of pantomime at Drury Lane, which dramatised his escapes from capture and his clever prison breaks. Another production, with songs, was performed at the capital's Bartholomew Fair. Sheppard epitomised the roguish robber, one of the capital's own. He was born at Spitalfields in 1702, put to an apprenticeship with a Clare Market carpenter and lived an innocent life until he fell into the company of bad women. He began by stealing silver from the houses where he worked, graduating to house-breaking and finally to highway robbery. He was betrayed by an associate of the self-styled thief-taker Jonathan Wild, and at the end of August 1724 he was lodged for execution in Newgate – whence women friends orchestrated his escape. Recaptured, he escaped again, but drink, it must be said, was his downfall. He went on a binge around his old haunts in Clare Market, where he was easily recognised. When he woke up, sober again, he was back in Newgate.

He was a star, a personality, the darling of raffish society. As he awaited the Tyburn cart and the noose, admirers and chroniclers (pressing coins into the turnkey's palm) were admitted to his Newgate cell to hear his story from his own lips. Professional hacks would offer money for such a life-story – or at least a fine ornate coffin when it was needed. In prison Sheppard had his portrait painted, and in return for an audience his callers, some of them nobles whom he asked to intercede with the king, were urged to try to procure a re-hearing of his case or an amendment of the sentence, alas without success. Perhaps they did not argue hard enough – perhaps not at all. Sheppard was hanged on 23 November 1724. He was twenty-three. Friends conveyed his body to a Long Acre inn and he was buried in St Martin-in-the-Fields churchyard. He lies, perhaps fittingly, in illustrious company, including Hogarth, who so relentlessly recorded the vice and viciousness of his age, Nell Gwynne, who rose above it, the painter Reynolds and the cabinet-maker Chippendale. So passed a legend.

Jonathan Wild, on the other hand, was reviled and jeered all the way to the gallows. A man of exceptional organisational skills, he ran with the fox and hunted with the hounds. He ran his own kind of mafia, a so-called prince of robbers whose amazing career ran concurrently with Sheppard's and who, on a May day less than a year later, followed him to Tyburn when it all went wrong. The Thief-taker General of Great Britain and Ireland was pelted with stones all the way to the gallows by the crowds jamming the streets. In notoriety his reputation exceeded that of Sheppard; his audacity, still, is unbelievable. From a respectable Wolverhampton home, after two years' trial he took a disinclination to marriage, deserting his young wife and son for London's fleshpots, where his high lifestyle soon put him in debt and in prison. There he cultivated the villains and began recruiting a criminal army that would eventually number seven thousand. Freedom brought him the occupancy of a public house in Cripplegate's Cock Alley – and entrance to a netherworld through his new companion, pickpocket, prostitute and general bad lot Mary Milliner.

His inn became a trading post for its customers' ill-gotten gains. When legislation made it an offence to receive stolen goods, Wild accepted the stolen articles as a 'recovery service', returning the items to their rightful owners for a fee. Such was Wild's apparent probity that the robbed paid up, picking up their property from pre-arranged venues. It was almost respectable. In time he affected the style of a gentleman. He had by then a complete mastery of the workings of the underworld, tampering with witnesses to prevent or abort prosecutions – in other cases ensuring conviction and death. He is said to have sent over a hundred souls to the gibbet, riding ahead of the Tyburn procession to give the waiting crowds a commentary on the condemned following behind.

In the early, most violent, period of the eighteenth century he had overall control of the capital's crimewave. His specially trained henchmen, in laced coats and brocade waistcoats, attended court balls, the opera and playhouses and

Thief-catcher and villain Jonathan Wild on the cart bound for Tyburn and the gallows. (Billie Love Historical Collection)

operated at fashionable levées; he had his own coterie of highwaymen and an entire industry of pickpockets and prostitutes. His sharpers were swindlers frequently setting up elaborate and ingenious scams to trick the wealthy. On a lesser scale they passed dud money into circulation at races and fairs, wherever the public carelessly foregathered. (There were at the time some forty mints turning out counterfeit coin.) In the capital female sharpers, dressed *à la mode* to attend masquerades and masked balls and ingratiate themselves into fashionable company, stole diamonds and other valuable jewellery. One noted male sharper posed, very plausibly, as a clergyman.

Wild's jaunt to Tyburn, following a convoluted court wrangle over some pieces of stolen lace, came only after persistent and prolonged lobbying and after he had attempted to cheat the noose by taking a massive dose of laudanum. At the gallows he was given some time sitting in the cart – until the mood of the mob became ugly, with calls for the executioner to get on with his job, and threatening his life if he did not. The Mr Big of London's early eighteenth-century underworld had finally run out of friends. He was buried (at two in the morning) in St Pancras churchyard, but his corpse was abducted a few nights later; the surgeons, it is thought, were keen to study such a complex character. His skeleton would be preserved in the museum of the Royal College of Surgeons as an object of curiosity. In his tumultuous life Wild had collected nineteen sword or pistol scars and his skull was held together by silver plates where it had been repeatedly fractured. The corrupt rewards system that had allowed his criminal empire to flourish would be discontinued when Henry Fielding took over as Bow Street magistrate in 1748 and, with his brother John, organised his own legal thief-takers (known as 'Mr Fielding's People').

It was jealousy, as we have seen, that took the unrequited lover the Reverend James Hackman to Tyburn after he was found guilty of the murder of the Earl of Sandwich's mistress Martha Ray; greed brought to a close the career of that other divine, the Reverend Dr William Dodd, when he misguidedly forged the signature of the Earl of Chesterfield – though he made a desperate bid to continue it by having friends cut him down after death and rush him to the Goodge Street undertaker's where vain attempts were made to resuscitate him. Political rebels paid a higher price, facing the full rigour of the state's displeasure before the mob at Tower Hill.

Tower Hill was the principal venue for beheadings. There was a social nuance in the punishment, as the foreign visitor Paul Hentzner detected; in *A Journey to*

England, published in 1598, he remarked on the three hundred people annually being executed in London, adding that 'beheading with them [the English] is less infamous than hanging'. It may have been poor consolation for those who emerged from the Tower to walk to the scaffold in the morning sunlight; they had included down the years such fulcrum figures in the country's history as the disobedient Sir Thomas More (1535), the Protector Somerset (1552), Archbishop Laud (1645) and the ill-fated Duke of Monmouth (1685) following the Battle of Sedgemoor, whose beheading was grotesque. The axe blade was so blunt that Monmouth rose from the block to give the executioner a talking-to. Two further attempts were then made to dispatch the duke – but so ineffectually that Jack Ketch (the real one) had finally to sever the head with a knife. The crowd, enraged, pelted the incompetent wretch, who only just escaped with his life.

Men like Monmouth met their end with the courage expected of their breed, even with a sublime equanimity. Making his way to the block in Lincoln's Inn Fields in 1683, William, Lord Russell, was calm. The Bishop of Salisbury, Dr Gilbert Burnet, accompanied him in the coach and wrote later: 'Some of the crowd that filled the streets wept, while others insulted. He was singing psalms a great part of the way, and said he hoped to sing better ones soon. As he observed the great crowd of people all the way, he said "I hope I shall quickly see a much better assembly".' At the scaffold he strolled round it a few times. After prayers, and again declaring his innocence, he undressed and laid his head on the block without the least change of expression. It needed 'three butcherly strokes' (by the same bungling Jack Ketch) to sever it.

The Stuart cause would bring more than its fair quota to the Tower and the scaffold: in 1716 the Viscount Kenmure and the Earl of Derwentwater; in 1746 and 1747 Lords Balmerino and Kilmarnock and the reprobate Lovat. They had known the risks, now they faced the penalty boldly – even blithely. Leaving Westminster Hall for the last time after his trial, Lord Lovat called out to his judges: 'Good day, my lords; you and I shall never meet again in the same place.' Gossip and gadabout Horace Walpole, advising a friend that 'London will be as full as at a Coronation', sat through the trial of Kilmarnock and Balmerino: 'The most melancholy . . . the most interesting . . . the most solemn and fine . . . sight . . . I ever saw,' he said, moved by the men's courage.

It was the social event of the year. Two-thirds of the old Westminster Hall was commandeered, with seating for the cream of the capital's society, who came to see their peers condemned. There was a box for the Duke of Cumberland, victor of sad Culloden, and one for the Prince and Princess of Wales. Kilmarnock accepted his guilt with impeccable fortitude; Balmerino behaved with contemptuous bravado. Both, as was expected, were found guilty of high treason and sentenced to be executed at Tower Hill on 18 August 1746. That day 'as the clock struck ten', they came forth on foot, Lord Kilmarnock all in black and supported by Foster, the great Presbyterian, and Mr Home, a young clergyman, his friend. Lord Balmerino followed, alone, in a blue coat, turned up with red (his rebellious regimentals). Kilmarnock was first, Walpole reports, showing 'a visible unwillingness to depart, and after five minutes dropped his handkerchief, the signal, and his head was cut off at once, only hanging by a bit of skin, and was received in a scarlet cloth by four of the undertaker's men kneeling, who wrapped it up and put it in the coffin with the body . . .'. Balmerino, brought out before the crowds to what Macaulay called the 'saddest spot on earth', seemed fearless, walking round the scaffold as if inspecting it for bad workmanship and testing the axe's blade and its balance in his hands – and so unnerving the axeman that he botched the job, taking three blows before he managed to sever the old man's head from his shoulders. For once the huge mob, some of them clinging in the rigging of ships in the river, was hushed, voicing neither the usual jeers nor cries of pity.

Lord Lovat was astonished at the number of people who had come to witness his departure. So congested was the scene that a stand collapsed, killing twelve of the spectators and injuring many more – to the old rascal's immense satisfaction. 'The more mischief the better the sport,' he chuckled. Reporting on Lovat's last moments (for the benefit of his ghoulish friend George Augustus Selwyn, who loved attending executions, sometimes in women's clothes), Walpole wrote:

He was beheaded yesterday [9 April 1747] and died extremely well, without affectation, buffoonery or timidity; his behaviour was natural and intrepid. He professed himself a Jansenist; made no speech, but sat down a little while in a chair on the scaffold and talked to the people round him. He said he was glad to suffer for his country . . . He lay down quietly, gave the sign soon, and was despatched at a blow.

At the undertaker's his head would be sewn on again before he was put in his coffin. Lovat was the last man to lose his head at Tower Hill. Beheadings would continue, but at Newgate, where the last took place outside the prison on 1 May 1820. The victims were the conspirators known as the Cato Street Five. There

Pamphleteer Daniel Defoe is punished for his views in the public pillory at Temple Bar. (By courtesy of the Guildhall Library, Corporation of London)

was at least a poetic justice at play: meeting in an old barn off the Edgware Road, as a reprisal for the Peterloo massacre they had planned to murder the entire Cabinet of the time as they dined in Grosvenor Square with Lord Harrowby. The heads of Lord Sidmouth, the Home Secretary, and Lord Castlereagh were to be collected in a bag, and a provisional government was to be proclaimed. There was much public sympathy with the plotters at the time, and later attempts would be made to castrate the men suspected of executing them.

Lesser ranks of the Forty-five's rebels were sentenced to be hanged, drawn and quartered on Kennington Common, Surrey's main site of execution. The betrothed of one victim died from the shock of seeing her beloved butchered before her eyes. Two Jacobite heads would be exhibited at Temple Bar; one was that of the Jacobite commander Sir Francis Towneley, an Englishman, who was first to face the knife at Kennington. He had ordered a new suit of black velvet from a local tailor for his execution, but, as was common practice, it was stripped from him to leave him naked as he was hanged. He was still alive as he was cut down and the executioner hammered desperately on his chest in an attempt to extinguish life before he started the butchery of the sentence. Again, the vast crowd had been strangely muted as they followed the first of the condemned from Southwark jail to the scaffold; the pie-sellers did a fine trade no doubt, but for once the atmosphere was far from fair-like. There was already growing in the capital a mood of sympathy and an indignation at the savagery of the rebels' sentences, and Cumberland, taking heed from it, thought it prudent to cancel a ball arranged for that evening.

There remained, none the less, for many more years an obsessive fear of the ousted dynasty. When all should have been long forgiven, another Jacobite rebel, Dr Archibald Cameron, died at Tyburn, the victim of a belated spite. His part in the Forty-five rebellion had been little enough, mainly attending the wounded of both sides, but he was the brother of the clan chief without whose support the uprising would have foundered from the start. Returning from exile in France – some thought to plot another insurrection – he was seized and taken to the Tower. His wife at the time was pregnant with their eighth child. Even the London judiciary, it is said, felt shame at his high-treason sentence: 'to be drawn on a sledge to the place of execution; there to be hanged, but not till you are dead; your bowels to be taken out; your body quartered, your head cut off, and affixed at the king's disposal'.

Like Lovat, Cameron died well and in some style, dressed in a light-coloured coat, red waistcoat and breeches and wearing a new bagwig. Along the route he bowed to acquaintances in the crowd and reached Tyburn at a quarter after noon. Unbound from the sledge (the usual transport for traitors) he stepped on to the cart amid the apparatus of death and looked around, smiling to the crowd. When the sheriff asked the attending clergyman whether he would be long, Cameron answered that it was indeed disagreeable to be there and that he was as impatient as they were to be gone. He told the sheriff that he freely forgave those who had been instrumental in taking his life away, and after joining the minister in prayers, gave the signal for the cart to be drawn away. His body was hanged for twenty minutes, then his heart was cut out and burned. But he was not quartered.

Earl Ferrers rode to his Tyburn hanging in his landau and wearing his wedding suit. (By courtesy of the Guildhall Library, Corporation of London)

He was not alone in exiting in style. Aware of their role as the principals in that most macabre of dramas and of their brief moment of fame, many met their fate in the high fashion of the day. One foreign observer, amazed by the whole carnival atmosphere, commented:

> The English are a people that laugh at the delicacy of other nations who make it such a mighty matter to be hanged. He that is to be takes care to get himself shaved and handsomely dresses either in mourning or in the dress of a bridegroom . . . Sometimes the girls dress in white with great scarves and carry baskets full of flowers and oranges, scattering these favours all the way they go.

But dress varied according to the victim's whim and outlook, and some, with a stark regard for the reality of their situation (and perhaps to cheat the hangman of his traditional perk of the prisoner's clothes) wore a shroud. Sixteen-string Jack (John Rann), the highwayman, who died at Tyburn in 1776, had a massive nosegay in the button-hole of his pea-green silk brocade coat and wore white gloves. Tied to his breeches were the sixteen ribbons indicating the number of times he had cheated the law. Innocents (not necessarily of the crime) wore a white cockade in their hats – or perhaps chose a white frock. Lord Ferrers came by his own landau and wore his wedding suit; the Perreau twins Robert and Daniel, hanged for forgery, perhaps unfairly, in 1776, arrived at Tyburn by mourning coach and dressed alike in deep mourning.

Even the coarse-grained Dick Turpin (who had a territorial right to die at Tyburn but opted for York) bought a fustian frock-coat and a new pair of pumps. Perhaps suddenly aware of the alienation his career had brought him, the previous day he gave five poor men ten shillings each to follow the hangman's cart as mourners; to others he gave gloves and hat-bands. On the way to execution he gracefully bowed to the crowds lining the streets. His end was not without pathos. He seemed reluctant to depart. On the hangman's ladder he talked with his executioner for about half an hour before 'turning himself off' and dying within a few minutes. He was tolerably good-looking and his last moments affected the less-hardened York crowd deeply. Like Wild, he suffered some disturbance in death. After lying at the Blue Boar Inn, his body was buried the following night in St George's churchyard. The night following the grave was robbed, and his corpse was later found in a surgeon's garden. Placed on a board, Turpin again made a triumphal procession through the streets – to the grave he had vacated.

What seems remarkable now is the amazing courage with which those whom society condemned to die accepted their fate and their central 'starring' role in the grotesque carnival of the hanging fair – not least, their striving in conduct and appearance to be worthy of the occasion, to put on a show. Even more shocking is the fact that for the drunken mob their macabre and sometimes bloody execution was just another good day's amusement.

CHAPTER XI
Wonders of All the Wide World

The capital, happily, had more innocent pleasures. The Restoration had ushered in an age of curiosity, and with it the intellectual climate for shows whose courageous entrepreneurs catered for the mind and spirit and provided a glimpse of a wider world as yet barely perceived by the toiling masses, and for the moment at least beyond the ambit of their often depressing lives. To stimulate the common fancy, and admittedly if possible to line their own pockets, those pioneering men ventured into the unknown, the realms of science and engineering, creating the kind of spectacles and exhibitions and exotic bazaars such as the capital had not seen before.

By the end of the seventeenth century Leicester Square was already on the way to becoming the hub of an exhibition and entertainment area spreading out to the Strand on one side and Soho on the other. And the Reverend Sydney Smith was of the opinion that 'the parallelogram between Oxford Street, Piccadilly, Regent Street, and Hyde Park encloses more intelligence and human ability . . . than the world has ever collected in such a space before'. He was a man always disposed to speak well of his friends – and his capital. But even the brusque Dr Johnson, drawn out by Boswell on the pleasures of London in 1769, observed: 'I will venture to say, there is more learning and science within the circumference of ten miles from where we now sit than in all the rest of the kingdom.' Learned societies were being launched like a contagion to disseminate the new scientific knowledge – and to enrol fresh cognoscenti.

Novelty and innovation would bring an outbreak of wholesome pleasures to the capital: fireworks explosions on the river or in the pleasure gardens (at every excuse); the morbid fascination of Mother Salmon's Waxworks, where waxwork figures 'handed out' the handbills at the door. The cry was for spectacle, for sensation, for revelation – and the great events locked themselves into the minds of those who witnessed them: the pomp and panoply of coronations, the even more majestic pageantry of the Lord Mayor's Show (still then mainly on the river) and the pioneering conquests of the intrepid early balloonists and parachutists as man explored his new dimension.

Such stirring events would be accompanied by an efflorescence in the arts. Under a benevolent Regency, architecture in the hands of Nash, the prince's favourite, among others, would rise on every side to delight the eye. Indeed, the prince, apart from his choice in women, had excellent taste that worked through to enrich England in its buildings and landscape; that favoured all the arts, and especially music, and accorded them a place in the life of the nation. He was a generous patron whose contribution was often obscured by his eccentric behaviour in other ways.

By the end of the eighteenth century the turnpikes had opened up the regions one to another and all of them to the capital itself. It was the finest hour, before the black gloom of industrialisation disfigured the land. Capability Brown would pick up the baton from men like William Kent who had already done much to soften and transform the countryside on the estates of the wealthy, blending park and garden seamlessly into the adjoining landscape. Horace Walpole rated Brown the best. And this, too, was the time of the Adam brothers; Robert in turn would pleasantly mellow the classical lines of the stately home.

Painting would defy the conventional, becoming stimulating and controversial under the rebellious brushes of trailblazers such as Constable and the reclusive Turner, the son of a barber and a butcher's daughter (and born in Covent Garden's Maiden Lane), who developed his own romantic style with bloody and tortured skies shot through by the play of light and his evocation of nature in her violent moods – only, astonishing as it may seem, to be discredited. The work may have reflected the man: he was a miserly, lonely figure, a man with 'no faculty for friendship'. Constable, equally obsessed and under the spell of Suffolk's wind-scoured skies, decisively advanced the cause of landscape painting, though he was never in his lifetime to be accorded his true merit. An amiable man, he later transferred his artistic loyalty to Hampstead, captivated by its cloud-capped beauty.

Art was in the ascendant. Reynolds, returning from Italy in 1750, had found fashionable women beating a path to his Great Newport Street studio to have their likenesses created by his brush; the beauties of the demi-monde were among them, including the mistresses of important men and the famous raven-haired courtesan Kitty Fischer, whose blue eyes had beguiled so many. Thomas Lawrence, a young and exceptional talent, drew the praise of Sir Joshua, one of the Royal Academy's founders in 1768, and would fall in love with his lady sitters one by one, portraying them as they wished the world to see them, but then had to content himself (under the Prince Regent's commission) with painting the allied generals in a tour of the courts of the continent. Canaletto had come and gone, the house-guest of the Duke of Richmond for a decade from 1745, suffusing his London scenes with a charming if duplicitous Venetian sunlight. The young artist Johann Zoffany would paint the contentment of the landed classes taking their leisure in their beautiful countryside. It would never be the same again. Man had made it and man might delight in it – but only for a time. Britain's wealth and domination in the world would be bought at the expense of it.

At Holland House Lord Holland and his lady welcomed the capital's wits and politicians, its writers and artists and scholars; conversation and repartee and argument flourished under their roof. Writers had declared a new era in literature, and it was a scene that Walter Scott, who loved London, came down from his Border fastness to embrace. He supped, unaffectedly, with the Prince at Carlton House, and with the Duke of Wellington, and recited his ballads to the ladies, old and young, while keeping secret his authorship of the *Waverley* novels. The prince and Scott took to each other at once and shared an admiration for the work of Jane Austen.

Music would blossom under the prince, who was himself a tolerable singer. Rossini came with his wife Madame Colbran and conquered at musical soirées in the salons of the capital's most fashionable hostesses and at Almack's, which was jam-packed for his concert; Mendelssohn, thought to be a continental playboy, young and head-turningly handsome, stunned audiences at the Hanover Rooms, the capital's main concert venue, and at the Argyll Rooms. There was a seriousness to life, increasingly recognised by the thoughtful minority, that underlay the bright dazzle of the pleasure society and the heedless barbarity of some of its sports. Minds were becoming attuned to an awareness of the breadth and splendour of existence and new pleasures structured with a cerebral excitement.

But old habits died hard; spectacle still equated with ostentation. The Pantheon, which had so outrageously sought to ban Mrs Baddeley, opening in Oxford Street in 1772, was splendour made manifest, one of the wonders of the capital. It was intended as a 'winter Ranelagh'. The rotunda took its inspiration from its like in Constantinople as well as from the one in the famous gardens: it

The sumptuous, if overwhelming, elegance of the music room at Vauxhall Gardens. (By courtesy of the Guildhall Library, Corporation of London)

had supper rooms, tea rooms, card rooms and small vestibules (presumably in place of those wicked alcoves). It was over two years in the building and so stirred one visiting foreign nobleman that he truly believed it must have been conjured by the wave of a fairy wand. Fifteen hundred people turned up for the opening night. Walpole was enchanted, describing it as 'the most beautiful edifice in England'; he also, somewhat ambiguously, thought its interior had 'the most beautiful stuccoes in the best taste of grotesque'. Charles Burney, father of the more famous Fanny, considered it quite 'the most elegant structure in Europe, if not the Globe'. Rowlandson was bedazzled and with Pugin would record its moments of high splendour. It staged fêtes, ridottos, concerts and the ever-popular, ever-intriguing masquerades for the capital's most fashionable people. It held twelve assemblies during the season at six guineas inclusive, but even so may have priced itself out of patrons. In a frantic effort to restore its appeal, Lunardi the balloonist, by now a celebrity, brought his balloon along for a guest appearance during the 1784/5 season – alas, to no avail. Cheaper prices brought in for a time a trickle of fresh patrons to popular exhibitions, but eventually the city's most dazzling monument to the 'beautiful life' succumbed; it became an opera house and, finally, slid to undeserved oblivion as a bazaar.

After the Pantheon's extravagance of line and décor the Egyptian Hall must have seemed mundane. Its focus, however, was significantly different: the widening of the horizons of the man in the street. Officially the London Museum, it took its popular name from its Middle-Eastern façade and housed a collection of 'Fifteen Thousand Natural and Foreign Curiosities, Antiques and Productions of the Fine Arts' assembled by William Bullock. The Liverpool man brought his curiosities to the greater audience of the capital around the turn of the century. Londoners poured in to browse and ponder (and giggle), encouraging the enterprising showman to expand into the larger Egyptian Hall exhibition in Piccadilly, with a further hodge-podge of artefacts that included in 1816 a display of Napoleonic memorabilia centred on the Emperor's carriage (bought from the Prince Regent for £2,500), luxurious and wisely bullet-proof. Eight hundred thousand people clamoured to see it, ten thousand each day. Among later attractions for patrons to mull over was a pharaoh's tomb with the detritus of a dig in the Valley of the Kings and other Mid-East *objets*. It was the place to bring country friends to gape and wonder. A moving panorama of the Mississippi – on a painted canvas three miles long – switched interest to the New World, and in 1844 the celebrated American dwarf General Tom Thumb was persuaded to show himself there. Thereafter – perhaps having sated too well the public appetite for the offbeat – the hall became a Mecca for magic.

But Londoners were a curious lot, and the exhibition, of whatever kind, was a form of communication for those who could not read. Knowledge was instantly and graphically conveyed. Panoramas were all the rage as Prince Albert set up his Great Exhibition in Hyde Park. From 1793 in Leicester Square Burford's show in its impressive circular turret would draw in the inquisitive to experience the inventive ingenuity of the artist Robert Barker's scenic painting. Spectators stood on a circular dais 30 feet wide at the centre of the scene, while the 'painting' hung on the inner circumference of the turret's wall. The method went on to become the medium for bringing alive the harrowing scenes of Britain's battle victories in what were the newsreels of the period. Thirty years on interest would shift to the Colosseum, the brainchild of Thomas Horner, in the south-east corner of Regent's Park, where patrons would have the whole landscape of the city (as viewed from the top of St Paul's) laid at their feet. In the afternoon they would see London by day, and in the evening, with flawless logic, London by night. This was only the start: there would follow cycloramas, dioramas, kineramas, cosmoramas and typoramas, each with their scenes and sounds more vividly evoked, so that one might experience, in perfect safety, the swinging motion of balloon flight, the terror and fury of foreign earthquakes and terrible storms – in the virtual reality of the time. Thackeray was quite dazed by such wonders: 'The awful booming of thunderbolts roared in our ears, dazzled our eyes and frightened our senses so, that I protest I was more dead than alive when I quitted the premises.'

Dominating the square by then was the towering edifice enclosing Wyld's Great Globe, 65 feet in diameter, and a dramatic presentation that placed man humblingly in the cosmos and delineated the physical features of his known planet. A 'world tour' was taken through tiers of ascending terraces, each with an assistant who, headmaster-style, indicated the salient contours with his pointer. It might have been a hard act to follow, but not, apparently, for James Wyld, the Member for Bodmin and a man with a passion for current affairs. His 'Crimea' exhibition a few years later took his informing genius a step further, when he presented a daily résumé of the news from the battlefronts, showing the relative positions of the warring factions. It was a brilliant innovation, a constant news update, that brought the passing public streaming in – artisans, legal clerks, ledger clerks in their shiny frockcoats, all the intelligent emerging classes that would one day coalesce into the concept of Middle England.

A broader understanding of the war-torn region would beckon soon after at the Oriental Museum, which would show the way of everyday life in Turkey, Armenia and Albania. The Great Globe itself, alas, would be only a ten-year phenomenon, denuding and somehow diminishing the square by its demise. Panoramas too would soon be passé. The crowd, ever fickle, had moved on. Such fickleness was something shrewd entrepreneurial minds took into account. The Colosseum had in-built inducements for those whose attention was not easily stretched: an aviary, a hall of mirrors, a museum of sculpture and later a cyclorama theatre. At the Royal Panopticon in Leicester Square everything was promised that would advance 'by moral and intellectual agencies, the best interests of society'. Its aim was a programme demonstrating practical science for popular consumption. Many-galleried and as exquisitely tiered as a wedding cake, a conflation of graciousness, it may in 1852 already have been out of kilter with the capital's new mood. It went depressingly downmarket to become the kind of attraction the hoi polloi demanded.

They loved the circus. Its early cradle in the capital was Astley's Royal Circus, an essentially equestrian show when it was started in Lambeth in the latter half of the eighteenth century by Philip Astley, an ex-cavalryman. He had earlier shown off his own riding skills in the fields around Southwark, before establishing what was also known as Astley's Equestrian Amphitheatre. Stunt and spectacle were the staples of what was one of the young Dickens's favourite haunts and one that would feature in his novels. The show's reigning star from 1808 was Andrew Ducrow, who was also a daring tightrope-walker. His bravado would quickly be capped by the matchless Louisa Woolford, who actually danced on horseback. A troupe of acrobats, illusionists and clowns, with the Great Grimaldi of their number at one time, kept lively the audiences of 'a house of public exhibition of horsemanship and droll'. Astley's would rise from the ashes of several fires to be part of the city's show scene until the end of the nineteenth century.

It was Islington, however, that could rightfully claim to have awakened interest in colourful equestrianism. In 1766 a handbill appeared proclaiming:

Mr Price will exhibit Horsemanship, this and every afternoon, if the weather permits, in a field adjoining the Three Hats . . . where Gentlemen and Ladies may be accommodated with Coffee and Tea, Hot Loaves and Sullybubs, the Loaves to be ready at Half an Hour after Four O'Clock every afternoon . . .

Syllabubs, sometimes a dish and sometimes a drink, were made, literally, under the cow's udder in big bowls of wine, brandy or cider, which curdled the fresh warm milk.

The show's promoter was Mr Dingley, who would do for horsemanship what Garrick was doing for Shakespeare. Mr Price, however, was soon upstaged and eclipsed by Mr Sampson, a former dragoon, who performed with breathtaking panache, standing on the saddle on one leg at the gallop. He also rode, hell for

Itching to amuse: posters advertise some of the tiny exhibition attractions. (By courtesy of the Guildhall Library, Corporation of London)

leather, hanging from the saddle so that his head brushed the ground. And that was just to warm-up the audience. He would dismount at full gallop, fire a pistol, and leap back into the saddle with his mount still at the gallop. He also rode two horses at a time and for a thrilling finale rode with his head on the saddle and his feet in the air. Soon this fearless horseman would have a bride of like talents (billed inevitably as The First Equestrienne), and their combined displays were given to the sound of music.

Dingley's wonderful cavalcade only came to grief when he had to ransom his horseman from a bizarre 'kidnap', a contretemps involving his rival Price, a prostitute, a sordid room at Bagnigge Wells – and the confiscation of Mr Sampson's breeches. He was replaced on the bill by Mr Coningham, a cultured gentleman who stood on the backs of two galloping horses while simultaneously playing the flute. It may have been enough to prevent the show's regulars from defecting to Dobney's, a nearby tea-garden where Price was starring and where, in 1772, one Daniel Wildman lived up to his name by giving an exhibition of beekeeping while balancing himself with one foot on his horse's neck, the other on the saddle, while the bees swarmed over his face and neck. Patrons could see it all for a shilling.

Even Ducrow could not have matched that. What he did do, as Astley's manager for many years, was present stylish re-enactments of such events as the victory of Waterloo, spectaculars (as in the pleasure gardens) with realistic sound effects and the smoke of battle. Pride and patriotism were fevered by such performances. Those feelings came to the fore too, uniting all sections of the populace more or less peacefully in its celebration of state and royal occasions. Fireworks, a perennial fascination, were an apt enhancement to those moments of history – to a greater or lesser degree, since it was an art in which England lagged until well into the seventeenth century. Once mastered, it was a passion fed with a fury by the pleasure gardens as they unleashed fusillades of maroons and rockets, and rockets on the backs of other rockets, simply to outmatch their rivals.

Human nature does not change, and animals and their antics were crowd-pullers then as now – and were used as such. They were exploited blatantly in the cause of commerce. The Strand's Exeter Change, a shopping flop at the start, was dramatically turned around by housing a menagerie on its top floor. A complex of the type that has recently been revisited, with units for seamstresses, milliners, hosiers, upholsterers (interior decorators) and the like, the roars from its wild-beast shows were heard by passers-by in the street, where a barker in Beefeater attire invited them to 'Walk up, walk-up'. The Change only fell from grace when it became the scene of a protracted butchery in 1826 when its popular elephant, a beast weighing five tons, which had appeared in Covent Garden pantomimes, became more of a danger than a diversion. After several squads of riflemen failed to finish off the rogue animal a cannon was called for and it finally arrived just as a keeper managed to end the animal's struggles with a harpoon. It all left a bad taste at the tills, and without its animal collection the Change soon closed its doors.

Yet another complex, the Soho Bazaar, opened by Queen Caroline in 1816, adopted the same ploy, drawing browsers – and animal-lovers – into an Aladdin's cave with every conceivable type of merchandise – pictures, fancy goods and every sort of gadget and knick-knack that was instantly appealing but once bought could be found no further use for. You could, while browsing the wares, also hire a maidservant or a governess.

The ultimate animal collection, of course, was to be found at the Zoological Gardens in Regent's Park. It had thirty thousand visitors within the first seven months of opening in 1828, and tickets were at a premium. It had bears, kangaroos, monkeys and many other species soon to be augmented by the addition of the royal menagerie from Windsor, and then by the animals from the Tower. The attraction was increased by the inclusion of giraffes, lions, elephants and hippopotami. It was for a time the only place to be, and the Great Vance of the music-halls sang: 'Walking in the Zoo is the OK thing to do'. The zoo's only real rival was the Surrey Zoological Gardens on a site east of Vauxhall Gardens. *Punch* considered it a 'good shilling's worth of beasts, flowers, music and fireworks' – an irresistible combination you might have thought. The visiting American novelist Nathaniel Hawthorne was unimpressed. The menagerie, he felt, was 'poor and scanty'.

The spice of variety was not only to be found in the pleasure gardens with their insatiable crowds. The Royal Aquarium was the surprising Mecca for many amusements, as well as the unlikely rendezvous for those seeking amorous intrigue. (It was here that the bored young wife Lillie Langtry met the peer who put her on the road to fame as the Prince of Wales's favourite.) For a start, palm trees softened the chill lines of the great hall. It had interesting sculptures besides the tanks of ocean creatures, and an orchestra, a skating rink, theatre and art gallery plus eating facilities, billiards and snooker saloons, and reading

Inside the Royal Aquarium, unexpectedly lush with palms and popular with lovers. (By courtesy of the Guildhall Library, Corporation of London)

and smoking rooms. Late on the scene, it opened its doors in 1876 at a cost of £200,000, determined to be mainly an educational enclave in the widening spectrum of capital entertainment. Its high aims, alas, perished in a skittish world, and in the last decade of the century it too capitulated to give popular audiences what they most craved: a kind of music-hall-cum-circus bill of scantily clad girls who did acrobatics and aquabatics (in a large tank), and even allowed themselves to be shot from cannons. It would return to serious matters in the early years of the new century as the Methodists' Westminster Central Hall.

Such then was the faltering pattern of enlightenment in which well-meaning men sought to broaden the minds of their fellow-beings. History may not concede that they wholly succeeded, but surely it will allow that they brought a civilising influence into society. How difficult was the task and the inevitable downward curve of their dreams is typified in the fate of the Adelaide Gallery. In 1830 the Gallery's learned professors launched into twenty-minute lectures on the approaching age while 'fearful engines revolved and hissed, and quivered as the fettered steam that formed their entrails grumbled sullenly in its bondage'. In his *London Life and Character*, Albert Smith continued:

> mice led gasping subaqueous lives in diving bells; clockwork steamers ticked round and round a basin perpetually, to prove the efficacy of invisible paddles; and on all sides were clever machines which stray visitors were puzzled to class either as coffee-mills, water-wheels, roasting-jacks or musical instruments. There were artful snares laid for giving galvanic shocks to the unwary; steam-guns that turned bullets into bad sixpences against the target; and dark microscopic rooms for shaking the principles of teetotallers, by showing wiggling abominations in a drop of water which they were supposed daily to gulp down.

So much for the serious studies. The delightful Smith again:

> By degrees music stole in; then wizards; and lastly, talented vocal foreigners from Ethiopia and the Pyrenees. Science was driven to her wits' end for a livelihood . . . The names of new attractions were covertly put into the bills, sneaking under the original engines and machines in smaller type. But between the two stools of philosophy and fun, Science shared the usual fate attendant upon such a position – she broke down altogether. Her grave votaries were disgusted with comic songs, and the admirers of the banjo were bored with lectures. So neither went to see her . . .

Smith says it all; the Gallery, after a brave fight, became devoted to the new craze for dance – and called itself a casino.

For those with a mind to it, the mid-eighteenth-century capital offered adventures into the macabre. Old bones – those in fact of Charles Byrne, the Irish Giant – were used to lure the select crowd into the medical ambience of John Hunter's Museum of Comparative Anatomy in the entertainment hub of Leicester Square. There Hunter and his assistants were in the habit of holding medical levées for patrons and friends who, over tea or coffee, listened to lectures

General Tom Thumb was at the Adelaide Gallery in 1844. (By courtesy of the Guildhall Library, Corporation of London)

TO BE SEEN,

At the WHITE HORSE INN, in FLEET STREET,

The Wonderful Short Woman,

BORN IN SALISBURY,

No more than Two Feet, Nine Inches high, straight grown, 31 Years

of Age, and gives Satisfaction to all that see her.

To be seen any Hour of the Day, without Loss of Time.

Note.——Gentlemen and Ladies may see her at their own Houses at any Time of the Day,

and the Price left to their own Generosity.

January. 1741.

Short notice: a handbill advises freak-lovers where to find the latest small wonder. (By courtesy of the Guildhall Library, Corporation of London)

on 'medical occurrences' and had the functioning of their organs explained to them.

Twenty years later in the Adelphi another medical man, James Graham, opened the doors of his Temple of Health and Hymen, furnished with 'medico-electrical apparatus' and his Grand Celestial Bed guaranteed to aid female fertility and for hire at £50 a night. It comprised a heavyweight slab of magnetic iron, on which was laid a mattress stuffed with the 'strongest, most springy hair, produced at vast expense from the tails of English stallions'. Its canopy of mirrors was supported by forty pillars of glass, each showing a golden nymph through whose lips there filtered soft orchestral accompaniment for the loving occupants. Before slipping between the magical bed's coloured sheets, the lovers (or patients) would be lectured by the great doctor on 'generation'. The bed, Graham claimed, produced perfect babies from the unions that took place in it – even previously barren relationships produced offspring 'when so powerfully agitated in the delights of love'. That agitation of the lovers was enhanced by the pressured cylinder simultaneously pumping 'magnetic fire' into the room – though the mirrors too may have played a part. The bed tilted after coition to assist conception. Among the desperate women who came to him in great numbers was Georgiana, the young Duchess of Devonshire, still not pregnant after five years of marriage.

Dr Graham also used milk baths (*à la* Old Q) and 'friction methods' to cure infertility and impotence in men. He was strong too on the benefits of mud baths, and recommended his patent elixir (at a guinea a bottle) and heightened the erotic charge of his establishment by having a bevy of young, diaphanously clad beauties wandering through it. One, for a time, was fifteen-year-old Emma, the future mistress of Lord Nelson. Given the pleasure he must have purveyed, it would be fine to be able to say that Dr Graham was no charlatan. He alas went bankrupt in a few years and ended his days undeservedly in a lunatic asylum. He would have been a gift to the tabloids.

His later condition, though, would have invited little sympathy; probably the contrary. The mentally challenged then, sad to say, suffered ridicule rather than compassion, and for a Sunday afternoon's sport Londoners in their hundreds would make their way to the city's infamous Bedlam institution, a swearing, singing, chain-rattling society of the damned (entrance fee: tuppence), where the unfortunate were taken (and sometimes manacled and whipped) and caged as objects of amusement. A large proportion of those who had lost their bearings in life were said (by one source) to be women in love, and hackney cab and stagecoach drivers whose condition was said to have been brought on by the persistent jolting of the pineal gland to which their work had exposed them. In May 1775, shortly before Bedlam moved from its old site beyond Bishopsgate, Boswell and Johnson went together to the asylum and found 'the general contemplation of insanity . . . very affecting'. Johnson on an earlier visit had been mistaken by an inmate for the Duke of Cumberland and berated for his inhumanity in the Highlands. How tenuous is the line . . .

Those bloodier chapters of history and its controversial figures might be more sombrely witnessed in the Fleet Street rooms of Mother Salmon's Waxworks, where a series of tableaux and figures (some made to function by clockwork) immortalised the nation's past and a representation of Charles I's execution was a

Pioneer balloonist Vincenzo Lunardi soars aloft from the Artillery Ground in 1784. (By courtesy of the Guildhall Library, Corporation of London)

reminder of how precarious was the nature of monarchy. The fact would be reinforced by the later, more famous, collections of Madame Tussaud, who would make models in Paris as the Revolution raged and the heads of her subjects were brought to her still bloody from the guillotine – some of them the heads of people she had known. Later, as a widow aged forty-two, she would come to England, bringing her exhibits with her to be shown round the country, and from 1835 at the Bazaar in Baker Street. She would prosper greatly, proof that blood and tears have ever their perennial fascination.

Before the end of the eighteenth century man would launch himself into a new dimension in a way the world had hitherto hardly dreamed of; the great topic of wonder and speculation would be the invention of the hot-air balloon. In 1783 the brothers Montgolfier had astonished Europe by ascending to 6,000 feet in their 60-foot-high craft, gaining for themselves the sobriquet 'the fathers of aviation'. But it was two other balloonists who brought the phenomenon of flight to the capital a year later: the Neapolitan Vincenzo Lunardi and the Frenchman Jean Pierre Blanchard. Lunardi soared into the skies from the Artillery Ground at Moorfields (before a milling crowd of 150,000) and made a flight of twenty-four miles – with a cat and a pigeon for company, a leg of cold chicken and a bottle of wine. Handsome and young, he was the secretary of the Neapolitan ambassador, and the perfect idol. He came down at North Mimms in his journey northwards to put out the shivering cat, and took off again, landing at Ware in Hertfordshire. (History is silent about the pigeon.) He returned to London a hero. Horace Walpole, almost alone, was critical: he had, Walpole felt, no right to risk the cat's life.

The following month Blanchard managed a further distance, and the new era of exploration seized the public imagination like a fever – and particularly that of the capital's fast set. Both men in turn were invited to dine at Devonshire House, where the Frenchman succumbed to the duchess's wiles and allowed himself to be inveigled into one of the Whig lady's greatest publicity stunts. On a cold December day the ticket-holding *bon ton* braved the chill of Grosvenor Square to watch the duchess release the balloon's mooring rope and send Blanchard aloft in his craft, now in the blue and buff colours of the party and emblazoned the 'Devonshire Aerial Yacht', for one of the duchess's most audacious political coups. The streets all around were jammed with sightseers and carriages going nowhere.

One thing by now was becoming startlingly clear: ascent by itself was not enough. Those brave men of the air, and those who would follow them, were not seen as the pioneers they were, but as performers providing spectacle and thrilling the capital with their daring. Crowds flocked to Newington Butts to see 'the first English female' take off: Mrs Sage, a buxom lady with some sense of occasion, stepped into Lunardi's gondola wearing a big velvet hat with ostrich feathers. With them (perhaps as chaperon) went one of Lunardi's friends. They landed at Harrow, where the lady was greeted by the schoolboys' clamorous cheers. Truly nobody (except maybe Walpole) was bored by balloons. But on occasion feelings ran high. In one attempt, before Lunardi's first success, one Dr Moret had announced his intention to take off from the fields of Belgravia. Expectancy was high, but it was followed by intense disappointment when the balloon caught fire on the ground – and then came the news that Moret himself had vanished, along with the takings. Denied the promised spectacle, the mood of the crowd became bitter and vented itself on a nearby tea-house, wrecking it completely. Just a month later Lunardi's red and white silk balloon would soar majestically into the blue.

In the capital's pleasure-gardens such flights would become a perennial draw – in Cremorne, Ranelagh and, of course, Vauxhall. Taverns with a bit of ground got in on the act, and many ascents were made also from Green Park and Greenwich Park. Dickens in *Sketches by Boz* describes a dual take-off: 'we retraced our steps to the firework ground, and mingled with the little crowd of people who were contemplating Mr Green. Some half-dozen men were restraining the impetuosity of one of the balloons, which was completely filled and had the car already attached.' Green and his wife were about to go up in one balloon while their son and his spouse crewed the other. 'Then the balloons went up, and the aerial travellers stood up, and the crowd outside roared with delight . . . and the balloons were wafted gently away.'

Run-of-the-mill stuff for Charles Green, one would have thought, in what was about his two-hundredth ascent. The year was 1836 but balloons could still stop the traffic. That same year, with Robert Holland, a Member of Parliament, and Monck Mason, lessee of Her Majesty's Theatre, he took off from Vauxhall in the red-and-white striped *Royal Vauxhall* balloon, having taken on board three week's provisions: 40lb of tongue, ham and beef; 40lb of bread and biscuits and sugar; 45lb of fowls and preserves; not forgetting two gallons each of port, sherry and brandy and a coffee-maker. As it happened, they came down the next day, in Germany.

A very ordinary-looking man – passing for a member of the resident orchestra perhaps as he walked through the pleasure gardens – Green had brought himself to notice during George IV's coronation celebrations when, with true showman's flair, he had filled his coal-gas balloon off the Piccadilly mains before making a flight from Green Park to Barnet. In 1828 he went aloft from the Eagle tavern in City Road on horseback, a feat he would repeat at Vauxhall some years later. The pony, in this instance, was nine hands high, gaily caparisoned, with its legs secured by ropes to the side of the car and its eyes blinkered. Sitting astride, Green's feet could touch the floor of the car. People were indignant that an animal should be treated in such a manner. Green had also travelled with more dangerous cargoes: from Cremorne he had taken off with a lady and a leopard in the basket. He was the first man to ascend in a gas balloon, and in 1838 achieved a height of 27,000 feet.

FLORA TEA GARDENS,
BAYSWATER,
Mr. HAMPTON'S

BALLOON ASCENT,

ALBION

Monday, July 1st, 1839.

Mr. HAMPTON, Respectfully announces to the Public, that his Sixteenth Balloon Ascent, Advertized for the 24th Instant, will positively take place on Monday next—when Tickets now outstanding will of course be admitted—and it is with much regret that Mr. Hampton was compelled to postpone the Ascent—but owing to the doubtful state of the weather in the Morning, coupled with the knowledge of the day previous (Sunday) having been so boisterous and wet, together with the urgent advice of his Friends, to whose decision he yielded, a postponement occurred. which had he foreseen so favorable an Evening would not have taken place.

Mr. H. proudly refers to his former Ascents as the best Proof of his readiness at all times to fulfil his Engagements with the Public, observing that neither danger or difficulty however great, has ever prevented him from making those Ascents, some portion of them even having been made under circumstances that probably no other Aeronaut ever encountered—Mr. H is now making arrangements for his

THIRD PARACHUTE DESCENT,

Which will take place in a few days at an Altitude of Three Miles, so as to be perfectly visible to the Entire Population of the Metropolis.

Doors Open at Two o'Clock. The Ascent to take place at 6 o'Clock.

Admisson 1s.   Children Half-price.

G. NURTON, Printer, 18, New Church Street, Lisson Grove, Marylebone.

Poster for a bold balloonist's ascent – and his promise of an imminent parachute descent from three miles high. (By courtesy of the Guildhall Library, Corporation of London)

The demand for spectacle would push the air pioneers into dangerous flirtations. Robert Cocking, another balloonist, died when his parachute jump went wrong. (The first such descent had been made in 1802 when M. Garnerin was taken up from North Audley Street and floated safely to earth at St Pancras.) Another aeronaut attempted to 'fly' down from a height of 5,000 feet into Cremorne Gardens, but crash-landed a trifle off-course in unfashionable Sydney Street, SW3. He had put his faith in bats' wings and a tail.

But the greatest spectacle of all – the concluding wonder of an era – remained firmly on the ground. The Great Exhibition of 1851, with its vast glass structure designed by Joseph Paxton, the Duke of Devonshire's gardener, whose shimmer the balloonists would have seen as they soared over the city that fine summer, was Prince Albert's brainchild – and he got most of the credit, especially from his still youthful queen. She was unable to stay away, and visited almost every day. With magnificent hyperbole the novelist Thackeray called it 'the vastest and sublimest popular festival that the world has ever witnessed'. Certainly it was a thrilling shop window for British ingenuity and inventiveness, a reflection of thrusting industry. By January over two thousand men were working on site in Hyde Park. Paxton's exhibition hall needed 293,655 panes of glass (weighing 400 tons) to cover some nineteen acres. It took 4,000 tons of iron and it was tested for structural safety by calling in the heavy-footed soldiery to dance and thump on its floors. It would house nineteen thousand individual exhibits, from the Koh-i-Noor diamond to the (admittedly imported) McCormick reaper.

There were objections to the desecration of one of London's green and open spaces for such a grandiose scheme. *The Times*, unhappy about the venue, argued (rightly, as it happened) that the park would become a 'bivouac' for vagabonds. And the Season would be ruined. In the event, the wealthy queued overnight for it to open on 1 May, being served breakfast in their carriages by their footmen. The exhibition closed in mid-October, after being visited by six million people, who paid a shilling each to view its wonders. And it made money, taking £356,000 at the gate. When it was all over there would hardly be a blade of grass left, and Paxton's wonderful glass blister – the Crystal Palace – would be deftly removed to the heights of Sydenham Hill to overlook the scene of its triumph and draw admirers for many years to come.

In the capital's other arenas the accent would swing to the spectacular in pure entertainment as the showmen and impresarios claimed the scene from the entrepreneurs. Circus, with its colour, thrills and excitement, captivated and captured the emotions, and it came seriously to town at Olympia in 1886 with the Paris Hippodrome, which staged stag-hunts and wheel-to-wheel chariot races and had over four hundred animals. A decade later the arena would be the headquarters for The Greatest Show on Earth, the Barnum and Bailey extravaganza with a big top over 500 feet long, and half as wide, with a three-ring layout and fifteen thousand seats. The menagerie tent alone was 250 feet long and 150 feet wide. And the show had a whole battalion of freaks. Between times the brilliant, home-grown showman Charles Cochran presented his prize-fighters, wrestlers and wild beasts.

In Queen Victoria's jubilee year (1887) Earls Court became a part of the old Wild West as Buffalo Bill (Colonel Cody) took it over for his famous show, later giving a private performance by royal command, when the queen witnessed Annie Oakley's remarkable marksmanship, a demonstration of the art of lassooing and a re-enactment of the Indians' attack on the Deadwood stage. A whole galaxy of royals accompanied the queen on that occasion and got so carried away that some of them jumped aboard the Deadwood coach to join in.

Islington's Royal Agricultural Hall, home of the Smithfield Club, yearly did a fast change from the rustic tweeds and the cattle browns of its December show to absorb the tinsel glitter of the World's Fair, an explosion of high spirits and razzmatazz that sought (decently) to continue the tradition and atmosphere of the indecent and defunct St Bartholomew's Fair. Here in the great farming hall each Christmas and New Year, as regular as pantomime, the seasonal fair opened on Boxing Day and ran for six weeks. Here the latest rides of the fairground industry, by long custom, made their début and whitened the knuckles of those who patronised them. For the less brave there were the moving waxworks, the freaks real and usually contrived, the exotic beasts like the horned horse, and performing crocodiles and pythons and much more to frighten and beguile those for whom it was a landmark in the capital year – and who came to wander mesmerised through its raucous din, its strident steam organs and the persuasive patter of its barkers.

It was here in 1896 that an event of some significance occurred. That year, the man acknowledged as the 'King of the Showmen', Randall Williams, had left his ghost show at home. His new 'ride' was the sensation of the fair: moving pictures. A couple of years later many more of the showmen had adopted the idea; there was Biddall's Royal Bioscope and Arnold Brothers with their Picturedrome, to name but two. Williams's showbill was modest by fairground standards, claiming merely that his show was 'a grand bioscope of animated pictures – the sensation of the 19th century, the whole of this magnificent exhibition is worked by Electricity generated on the premises by our own magnificent [steam] engine'. It was, simply, 'the Greatest Scientific Invention of the Age'. Perhaps it was. It would have the power to embrace and encapsulate all that had gone before. It became the cinematograph.

CHAPTER XII
A Theatre in the Streets

The ordinary Londoner's theatre was in the streets, a passing pageant of colour and smells and squalor. All life was lived there. The fashionable people, the *bon ton* and the expensive courtesans paraded in the royal parks and in the Mall; in the teeming, claustrophobic courts and stinking alleys, the capital's poor and huddled masses bickered and sweated and loved and drank to excess, living out their lives without hope or dignity in the common glare in their tinder-box ghettos.

It was the under-privileged who formed the bulk of the capital's population, markedly during the Restoration years and for a long time afterwards. A great many were people on the lowest rung. Some practised as beggars, some stole or prostituted themselves to survive; it would have been surprising if some had not succumbed to these softer if more dangerous options. They thronged the streets by day and more menacingly by night, a social segment in constant flux, swollen dangerously from time to time by the demobilisation of soldiers and the sudden redundancy of seamen, often cast adrift without pay.

Disorder was common in the streets, but so was diversion of every sort. Girls trailed lethargic asses whose milk (fresh from the teat on the doorstep) was said to be beneficial to babies; oyster-sellers trundled their barrows (selling by weight); young mop-selling maidens touted their merchandise bundled on their heads; fruit-sellers made their rounds similarly burdened; and so came tinkers and pot-menders, bellows-repairers and rush-seat menders; hot-food vendors with their 'hot pudding pies' and 'hot codlings' (apples); sellers of sea-coal and discordant knife-grinders; and chimney-sweeps trailing sooty child assistants . . . There was scarcely a single commodity that did not come calling at the citizen's door, or into the shadowed confines of the court it spilled into.

Dealers brought dead men's shoes, sad and misshapen, and garments that had gone beyond the threadbare; doormats and toasting forks, trinkets and tatty jewellery; combs and tumblers; matches and fire-irons; singing-birds (larks, thrushes and canaries); and ropes of onions; eels and cucumbers; fish of all kinds and hot sheep's feet; cherries on sticks and hot baked Wardens (stewed pears); and the afternoon brought the toll of the muffin man's bell. Cluttering the kerbside were the barrows of the toy- and doll-sellers with those of the gingerbread and roast-chestnut men. Dustmen clanged their warning bells; criers and bellmen of the night watches imprinted their footfalls on the silent cobbles, carrying halberd and lantern, calling time and weather.

The stench and the calls of commerce mingled with the cries of the city's itinerant entertainers: tumblers, acrobats, jugglers, strongmen and stuntmen who vied on street corners or close to an inn for the passer-by's attention (and an appreciative coin); fiddlers unstrung by drink bowed merry jigs on their battered instruments between one fair and the next, while ballad-sellers sang their seditious words (to teach the tune). They sang of murders and important hangings – the belated news bulletins of their day – and cruelly satirised both personages and public occasions. Their highpoint was the seventeenth and eighteenth centuries; their publishing lair the den of Seven Dials.

This then was the world of the hoi polloi, their amusement the kaleidoscope of life as it unfolded around them and such joys as it afforded them. For many, menial self-employment was the only option that offered them an honest role and the means of survival – by the smallest of margins. Henry Mayhew, that great recorder of London life, in his mid-nineteenth-century survey *London Labour and the London Poor*, estimated the city had thirty thousand costermongers finding their livelihood on the streets. Some may have lived in the hope of a better world, although religion was not strong in their ranks: when the Methodist George Whitefield preached before a Whit Monday crowd of ten thousand at Moorfields Fair in 1742 he was pelted with stones, rotten eggs and dead cats.

For most their solace was in the alehouse; their playhouse the 'penny gaff', the canvas booth hastily and illegally erected on waste ground or in the corner of some crumbling warehouse by itinerant players for a performance of two twenty-minute melodramas divided by an 'interval' of clowning or comic songs. Men from Italy would bring organs on carts – the barrel-organ, with grinder and monkey – to add to the cacophony of trumpets and fiddles and bagpipes and its own near-relation the hurdy-gurdy. Punch (with Judy) reached London about the same time – the mid-seventeenth century, and again from Italy – to be followed through the streets by troupes of mesmerised children. Other marionette and puppet shows would emerge to almost rival the old wife-beating

A puppeteer pulls the strings in a Regency street entertainment for all ages. (Billie Love Historical Collection)

rascal. But Punch had an appeal beyond class and circumstances and to all age groups and, surprisingly, found his best pitches in Regent Street and Leicester Square: Hickey (of the celebrated *Memoirs*) was an addict, and Pepys could never resist a puppet show. Like the dancing bear, Punch would be around for some time to come.

Like the itinerant musicians and the ballad-sellers, the strong men and the stuntmen, the gingerbread men and the beggars, the puppeteers gravitated to the city's big occasions and to the fairs that periodically gathered all the elements of the capital's street entertainments into a grand orgasmic convulsion of merriment that gave full vent to the passions of that simmering society. The fair was a safety valve, a salve for the bitterness that life inflicted; it kept the lid on discontent until the next time.

Some fairs were less unsavoury than others, though none was remotely respectable. A clue to their scale of dissipation following the Restoration can be found in a mention of St James's Fair in 1688, as it was squeezed out of its normal site by building development. It was relocated in 'the greate Brooke Feilde Market for Livestock [Shepherd's Market]'. There, we are told, the fairgoers would enjoy 'Musicke, Drinkinge, Rafflinge, Gaming, Lotteries, Stage Playes & Drolls as well as Prize-fightes, Bull-fightes, Beare-baitinges & other cruel Sports . . . with all manner of Boothes and Gingerbreads in the shape of Tiddy Dol . . .' Added to which the fair already had a reputation as a rowdy, lewd occasion, with drunken prostitutes 'uncovering their nakedness'. Things, one might have thought, could not possibly get worse. But they did.

Bartholomew Fair was a low-life festival that drew people from all classes to its brash, raucous excitement. Wordsworth, taken by that fervent Londoner and essayist Charles Lamb, described it as 'this Parliament of Monsters, Tents and Booths'. It took over Smithfield in August for a fortnight or more of daring, drunkenness and lechery that lived up to the reputation the playwright Ben Jonson had given it. In the later seventeenth century its handbills were promising such feats as 'Excellent Dancing and Vaulting on the Ropes' by Jacob Hall the aerialist (and the man who shared Lady Castlemaine with the king) and 'Flying over Thirty Rapiers'. In 1770 it was still on a high, lively and licentious. Young royalty went along, discreetly, with the young bloods of the capital, who left their normal haunts of Covent Garden and St James's in the hope, no doubt, of amorous dalliance with some compliant doxy among the fair booths or nearby in the bordellos of Cock Lane. The fair's theatrical booths, it should be said,

The Female Blondin (aka Miss A. Young), watched by thousands, crosses the Thames. (By courtesy of the Guildhall Library, Corporation of London)

played host to the best actors in town, whose own playhouses, unable to compete, closed for the fair's duration. Some of the productions, indeed, were extravaganzas, with the mechanics of the scenery more interesting than the substance of the play.

The legendary Richardson, however, kept his feet and his show on the ground. A regular at all the capital's fairs, this great showman, illiterate and often tetchy, who had begun his working life cleaning cow-stalls in Islington, kept his cavalcade endlessly on the move. His 'theatre' was a splendid set-up with upper and lower stages – one for dancers, the other for paraders and actors. His shows had fine orchestral backing and well-painted scenery; the performance started with a play (usually a tragedy), and he would throw in an inventive pantomime and a comic singer to lift the gloom. The spectacle belied the man, who dressed as soberly as a Quaker in a long blue frockcoat, and black vest with breeches of a dark velveteen. He bought a new suit yearly – always on the same date.

Pepys loved any fair, but Bartholomew's particularly: the puppets, the dogs that did Morris dancing and the mare that 'counted' money. The freaks too were an endless fascination: the woman with three breasts, all of them or just one giving milk as required; the midgets and fat boys; the giants and giantesses; the five-legged bull; the three-legged man; the Siamese twins; or something even sadder and more grotesque. During the Smithfield fair of August 1842 the following handbill was widely circulated:

EXTRAORDINARY PHENOMENON!!! This Greatest Wonder in the World. Now Exhibiting Alive at the Globe Coffee House . . . a FEMALE CHILD WITH TWO PERFECT HEADS . . . Born at Wandsworth, Surrey, April 17th 1842. The public is respectfully informed that the child is now Living; and hundreds of persons has been to see it, and declares that it is the most wonderful Phenomenon of nature that they'd ever seen. Admission 1d each. No Deception; if dissatisfied the Money Returned.

The sad truth was that freaks were fun and endlessly fascinating. The normally sedate Evelyn, a deeply pious man, was much taken by such oddities – as he would have been by the stuntman called the Turk, who did amazing feats on the tightrope, including dancing on it blindfold. A performer who brought a hush to the roistering crowd was another Richardson, a fire-eater who 'chewed' hot coals, blew a hot coal on his tongue into life with a bellows and cooked an oyster on it – before swallowing the entire mouthful. As a pick-me-up he gave himself a libation of flaming pitch, sulphur and wax. At Bartholomew's in 1816 fairgoers were silenced by the astounding feats of a female Samson; billed as the 'French Female Hercules', Madame Gobert would sit several people on an average-sized table and then lift it (and them) by her teeth. She took a 400lb anvil on her stomach, inviting four of her 'forge' assistants to hammer it unrelentingly. Then she would lift the anvil by her hair and swing it around – on her tresses.

Southwark's yearly fair replicated the same irrepressible behaviour, cramming itself into the courts and crannies of what is now the Borough High Street. The populace flocked over London Bridge in droves to revel in its wild atmosphere and gross excesses. Here Hall's rival, the celebrated high-wire performer Robert Cadman, seems to have been the favourite, but Evelyn was entranced too by the dancing asses and the monkeys who somersaulted on the high wire with baskets of eggs and jugs of water, without spilling a drop or even cracking a shell. There were of course freaks aplenty to satisfy the diarist's curiosity, as well as Chinese birds that played cards and could tell the time by the clock, along with the usual sword-swallowers and bare-knuckle fighters and hasty-pudding eaters. Every oddity in the whole wide world, sooner or later, would find its way to the fair.

The dancing duo of a bear and a monkey take their turn around town. (By courtesy of the Guildhall Library, Corporation of London)

Periodically the capital would find itself pitched into the unexpected revelry of the most spontaneous carnival of them all, the famous Frost Fair, held on the frozen Thames – something no longer possible with the now faster-flowing river. In its novelty it outmatched all others, turning the river and riverside into a winter pleasure garden. Booths, made of warm blanket cloth, were set up on the ice for the gratification of every whim and human activity, including that which required the ultimate in mutual warmth and consent. Boats became sledges and whizzed, horse-drawn, over the ice. Formal streets evolved and hackney carriages plied for hire from the watermen's stairs (and to their fury). The Merry Monarch, who loved watching the frantic jollity of the fair from his palace windows, in the great frost of 1683/4 led the queen and lesser royals on to the ice and accepted a slice off the ox roasting beside Whitehall. Someone organised a foxhunt and the king, nothing loth, took part. The feasting was prodigious as the folk of the capital seized the opportunity to indulge themselves with 'rabbit, capon, hen, turkey' and 'hot codlins, pancakes, duck and goose'. There were donkey rides for a shilling, and horse racing and coach racing, with much carousing and betting on the outcome. Evelyn, moving in the highest circles, crossed the river dry-foot to dine at Lambeth with the Archbishop of Canterbury, when the ice was 'now become so thick as to beare not only streets of boothes in which they roasted meate, and had diverse shops of wares quite acrosse as in a town'.

The Frost Fair of 1788/9 was strung down the river from Putney Bridge to Rotherhithe, while that of 1813/14 was the greatest of them all, as though to celebrate the ever-growing importance of the city, now the largest in Europe, with a population swelling to a million. It had also succeeded in becoming the world's leading financial centre. There was a renewed flurry in the streets, though such activity had always characterised the capital. It was something the eighteenth-century writer Tobias Smollett brought wittily to attention through his character Matt Bramble: 'The foot passengers run along as if they were pursued by bailiffs. The porters and chairmen trot with their burdens. People who keep their own equipages drive through the streets at full speed. Even citizens, physicians and apothecaries glide in their chariots like lightning.' Watermen's wherries still busily criss-crossed the Thames and waited by the river-stairs, their oars often a faster mode of travel than by coach through the dusty, congested streets. As the Prince Regent came to the throne in 1820, in his booming capital there were still three thousand wherries on the river, even though the streets had well over a thousand hackney coaches and countless sedan chairs (at one shilling a mile); the latter were the choice of the quality – and of ladies discreetly on their way to their lovers.

As the notorious central fairs of the capital dimmed and faded (or, more usually, were summarily extinguished), determined merrymakers took themselves to the fairs of the fringe – at Camberwell and Peckham and Mitcham; at Bow and Edmonton and Enfield, all already in both trading and moral decline. They surged in cavalcades to Stepney and Fairlop and Greenwich in every type of wheeled conveyance, including coal-carts – and from the second quarter of the nineteenth century by the pleasure steamers beginning to operate on the Thames. For the big Easter and Whitsun fairs steamboats would leave Nicholson's Wharf and Hungerford Market Pier every fifteen minutes. Passengers queued for up to three hours to get aboard.

A horse-drawn monster organ jangles a tune for the passing hoi polloi. (By courtesy of the Guildhall Library, Corporation of London)

Each fair sang its own praises; each had its own attractions, though none was more bizarre than Charlton's Horn Fair, an occasion of cross-dressing and gender-bending that quite disconcerted the touring Defoe. As if that were not enough, the wearing of horns was almost obligatory. The women that day, it is said, had a licence to be bold. Soon, though, the behaviour of the fair crowds, never genteel, deteriorated into a vicious debauchery that even the most broad-minded among the masses found unacceptable. They left the fair to the riff-raff and the untender mercies of the magistrates. The outcry was muted. In any case the river steamers by then were opening up a fresh world of fun and more innocent amusement. They left from London Bridge and Tower and Westminster piers for Gravesend, Sheerness, Margate and Southend – and reached upriver to

A breakfast stall at the kerb, where passers-by could grab a bite in the street. (By courtesy of the Guildhall Library, Corporation of London)

Richmond, folding down their tall, majestic smoke stacks to glide under the bridges. Less than reliable at first, it would be the mid-century before they really established themselves as fully part of the capital's pleasure scene and that great new escape from the smog-bound streets, the seaside. Often they operated from insecure piers and landing stages hastily erected by the companies themselves, causing concerns about safety in the Press – though not apparently among the boat-owners. The competition was fierce – with all the cut-throat risks and cost-cutting that implied. Trippers were crammed aboard till the vessels sat dangerously low in the water, and they often tipped to the portholes as passengers fought to disembark.

Their day, however, would be brief. They would be eclipsed by the railway, opening up the coast of England's south-east corner with greater speed and ease. The response was startling, catching even the buoyant railmen unprepared. When the first London–Brighton excursion left London Bridge (at 8.30 a.m.) in 1864 its forty-five carriages were pulled by four engines; at New Cross a fifth engine was added, along with a further six carriages; and at Croydon, yet another six coaches joined – plus another locomotive. Two thousand people were off to the seaside – and Brighton awaited them *en fête*.

Some preferred 'excursions' closer to home. Voltaire, during his brief sojourn at the White Wig Inn in Maiden Lane in 1727, presumptuously suggested that the Londoner's choice on a Sunday was to go either to church or to a prostitute. In fact, most did neither. They headed out from their smoke-grimed alleys to the heady air of the immediate countryside – to the wide open spaces of Kentish Town or to Hackney with its slightly racy reputation and its bird-shooting, bull-baiting and hare-coursing, all with their opportunity for betting. Pepys joined the trippers one fine June day in 1664: 'With my wife only to take ayre, it being warm and pleasant to Bowe and Old Ford; and thence to Hackney. There light and played at shuffle board [shove ha'penny], eat cream and good cherries, and so with good refreshment home.' Hackney then was a village with the houses of a number of the city's businessmen and merchants.

Others resorted to the relative peace of Copenhagen Fields, with their tea gardens, a favourite with lovers as well as genteel families. There was, of course, all the fun of the Sunday fair at Battersea Fields (taking refreshment perhaps at the louche Red House tavern), with its hawkers, conjurers, donkey-rides, horse-racing, comic singers and shameless dancers and roundabouts – and lots of gambling booths. Thousands came by river-steamer to the revels that some likened to the goings-on in Sodom or Gomorrah.

Seriously wagering men went to the races on Bromley Common or to Epsom or even to mingle with the nobs at Newmarket, recognised back in the reign of James I as the headquarters of the Turf, and on the evidence of Defoe's kingdom-wide tour a vast unruly gathering where Tattersall did his horse deals in the street and bets were laid in the coffee-room. The aristocracy watched from their carriages, but after the 'off' the more enthusiastic mounted spectators followed the runners up the course, yelling and screaming their encouragement.

Greenwich Park was popular, especially after the start of a regular steamboat service in 1854, as were many more of the down-river destinations with their weekend amusements. Up-river there was Eel Pie Island, where the steamers from Westminster Bridge called 'to land great numbers of holiday folks, desirous of the delights of pure air and solicitous to banquet upon eel-pies'. Those who rose late would find their way to Islington's Highbury Barn, with its ambition to be a 'North London Cremorne' and its huge 4,000 square feet of open-air dance floor. Londoners went there in their hundreds on Sunday evenings to dance the hours away. It was the place to be, much, one supposes, to the chagrin of once-fashionable Hampstead Wells, where they had flocked to sip the waters and promenade and dance in the Great Room – until the Room lost its cachet. It had become so popular that when Fanny Burney's heroine Evelina was accosted by a young man desirous of 'hopping a dance' with her, she knew she could only decline.

CHAPTER XIII
The Sport of Gallants

Sex was easily and abundantly, if not always freely, available in Restoration and Regency London. The need was serviced by battalions of committed ladies in the red-light districts as well as by bands of adventuresses – moonlighting milliners, shopgirls and seamstresses – who patrolled the shady nooks of the city's many (aptly named) pleasure gardens. The main areas of availability were, outstandingly, Covent Garden and St James's, the Haymarket (somewhat downmarket) and Southwark, with its long history of comforting men since the time of the Roman legions. Beyond the pale – and beyond the writ of the City's administration – lay Lambeth Marshes, an outreach of the most noxious decadence where every appetite could be appeased and pornography smuggled in from France was guaranteed a ready sale. In the east, in the lanes and alleyways that led up from the river, from the Tower to Limehouse, into Ratcliffe Highway, men home from the sea found willing arms and the attentions of which they had been deprived. In the bawdy houses of Smithfield – in Hosier and Cock Lanes – men working the capital's great stock market took their moments of pleasure with poor wretches abandoned in every way. In a hell-bent, hedonistic society pursuing pleasure and gratification of every kind, there were countless madams who made sure it could do so – and became wealthy in the cause. Their bordellos – often quaintly named 'houses of resort' – teemed with activities from the basic to the erotically charged that sought to rekindle sated appetites. In the theatre actresses, as we have seen, daringly advertised their attributes, exposing acres of inviting bosom, inflaming desire and causing the kind of arousal that sent rakes hastening to the nearest bawdy house. In such a licentious climate, inevitably, the innocent fell prey to the sensualists.

Pepys may have sought solitary pleasure in his fantasies about Lady Castlemaine 'without whom all is nothing' – he was devastated on hearing that she had taken on Charles Hart, the leading actor of the King's Company and seducer of the youthful Nell Gwynne – but he compensated for his distress by fondling his own maids (and other people's), even as they stood beside him in church. Typical of his sometimes tentative advances was his confession in 1667 as he sampled the sermon at St Dunstan's in the West in Fleet Street:

> I . . . stood by a pretty, modest maid, whom I did labour to take by the hand and the body; but she would not, but got further and further from me, and at last I could perceive her to take pins out of her pocket to prick me if I should touch her again . . . And then I fell to gaze upon another pretty maid in a pew close to me, and she on me; and I did go about to take her by the hand, which she suffered a little and then withdrew.

Like Boswell, Pepys consistently played below his class, fascinated but frightened by bordellos and finding his mistresses where his wanderings took him – the first in the emporium of Westminster Hall, where he wooed a haberdasher named Betty Lane.

The diarist usually took his paramours to a safe distance whenever possible, and after preliminary local trysts took his haberdasher by boat across the river to a room in the King's Head tavern, with its view of the Lambeth Marshes. Having fed her and plied her with drinks, he found her 'wanton and bucksome' but discovers 'she dares not adventure upon that business' – a disappointment obviously, since in an earlier meeting she had permitted his intimate fondling and teased him with her own caresses, jibbing only as they came to the last bastion. But all bastions fall, and soon, with Betty now conveniently married, plump and warm and shedding all former reluctance, the pair were soon over the water to their old haunt, feasting and taking their pleasure, twice 'doing what I would with her', before setting foot back on Westminster soil. Once set on his course, neither woman nor maid was safe from him. His *modus operandi* would remain much the same: eats, drinks, a tavern room and much tousling and fondling, to which none of his conquests seems to have objected, and indeed, may have enjoyed. He exploited his power to promote naval personnel, including the carpenter husband of a Mrs Bagwell in a quid pro quo that saw a protracted period of 'negotiation' before Mrs B., a pretty woman, gave way 'after many protestings' in the spartan comfort of an out-of-the-way tavern in Moorfields and granted him 'what I would, with great pleasure'. Further meetings and further promotions followed ('This noon Bagwell's wife was with me at the office, and I did what I would'), while his understanding with Betty

The procuress Mother Needham 'recruits' an innocent girl off the country stage. (By courtesy of the Guildhall Library, Corporation of London)

(now Mrs Martin) continued at home and away. ('Thence to Mrs Martin's lodging and did what I would with her.') Married ladies were always safer game, not least because they had husbands who could be held responsible for any unfortunate pregnancy.

Our diarist was now an addict to the sensual pleasures, itching with desire that allowed him no rest till he had visited one or other of his ladies. But he cast around for adventures elsewhere, eschewing the stews while playing with his maid's breasts, flirting with barmaids with amorous intent, and finally debauching Betty's sister in a room of the Dog tavern that had neither bed nor couch, 'paying' twenty shillings for the uncomfortable privilege. He behaved with more delicacy in the company of Mrs Elizabeth Knepp, a flighty young actress whom he took to the Cock alehouse in Fleet Street and wined and dined, and on outings around the capital during which she allowed his roving hands free licence.

Pepys was fond of 'frolicking'. He loved travelling by coach, particularly with warm female flesh pressed against him. He was adept at stealing a hand under a petticoat, and he was in his element in darkened vehicles where he could suborn a complaisant companion's hand into his own lap. In time they would come to understand what was expected of them. Few things gave him more delight than being crushed in a coach with the little actress on his knee singing his favourite song, the Scots ballad 'Barbary Allen' to him while he toyed with her breasts. She would sign her notes to him as the song's heroine, he would respond as 'Dapper Dickey'. The diarist's circle of opportunity would widen with the acquaintance of ladies who enjoyed the flirtation but seem mainly to have declined carnal involvement.

It is easy to forget that Pepys, now Secretary to the Admiralty, was a considerable figure in the state affairs of the day, in particular during the Dutch war of his *Diary* decade, and that he existed on the fringe of the royal circle and earned the king's personal praise more than once. He moved in that ambit of pleasure in which the royal mistresses were publicly owned and the king walked the dogs almost daily in St James's Park in the company of his current favourite and paused to feed the ducks. Given his nature generally – his love of fairs and playhouses and the sheer joy of just walking the streets of his capital – it would have been surprising had Pepys's own hormones not been charged by the high-octane atmosphere around him; more astonishing is the modest level of his sexual ambition. In time, though, his success, albeit still secret, led him to adopt the manner of a Restoration gentleman and he began to wear a sword and to have the swagger of a gallant.

It is likely that Pepys's tavern assignations, like those of the later Boswell, indicate a common practice in that free-and-easy society when the amatory companion was socially inferior. Boswell, however, staggering guiltily between church and strumpet, was drawn to whores, perhaps because of the uncomplicated nature of the transaction. His own pursuit of a 'handsome actress of Covent Garden Theatre' was, too, more confident, certainly more rewarding. After a protracted play of reluctance on the lady's part, he brings his amour to agreement. They are discreet; they meet in Covent Garden (after the performance) and dash away by hackney coach, blinds drawn, 'to the destined scene of delight' – in fact, a not-too-distant Fleet Street hotel. There, his *Journal* tells us, in order 'that Ceres and Bacchus might in moderation lend their assistance to Venus, I ordered a genteel supper and some wine'. He is the confident amorist, conscious of his 'qualifications as a gallant'. Indeed by morning his bedfellow, who had agreed 'to permit me the full enjoyment of her person', had done so five times but declined his dawn request to make it the round half-dozen. Even so, Boswell's joy is unbounded: 'What a loose did we give to amorous dalliance!' His delight is incandescent: 'from my dearest creature's kindness, [I] had a most luscious feast'. He had never before enjoyed a 'voluptuous' night remotely like it: 'Five times was I fairly lost in supreme rapture.' His companion's nature, her sense of delicacy mingled with a delightful wantonness made him 'enjoy her with more relish'. He confides to his *Journal* that surely now he may be deemed a 'Man of Pleasure'. Later he congratulates himself that the whole affair has cost him only eighteen shillings. Alas, there would be an extra consequence: the gonorrhoea his actress gave him.

Sex was never far from Boswell's mind. In church during divine worship he would be 'laying plans for having women'. On coming south to the capital he had astonished himself by his abstinence in a city with an abundance of 'free-hearted' ladies, from the costly madam at fifty guineas a night down to the nymph strolling the Strand in her white-thread stockings, whose fee for her person was but a pint of wine and a shilling. In truth he had initially been high-minded, slightly pompous even, about the qualities required to win his involvement: there was, he believed, no 'higher felicity' that a man might enjoy than 'reciprocal amorous affection' with an amiable woman. In such a union the lover was accorded pleasures both of mind and body. He could not possibly see himself making an 'intimate companion' of some ill-bred, ignorant creature. Nor did he see his delicacy in amour being satisfied in the sordid voluptuousness of the brothel. As it happens he was wrong on several counts.

He would become increasingly fond of paying his addresses to the Paphian Queen and 'experiencing the melting and transporting rites of LOVE'. He would descend from his high ideals frequently, prudently engaging in armour, which denied him full satisfaction. However, needs must: he goes to St James's Park, a well-known rendezvous, picking up 'a low brimstone [a hot-head]', and performs 'most manfully'. Satiated, he wallows in self-loathing, determined that should 'the Cyprian fury . . . seize me, to participate my amorous flame with a genteel girl'. It is a vain hope; he would remain given to 'low debauchery'.

Boswell gets pleasure from a woman's body; he is whole-hearted in his worship of it and there is nothing perverse in his delight; he violates no virgins. The same might be said of another frank diarist, his eighteenth-century contemporary William Hickey, who returned from India to write his famous *Memoirs* in retirement in Beaconsfield, in Buckinghamshire. He too emerges as a man in love with women and in pursuit of pleasure from and with them. St James's Park figures again in his story: 'My first venereal attempt was made on a dark night in St James's Park, upon the grass, about Christmas of the year of 1762 . . . and grievously disappointed I was.' His first serious pick-up was under the Piazza in Covent Garden, earning him 'great credit for my vigour'. Hickey's attachment 'to women of loose and abandoned principles' he attributes to his early encounters with the encouragement of Nanny Harris, his mother's servant/companion, who had debauched the thirteen-year-old son of the Duchess of Manchester before joining the Hickey household. Of these early embraces he later confessed: 'I then had no idea of the spot on which I found my hand, or the delicious pleasures I was shortly to derive from it.' While he was still only thirteen he would take to the theatre (and a box) his first whore: his old wanton love Harris, who had left the Hickeys to enter the keeping of a young gentleman of fortune. Hickey also had Pepys's penchant for maid-servants, pursuing one for six months before 'I partook of her favours'.

More than Boswell or Pepys, he was at the social core of an astonishingly libidinous society, in which ladies satisfied their desires as eagerly as men. Sexual pleasure, sometimes thought of as a preoccupation of our own time in the early twenty-first century, was a constant in fashionable circles from the Restoration to the Regency and beyond. In the mid-seventeenth century women were thought to be the lustful sex, and certainly if there were such a condition as womb frenzy, as one pornographer believed, which could be cured only by urgent copulation, there were ladies whose behaviour gave credence to his theory. The extravagant Italian opera singer Caterini Ruini Galli ruined three lovers, physically and financially, including a Russian ambassador and a husband, before ending up in a Haymarket house of resort; Lady Dorothy Seymour Fleming was a constant visitor, alone, to the capital's notorious bagnios, and forgot to change her lifestyle when she married Sir Richard Worseley, who cited a whole platoon of aristocrats when he divorced her. Lady Dorothy would go back to doing what she did best.

Kitty Clive: Walpole's platonic friend. (Billie Love Historical Collection)

In Regency times especially life was played to the full, with a heedless nonchalance it would be hard to imagine now – and nowhere more so than in the tortured lists of love. Ladies of the *bon ton* clearly enjoyed an equality with men in their amours. Hickey makes clear in his *Memoirs* the amiability (and availability) of women in readily offering comfort to male friends. A casual bout of passion was of no great consequence. As we have seen, when the admittedly notorious Lady Harrington gave Casanova a lift home from a pleasure garden in her coach one night, the great lover's overtures in the gently jogging vehicle were not parried.

Ladies passed from hand to hand and bed to bed with perfect impunity – technically whores perhaps but still ardently pursued as desirable attachments. Men fell madly in love with them, cuckolding each other – often their best friends; sons followed fathers into the beds of mistresses. If there was a chasm between the classes socially, it was less obviously so sexually. The young buck who patrolled the shadowy avenues of Vauxhall Gardens to prey on flighty and perhaps not-so-innocent womanhood had the same goal and instincts as the low-life Lothario. In the demi-monde circles in which he moved and which ambivalently fringed the decadent aristocracy the one could satisfy his desires in some style in a suitable liaison or more circumspectly with some compliant female companion in the many houses of pleasure that then existed, while the other sought solace in the downmarket stews of the Haymarket or Covent Garden – even perhaps in that colony of perversions, Lambeth Marshes. For poor lovers the capital's lodging houses were convenient; places, someone said, 'adapted for whoredom'. The price of a bed was tuppence; a double threepence. Strangers, men and women, sometimes slept in the same bed. One source, a survey of such places, reckoned, unsurprisingly, that they encouraged immorality: 'The people who slept in the rooms I am describing were chiefly young men, almost all accompanied by young females. I have seen girls of fifteen sleep with "their chaps".'

There was in fashionable society an all-pervading, almost palpable undertow of eroticism: bosoms were universally and blatantly bared in enticement. Dr Johnson himself was not immune. Invited by his friend Garrick to come backstage after a performance, he afterwards told the actor: 'I'll come no more behind your scenes, David; for the silk stockings and white bosoms of your actresses excite my amorous propensities.' Sensual intercourse between the sexes, he maintained, was all in the mind. Walking home late and accosted in the Strand, he would have to fight against temptation, and admitted to Boswell, according to his *Life of Johnson*, that on first coming to London he was 'not so strictly virtuous'. His biographer adds: 'It is well known, that his amorous inclinations were uncommonly strong and impetuous. He owned to many of his friends that he used to take women of the town to taverns' and that in the fight against temptation 'he was sometimes overcome'. The great man was forgiving of adultery if for wantonness of appetite a man stole away into the quarters of his wife's chambermaid. The wife should reclaim the husband, he said, by studying how to please him, a remark that can hardly have gone down well with the bluestockings of the time.

What friendship might fail to provide, money would buy. For the rake with a fat wallet the choice was limitless. One foreign visitor, Georg Christoph Lichtenberg, noted that there were women to suit every fetish: 'dressed, bound up, hitched up, tight-laced, loose, painted, done up or raw, scented, in silk or wool . . . what a man cannot obtain here, if he have money . . . let him not look for it anywhere in this world of ours' – all were available in the streets, in ghettos such as Lewknor's Lane, 'a rendezvous and nursery for lewd women', where the Roundheads had surreptitiously sought their pleasure and where Wild had once had a house of ill-fame.

Houses of prostitution were scattered through all areas of the central city, and were open for business as usual on the Sabbath, even if music and card-playing were banned and the theatres had to remain closed. Among the most notorious in the eighteenth century was the Maidenhead (bearing the sign of) in Ram Alley, a narrow passage near the Temple, in which every house was a brothel, as were at one time all those of Covent Garden's Tavistock Row. Bow Street would likewise become a pulsating hive of questionable pleasures. The capital's sex industry indeed would find its epicentre in Covent Garden. Here Mother Cocksedge's establishment would prosper exceedingly next door to the house of Sir John Fielding, the blind magistrate. The Garden was already in decline from around 1700 as the well-to-do began to flee, leaving their grand houses to fall into disrepair and be let out as tenements, or, as Addison put it, leaving the 'once elegant boudoir of some long-dead Duchess' to be 'inhabited by seven or eight wretched human beings', and the area would become a den of iniquity in which every whim could be satiated. It offered ladies of pleasure (in some abundance) and the premises in which their services could be engaged; houses of resort (molly houses) to which homosexuals adjourned; posture ladies with whom flagellation could be sought – or inflicted on a willing female form. In 1770 it would still be described as 'the great square of Venus', with its precincts 'crowded with the practitioners of the Goddess'. Pleasures clustered also by the river; in Ratcliffe Highway there were all the services a sailor required: beer halls, gin palaces and the bordellos and lodging-houses he was lured to by the girls who crowded round the gangplanks of newly berthed vessels.

Coffee-houses could be accommodating, and where the sign showed a woman's hand holding the coffee-pot this was a covert signal of other services within. In the mid-eighteenth century the Bedford Head coffee-house ladies were priced according to class and their individual proclivities. Under its roof there gathered nightly the capital's literati, such as the poets Alexander Pope and the profligate Charles Churchill, but also people of the rank and fame of Sir Henry Fielding and Oliver Goldsmith, Dr Johnson and Garrick as well as the painter and satirist Hogarth, whose supper at the Rose tavern in his *Rake's Progress* (1735) shows its characters clearly in wanton, pleasure-seeking mood. The tavern where Pepys had once popped in from the theatre to enjoy 'half a breast of mutton off the spit' had strippers who cavorted naked on tables or on the floor, and in Hogarth's work a posture moll is seen undressing for business. A regular at the Rose tavern was Kitty Fordyce, who had fallen on hard times after being in the keeping of three gentlemen, one of them a lord. Another was Elizabeth Thomas, a beauty hotly pursued and not unrewarding to those she favoured: her charge in the mid-eighteenth century was one guinea, with a half-crown for the maid.

Richard Haddock, one of the Garden's purveyors, ran his brothels under the guise of legitimate commerce. His girls ran coffee-houses, chocolate-houses and fashion shops as a front for their real activities, and indicated their availability by the sale 'to gentlemen of two-penny glasses of *usque baugh* in the back room'. In Mother Cole's millinery shop in Russell Street it was said (by Twigg) that 'three lovely young Harlots served the Gentlemen in a spacious Drawing-room at the back'. Fox was allegedly a client. Such services, indeed, were often available behind such ordinary shop-fronts as those of haberdashers, perfumers, hosiers, barbers – and even on the premises of cheese-mongers, grocers, tailors and watch-makers. Lady barbers, it was said, would sometimes oblige for half a crown. Such favours were even available in the King's Bench debtors' prison, where a fork stuck in the cell door with the prongs up-turned indicated the

Peg Woffington: Garrick's one-time mistress. (Billie Love Historical Collection)

business in progress, perhaps a conjugal visit but just as likely an illicit encounter.

The Shakespeare's Head, like many taverns, was a resort of convenience which Boswell put to good use: meeting a couple of 'pretty little girls', and pleading poverty, he proposes that they all 'be gay and obliging to each other'. They retire to one of the tavern's rooms, where, he tells us, he solaced his existence with 'one after the other, according to their seniority . . . enjoying High Debauchery with genteel Ceremonial'. (Manners in all things.) The tavern, well-known as the haunt of wits and literary gents and poor harlots, reportedly allowed a great deal of horseplay between the sexes. Condoms, as in many taverns, would be available.

Celebrated toasts of Covent Garden in the 1760s included the dancer Nancy Cooper, Betsy Weems (who had an artificial eye that frequently got lost in her more frantic cavortings) and Lucy Cooper, who almost starved in the King's Bench prison until the kindly Hickey raised a collection of fifty pounds for her. Few were better acquainted with the high and low harlotry of Covent Garden than Hickey. He claims that he was drinking with the fast set and visiting brothels accompanied by 'the most lovely women of the metropolis' before he was fourteen. But he never gambled. He had the demi-mondaine Fanny Hertford as his mistress at nineteen, but the grand passion of his life was another of the demi-monde, Charlotte Barry. He was no stranger to the 'absolute hell upon earth' of Wetherby's (in Little Russell Street):

> Upon ringing at the door, strongly secured with knobs of iron, a cut-throat-looking rascal opened a small wicket, which was also secured with narrow iron bars, who, in a hoarse and ferocious voice, asked: 'Who's that?' Being answered 'Friends' we were cautiously admitted one at a time, and when the last had entered, the door was instantly closed and secured, not only by an immense lock and key, but by a massy iron bolt and chain.

Elizabeth Wetherby ran a low-class establishment which attracted the cream of dissolute society – highwaymen, gamblers, rakes, pickpockets, swindlers, whores (including Lucy Cooper) – and gentlemen of quality. The entrance fee was the price of a cup of coffee. Lucy, once the mistress of Sir Orlando Bridgeman, one of the Hellfire set, and of as many others as took her fancy, was said to be 'lewder than all the whores in Charles's reign'. Another of the available ladies was Polly Talbot, once a conquest of Old Q, William Douglas, Marquess of Queensberry.

At Maltby's the fast set met for 'a drink and a doxy', and Tom King's was then the 'fashionable rendezvous for all trades, spendthrifts and strumpets'. Mother Whyborn (Elizabeth Wiseborne), herself a well-known bawd, had studied to please in the Italian style. She had taken over the role of Mother Cresswell, from whom she had otherwise learned the trade. She was a regular churchgoer and had virginities routinely restored – for the pleasure of quality customers and no doubt the profits of the house. Moll Davis, one of the Merry Monarch's former mistresses, was a close friend. Mother Whyborn had among her clients the poet and playwright John Gay as well as Alexander Pope; in her stable, beside Drury Lane, was the legendary Sally Sainsbury, who had begun her career by befriending apprentices at half-a-crown for half-an-hour and rose to entertain a string of aristocratic lovers and (she claimed) the Prince of Wales (later George II). Sally's downfall came in the middle of the night in the Three Tuns tavern (unashamedly a house of shame), when she stabbed the carousing Hon. John Finch in a quarrel over theatre tickets. Distraught, she begged his forgiveness and with his famous 'last' words the dying man acted most nobly with the utterance: 'I die at pleasure by your hand.' In fact Finch recovered, Sally, despite the intervention of powerful friends, went to Newgate on the reduced charge of assault, with a fine of £1,000. She died in prison. Six gentlemen of rank carried her bier to St Andrew's churchyard in Holborn.

One of the most prestigious bordellos was that kept by Elizabeth Gould, a Covent Garden procuress whose establishment affected the French style in which the wealthy might take their sophisticated pleasures. At the time the focus of such luxury activity was on the move – westwards to converge on the fashionable area of St James's. But the City's bankers and merchants and men of trade, with new money but without pedigree, still felt more comfortable mingling in Covent Garden than with the members of the *bon ton* (most of whom owed them money), who would have snubbed them anyway. Gould's staff were well trained and immaculately turned out; the food and wines were the very best. Her young ladies were chosen for their discretion; they were also required to have an understanding of 'a gentleman's needs'. Their night-long company cost about £10, though there might be extras. Elizabeth Dennison, sometime mistress of Sir Francis Dashwood and Philip Stanhope, and her husband Richard opened an upmarket establishment in about 1730. Given her connections, failure was hardly an option and her girls could mix at any level and were absolutely the 'best pieces' and among the most beautiful of the capital's courtesans.

Mother Elizabeth Needham (one of many aliases) had once been the doyenne: her neighbours in her de luxe house in St James's were mainly the aristocracy and the king's mistress, Lady Castlemaine. She kept her delightfully named 'house of civility' in Park Place, the fringe of St James's, from 1709. An orange-girl who had graduated into sin at the age of fourteen, she had made rich conquests – and big money, which financed her St James's house. She was a handsome woman and, as the best-known procuress, waited in inn yards to recruit her girls fresh off the stagecoaches from the country. Hogarth's painting of her in action in 1731, in *A Harlot's Progress*, sees the wicked old bawd interviewing (supposedly befriending) a fresh-faced country lass who has just stepped off the York stage . . . The girl's future is almost inevitable.

Among Needham's common calls was Cheapside's Bell Inn. She was a hard-bitten lady, hiring out to the girls the clothes they wore (at a steep price); backsliders in deep debt found themselves in the debtors' prison. Those working in the bordello were expected to double as house-servants, and moments after doing the dusting might find themselves in bed with the Prince of Wales. A year after Hogarth immortalised her in his famous sequence, the great madam found herself clamped in the pillory for her activities, dying soon after from her treatment by the mob. An unknown pen lamented her passing, none too sorrowfully:

> She who drest you in Sattins so fine
> Who trained you up for the Game,
> Who Bail, on occasion would find
> And keep you from Dolly and Shame
> Now is laid low in her Grave . . .

Her role would be assumed by Jane Douglas, whose ladies entertained Prince William, the Duke of Cumberland – and other members of the military – as well as the captains of East Indiamen, who brought her young ladies 'treasures' from their distant voyages. The capital's intelligentsia came, along with Hogarth who sat drawing in a corner. Douglas was genteel and took her own lovers from the ranks of the aristocracy. From a highly respectable Scottish family, she had been operating in Piccadilly from the age of seventeen, later moving to St James's; her house had a long history of entertaining princes, peers and the highest in society. Women of rank visited, incognito. Her girls, she ensured, had 'sexual expertise', the house-servants wore a splendid livery and the establishment served gourmet food. In a reversal of the then trend she moved to Covent Garden when she discovered that so many of the capital's young actresses were willing to supplement their incomes. Few requests were refused; few left unrequited. One of her clients, a well-known physician, came but once a year – to indulge in a spot of voyeurism and have a couple of her ladies dance naked for him. Douglas was an excellent business woman; buying her condoms from a firm in the Strand, she sold them to her clients done up in dainty silk bags tied with ribbons – at a suitable profit. She also supplied aphrodisiacs. Nothing came cheap at Mrs Douglas's.

Bagnios usually had convenient retiring rooms that enjoyed a high occupancy. They had been around since the twelfth century, then serving mainly as houses of ill-fame, and the centuries had not changed their main function. The word, with the Restoration, became synonymous with brothel. Typical of the arrangements they encouraged was that enjoyed by Casanova during his stay in London: he negotiated a fee (six guineas) and took the lady to the theatre and then supper and thence to bed. On an encore assignation at Mrs Welch's St James's bagnio he hired one of her rooms for an hour. Mrs Welch, one may assume, was operating at the top end of the industry, since it was here that the great lover had his well-publicised encounter with the courtesan Kitty Fischer, dripping in diamonds and waiting for a duke to take her to a ball. But there was time to spare and it was hinted that the lady was available. The air must have been electric – and Casanova was about to face his most humiliating put-down. Offering ten guineas, he was witheringly rebuffed. Only later was he told that gentlemen were expected to pay such celebrated ladies with a banknote and that Kitty accepted nothing less than those of a £50 denomination. Casanova's story was that he turned down the offer, but then, he would say that, wouldn't he? The bagnios were undeservedly popular for such chance intrigues. One of the most fashionable for a time was that opened in Covent Garden by Betty Careless (real name Carless), 'a peerless Beauty, the gayest, most Charming, Wittiest of Courtesans', who had earlier been under the protection of Captain (Mad Jack) Montagu, later Earl of Sandwich.

But the groves of pleasure moved relentlessly westward and the good whores followed. The ambience was upmarket. King's Place, just off St James's Square,

Rakes frequently got involved in rioting in red-light Covent Garden. (By courtesy of the Guildhall Library, Corporation of London)

catered for the highest in the land. The Royal Oak tavern nearby had rooms where 'mollies' could act like married couples; within a stone's throw of St James's Palace was the King's Head tavern, mainly a brothel; and the King's Arms, also in Pall Mall, was described by Walpole as 'a notorious house of ill-fame'. In a perversion of taste the houses of pleasure were known as nunneries, and their madams called abbesses. One such, a Mrs Catherine Windsor, in 1775 was providing accommodation for couples in need, a place of hasty consummations. She had some 'fine pieces'. Fox visited, and she also had the patronage of his friend the Prince of Wales and of his brother the Duke of Clarence. Mrs Jordan, it was rumoured, augmented her Drury Lane earnings with visits to Mrs Windsor's. She was, it is said, uninhibited in bed.

Black Harriott, an ex-slave and a white man's mistress, graduated to a house in the Place; when her white man died, she had a score of peers calling, plus 'fifty rich men' whose exertions left her richer by a £50 note each time. Among those visiting her was the rake-hell John Montagu, Earl of Sandwich, aka Jeremy Twitcher, lecher and luminary of the Hellfire Club and the Medmenham Friars. Mrs Sarah Dubery, who had a Temple of Venus in Stanhope Street, also moved with the times to St James's to cater for diplomats from foreign shores with a stable of the very best impures and a few moonlighting actresses, including the versatile wire-walker Isabella Wilkinson. Mrs Dubery conscientiously comforted the quality for more than thirty years, and found patient partners for Old Q, who in his later years, despite the asses' milk, suffered (for him) a sad loss of performance. At any one time he would have no fewer than seven procuresses looking out for fresh and nubile flesh.

Charlotte Hayes's grandly named 'house of celebrity' was established in the Place from 1767. Born in a Covent Garden slum about 1725, by 1753 she was taking her 'best pieces' to participate in Dashwood's Medmenham orgies and to make up any shortfall in the female numbers: of the Hellfire Club's forty members, fifteen were considered to be 'Ladies of Quality'. Active male members included the Dukes of Dorset and Argyll; the Earls of Bute, Lichfield, Stafford and Kinnoull; and a goodly sprinkling of peers. Hayes moved with some ease in such decadent circles and had her own box at the opera (an essential of the trade); her girls wore the best French underwear and could have their virginity 'restored' several times. Rich Jews came to forget their money worries in the arms of some skilled and amply bosomed companion, and the house supplied only the best 'cundums', made in Marseilles.

It was here at Charlotte's that the ex-milliner actress Frances Barton, famed for the provocative exposure of her bosom to the male gaze, was groomed for her profession. She had married a Guards trumpeter named Abington, but continued to take lovers, plucking them widely from the parliamentary ranks. One lover was the poet Byron's father, 'Mad Jack' Byron, a hero in the boudoir as in battle. By 1770 Frances was famous. As a live-in guest in the Mayfair house of the Marquess of Lansdowne she had a stipend of £50 a week, with an elegant carriage, but might still be seen at Hayes's or entering one of the capital's bagnios. Hayes's own career was controversial. It was capped in 1772 by an event extraordinary even in that dissipated society: her staging, before a specially invited male audience, of the Feast of Venus, whose climax was reached in a Tahitian dance in which the nude and youthful partners, willowy girls and energetic young men, made athletic and rhythmic love to the sound of music. The performance, with Charlotte herself as its central figure, ended in a two-hour orgy in which the audience joined. Afterwards a banquet was served.

Just as Charles II in a 'voluptuous and sensual' life had led the mad dance of his reign following the Restoration, so the Prince of Wales a century or so later would set the tone for the Regency. The web of pleasure and intrigue was close and intricately woven and reached into all corners of society. Men of wealth were prepared to pay for their pleasure and, as we have seen, there were ladies around who ensured that they did. In the mood of the capital restraint had no place – whether in the White House's mirrored boudoirs or in the heady freedom of the Argyll Rooms. Byron was particularly well qualified to judge the dementia that drove the fashionable throng:

> Behold the new Petronius of the day,
> Our arbiter of pleasure and of play!
> There the hired eunuch, the Hesperian choir
> The melting lute, the soft lascivious lyre,
> The song from Italy, the step from France,
> The midnight orgy, and the mazy dance,
> The smile of beauty, and the flush of wine
> For fops, fools, gamesters, knaves and lords combine,
> Each to his humor – Comus all allows
> Champaign, dice, music or your neighbour's spouse.

A man would lay down his wife for another – in payment of a gambling debt he could not honour. Mistresses changed hands on a similar basis. Several ladies of the Devonshire House set in the later eighteenth century were said to have accepted new lovers in this way, and Georgiana, the Duchess of Devonshire, hints as much in her novel *The Sylph*, published anonymously. Ladies who gambled and lost could be – and were – blackmailed into sleeping with a friend to secure his silence or the money that would free them from embarrassment. The duchess herself ran up dangerously high gambling debts. Another member of the circle, Lady Melbourne, a dark-eyed beauty who turned men's heads, distributed her favours generously but discriminatingly between her husband; Lord Egremont (to whom, it is said, she was passed by Lord

Bawds and pickpockets at work underneath the arches in Covent Garden. (By courtesy of the Guildhall Library, Corporation of London)

Coleraine for £13,000, which she shared); and the Prince of Wales, among others.

The *bon ton* behaved badly, exciting in 1776 the fury of the *Morning Post*, which was moved to comment: 'The excess to which pleasure and dissipation are now carried amongst the *ton* exceeds all bounds, particularly among women of quality.' That same year, the radical Richard Price, a man in evangelical overdrive, also warned the nation about its conduct: 'We are running wild after pleasure and forgetting everything serious and decent in Masquerades. We are gambling in gaming houses: trafficking in boroughs: perjuring ourselves at elections: and selling ourselves for places . . .' The newspapers were calling the Prince Regent's parties 'promiscuous assemblies' and hinting at scandalous 'midnight bowers and miscellaneous companionships'. The *Post* had a point: the young duchess had a close friendship with the Prince of Wales which might easily have been misconstrued – and to the fury of Mrs Fitzherbert, who would have more reason to direct her wrath at Lady Jersey, at forty-one the mother of nine children but still beautiful, and who temporarily stole the prince away in a very public and notorious affair. Georgiana's own husband had kept a former milliner in a discreet but convenient cottage and later shared the bed of the duchess's best friend. Years later the duchess herself would stray into the arms of a cold-hearted and calculating politician and future premier, Charles Grey, and have his child, while her sister Harriet, Countess Bessborough, would take as a lover the twenty-year-old Lord Granville Leveson Gower, who drank and gambled, but was romantically handsome and was known to have turned down the favours of that fashionable impure Harriette Wilson.

Harriette also tried to seduce Byron but was rewarded only by his friendship. She was witty and amusing and her chosen lifestyle was typical of that of her kind. She was the mistress at fifteen of the Earl of Craven but quickly tired of his attentions (or lack of them) and moved on. One of the great toasts of the beau monde, she drove in Hyde Park with her sister courtesans in her carriage at five, the fashionable hour. Her carriage was lined with pale blue satin and was attended during her drives by a bevy of admirers. Her men visitors called by appointment and observed the most civilised conduct. Her first love was the threadbare aristocrat the Marquess of Lorne; later the Marquess of Worcester took her under his protection, a delightful euphemism implying (but by no means guaranteeing) monopoly of the lady's bed, and would hardly leave her side. He wished to marry her but she rejected him – for his own good. Slender-waisted and with voluptuous breasts, and so constantly importuned, Harriette was fastidious about where she bestowed her charms, insisting 'I will be the instrument of pleasure to no man. He must make a friend and companion of me, or he will lose me.'

Nowhere is the function – and the irreverent flavour – of the opera more amusingly conveyed than in her delightful *Memoirs*, which rival those of Hickey in their candour. Its role as an 'auction house' for amatory favours is made plain. When she took her box at the King's Theatre in the Haymarket, the Royal Italian Opera House, the wives of the nobility could only watch balefully as their husbands and sons lined up to pay her court. Her sisters, from her box, distributed their sexual favours for 'later' and changed partners at an astounding rate, negotiating the terms for their protection in longer-term liaisons with this or that sprig of the aristocracy. She herself, after leaving Lord Lorne, was pursued by titles, and became besotted with Lord Ponsonby ('I was made for love'), who adored her.

It was from such women that the inexperienced young rakes learned the arts of love, and her *Memoirs* are highly revealing of the interchange between the sexes and different sectors of society and of the sophisticated world of the fashionable courtesan: the coquettish and easily shifting accommodation of lovers and the etiquette of assignations. Harriette took on her most famous 'friend', the Duke of Wellington ('he groaned over me by the hour'), while Lorne was conveniently in Scotland – after seductive persuasion by the well-known procuress Mrs Porter of Piccadilly, where the duke was apparently a regular client. What also emerges is the stark portrait of a shallow society and the ambiguous role of the courtesan in it. Of one of her suitors, in the Guards, she says: '[he] insisted on falling in love with me, merely to prove himself a fashionable man. [He was] a sort of man who would rather have died than not been a member of White's club, at the door of which he always wished his tilbury and neat groom to be found, between the hours of four and five.'

Women like Harriette formed 'connexions' with men who could afford them; one sister agreed an arrangement with a 'little Portuguese' count for £200 a month in advance and the use of his horses and carriage. The really fashionable impures, however, known to have the arts and wiles that pleased men, were beyond the reach of all but a few; the famous Laura Bell, in the mid-nineteenth century, reputedly had a fortune lavished on her by the Nepalese prime minister after a night of passion; Lord Hertford, an ardent sensualist, was rumoured to

Downfall of a debauchee as a drunken rake is skilfully relieved of his watch. (Museum of London)

have paid £40,000 to the Countess Castiglioni for the same – and may well have taken his money's worth since the Countess had to spend three days in bed recovering. Perdita, on the other hand, the Prince Regent's evanescent passion, was promised £20,000 and succumbed – but in the event faced disappointment when the prince eventually reneged on the deal. His friend Fox, a charmer and a ladies' man, who seduced only courtesans, managed to negotiate for her an annuity of £500, and earned her lasting friendship.

Some rose from the beds of their protectors into the sullied ranks of the aristocracy. Lavinia Fenton, as Polly Peachum in the first production of Gay's *The*

Beggar's Opera, took the eye of the Duke of Bolton, who set her up as his mistress at £400 a year, and later, on his wife's death, made her his duchess. Fox honourably married his mistress of many years: Elizabeth Armistead, a Cockney shoemaker's daughter, one of the most glamorous courtesans of her time, had 'finished' her education in the noted Mrs Goadby's nunnery and had comforted the Prince Regent (later George IV) before permanently ending up in the bed of his friend. Both men were emotionally rather than physically demanding in their attachments. At one time the two had shared the favours of three ladies, Perdita, Grace Dalrymple and Mrs Armistead. Once, when their visits to the last coincided, both took the situation good-humouredly, Fox presumably withdrawing. Elizabeth Anne Howard, who lived with a wealthy lover in St John's Wood, became a countess in the cause of solacing Prince Louis Napoleon (Napoleon III) and making him substantial loans. Lord Cleveland was said to have once paid £1,000 for a single *pas de deux* with her.

But treachery was rife. Mary Ann Clarke, kept by Prince Frederick, Duke of York, the Commander-in-Chief of the Army, cost him a promising career and heaped scandal on his head in 1809 when his payments to her of £1,000 a month were stopped. To keep up appearances in her grand house with twenty servants and three chefs, the beautiful courtesan started selling commissions in the Horse Guards by adding names to the list of those put forward for the duke's approval. The lovely Clarke had her dazzling day in Parliament when an inquiry was held, and such was her charm she walked away from the maelstrom with a pension, provided she left Britain. Constancy too was strained: Hickey relates being introduced to women of a very superior sort who were 'mostly in keeping', but 'as is almost always the case, were unfaithful to their immediate patrons, always having one or more gallants for their own private gratification'. He had access he says 'to the finest women then upon the town', including Madame La Tour (then in the keeping of Sir Penistone Lamb, later Lord Melbourne), which did not cost him a shilling. In fact he frequently preferred 'going to a bagnio with the most hackneyed and common woman'.

In the capital's hierarchy of harlotry the ladies of the demi-monde looked down on their ragged cousins of the pave, the girls Mayhew's survey found crowding the Haymarket from noon to midnight, some of them as young as thirteen, and most from the lower strata of society with little choice in their vocation. He found: 'They prostitute themselves for a lower price, and haunt those disreputable coffee-houses in the neighbourhood . . . where you may see the blinds drawn down, and the lights burning dimly within, with notices over the door that "beds are to be had within".' This was not the scene of pleasure but the sad, forlorn face of poverty that disgraced the great city. Their presence fulfilled a social need – the brisk, sometimes brutish, bout of gratification devoid of warmth or pleasure.

In the mêlée of the capital's streets any well-dressed male might feel his hand taken by that of a young girl, with the plea 'Come, let us drink a glass together' or simply the stark promise 'I'll go with you if you wish'. Men stepping into the night from the clubs of St James's would be accosted from the shadows by ladies looking for trade; in notorious Norton Street men were sometimes dragged off the street by the scantily clad ladies who dashed out from its brothels; in the Strand as dusk fell, a man would find a coquettish companion suddenly at his side. Such casual encounters are described by Boswell in his *Journal*. Having picked up 'a strong jolly young damsel' in the Haymarket, he marches her to the Westminster Bridge, and then 'in armour complete [a condom] did I engage up in this noble edifice'. He was much taken with the idea of 'doing it there' with the Thames rolling below them. (The old Westminster Bridge had alcoves – actually semi-octagonal recesses – to provide covered shelter for pedestrians.) For such a moment of dalliance the fee might be only sixpence; for a bed and a little playfulness two guineas and half-a-crown for the maid was the common tariff in Harris's famous *List of Covent Garden Ladies*, although it ranged from ten shillings to five guineas (for a girl who enjoyed 'frolics' with petty officers).

At the end of the Regency there were reputedly some thirty thousand prostitutes on the streets and in the capital's brothels. The rakes who used them, one ventures to say, were mainly men without the warm humanity of a Boswell, a Hickey or a Pepys – callously dissolute men who used women ill, perhaps, as has been suggested, from an inward fear and hatred of them. In a brutish society they were predators pure and simple, casting a bleared and jaundiced eye over the 'fresh pieces' the old procuresses paraded for them in the lobby of Drury Lane, a gaggle of young innocents ripe for the plucking. Some madams even took their young bawds to Brighton in pursuit of the Prince Regent's entourage.

There is, alas, no equivalent Harris *List* for rakes. They were a motley crew of braggarts and sensualists who haunted the opera and the theatre and the night-houses of the city. They cut a dash undoubtedly; some were utterly depraved.

The 'macaroni preacher', the Reverend William Dodd DD, LLD, a swell in the foppish style, who made his exit for forgery at Tyburn, had regularly enjoyed the company of Polly Kennedy, sometime mistress of the 2nd Viscount Bolingbroke. Bolingbroke personified the predatory rake, boasting that he would 'seduce any innocent girl whatever'. Another was William Stanhope, Earl of Harrington and 'a goat of quality'. His conquests included the opera siren Caterini Ruini Galli, Kitty Brown of the 'pointing bubbies', Kitty Fischer, the actress Mrs Houghton, and Jane Courteville, left at a loose end by the death of the Duke of Dorset. The earl ('Lord Fumble') was said to visit Mother Prendergast's house on Sundays, Mondays, Wednesdays and Fridays, seeking the company of two companions at a time; Lady Harrington's lifestyle was one of equal variety. About 1754 Frederick Calvert, the 7th Earl of Baltimore, was keeping a harem of 'five white ladies and one black', all chaperoned by his wife. Perhaps he took Sundays off. Lord Chesterfield, whatever the advice he gave in *Letters to his Son*, also liked two ladies at a time, and loved having his eyelids licked.

That seedy world of profligacy and the exploitation of the innocents is magnificently captured by the under-valued Hogarth in *A Rake's Progress* and in *A Harlot's Progress*, a series of six paintings begun in 1730. In plate one of the latter, a 'progress' from coach to coffin, the gentleman watching Mother Needham cozening the fresh-faced girl just off the country stage is the serial seducer Colonel Francis Charteris, the man they called the Rape-master General of Britain, a 'huge raw beast' willing to pay twenty guineas for a virgin. He was a thoroughly bad lot, a monster with a voracious appetite for sex and a cheat at cards. Nothing in petticoats was safe from his attentions, and he was constantly on the lookout for innocents to add to the tally of over a hundred he had already seduced. He sent out his servants to scour the country round for fresh and lusty country girls with buttocks 'as hard as Cheshire cheeses, that should make a Dint in a Wooden chair, and work like a parish Engine at a Conflagration'. At his Scottish home he kept a seraglio, no doubt against the possibility of lean times.

His penchant for debauching maid-servants would finally bring down Mother Needham and her unsavoury empire, after he was found guilty of the rape of one of his housemaids. The girl had been sent to him, no doubt knowingly, by the famous procuress, who was found guilty of keeping a disorderly house and sentenced to stand in the pillory. Charteris was sentenced to death, but spent only a short time in Newgate before being given a royal pardon. There was public outrage at the decision. Mother Needham, powerless in the pillory before the mob, was pelted near to death and died soon after. Charteris lived to continue his lechery into old age. His fate, one feels, should have been different, like the rake in Hogarth's eight-sequence series, destroyed by a pleasure-bent, uncaring capital.

CHAPTER XIV
A Return to Puritanism

Vice did not end with Victoria; after a time it merely hid its face. The expensive courtesan still supported her sophisticated lifestyle by pleasing men and providing what was agreeable to them. In Hyde Park the female occupant of a fashionable equipage would be surrounded by her ardent admirers, her profession established. Laura Bell, the Irish shopgirl – by the age of twenty driving her own barouche with a magnificent pair of whites – would continue to have her phaeton surrounded by ambitious beaux when she drove in the Park; when she went to the opera, it was like an attendance by royalty. The entire house stood to watch her leave, and she broke, unendurably, a great many hearts when she chose to marry, in 1852, an officer and a gentleman, Captain Augustus Thistlethwayte, whose habit in summoning a house-servant was to fire a pistol shot through the ceiling of the room. In the mid-Victorian age the best whores still rode in Rotten Row, and the villas of St John's Wood became increasingly the residences of kept ladies and other comforters of men. Skittles, they say, who rode with such style and so fearlessly to hounds, was the last of the great Victorian courtesans – the last lady who did it in style.

A glimpse of that lingering naughty world that lured men into the haunts of pleasure is sensuously revealed in the portrait of a fashionable night-house evoked in a poem that appeared as late as 1873 in *Beeton's Christmas Annual*. (It was promptly banned by W.H. Smith and sold a quarter of a million copies in three weeks.) The annual's editor was Mrs Beeton's less-famous husband.

> . . . a bravery of gilt, a mass
> And wealth of waving hair, and glittering glass;
> A hundred rainbows cross and intertwine,
> A thousand wicked eyes enchanting shine.
> Lips, full of sin, yet plump and ripe withal,

Shape naughty kisses, and for liquids call,
Hands, gloved divinely, creep beneath men's arms;
Whilst shapely ankles tell of hidden charms;
Toilettes, too ravishing for mortal pen
Flit everywhere, and prey on helpless men.
Houris in *eau de Nile*, and salmon pink,
And peacock blue, distract and daze, and drink.
The utter stranger greet they with a smile,
So artless seeming, yet so versatile;
As some in distant corners toy and sport,
While shop-boys, trying tip-top swells to be,
Have robbed the till and call for S & B.

There was still a kind of ambivalent half-world where the fashionable new womanhood met, a world that Gronow, as old age crept on him in 1862, was unsure about:

I do not mean to say that there are not now . . . beautiful and amiable women, combining good sense and high principle; but there are too many who seem to have taken for their ideal a something between the dashing London horse-breaker [impure] and some Persian *artiste dramatique* of the third-rate theatre; the object of whose ambition is to be mistaken for a *femme du demi-monde*, to be insulted when they walk out with their petticoats girt up to their knees, shewing (to do them justice) remarkably pretty feet and legs, and to wearing wide-awake hats over painted cheeks and brows, and walk with that indescribable, jaunty, 'devil-may-care' look which is considered 'the right thing' nowadays, – to make sporting bets – to address men as Jack, Tom or Harry, – to ride ahead in the Park . . . to talk of young men who 'spoon' them and discuss with them the merits of Skittles and her horses, or the last scandalous story fabricated in the bay window at White's, the very faintest allusion to which would have made their mothers' hair stand on end with dismay and horror – this is to be pleasant and 'fast' and amusing. The young lady who is weak enough to blush if addressed rather too familiarly, and so unwise as to ignore the existence of *les dames aux camelias*, is called 'slow' and distanced altogether: in the London steeple chase after husbands she is 'nowhere' – an outsider – a female muff.

There remained discreet arrangements, like that enjoyed by Samuel Butler, the author of *The Way of all Flesh*, who visited Madame Dumas in Handel Street every Wednesday afternoon (paying £1 for his visit). Madame Dumas did not solicit in the arcades or the assembly houses; gentlemen called on her at her rooms. But out in the streets, and notably in the Haymarket, the pavements still thronged with available ladies of the lower sort, some, as we have seen, mere children. Prices were low. There were, in 1859, nearly three thousand London brothels that the police were aware of, though other estimates suggested a figure double that, and the capital may have had as many as eighty thousand ladies in the business. It would remain an activity observable in the streets. Poverty, as always, swelled the ranks: shopgirls, seamstresses, milliners, all those scandalously low-paid and sweating over collar-bands and button-holes and hat linings, and surveying the futility of their lives, must have considered joining the band. Many doubtless did.

Society, however, was becoming sated with pleasure, perhaps disillusioned with a world of glitter but of little substance; a mood of piety was creeping in, led partly and surprisingly by the penitent woman who had lately been the toast of the capital, Laura Bell. From about 1860 Bell performed an astonishing career-switch by becoming a committed and eloquent preacher – thought by many to rival even Spurgeon. With her hands bejewelled in diamonds she spread the Word; the good and the godly, including her friend Mr Gladstone, came to the tea parties at her Grosvenor Square home.

The new Puritans would gradually work their change – organisations like the Society for the Suppression of Vice, for instance – while the pervasive evangelical movement gained ground and did good, dimming the last glow of the old, Regency England, stridently striving to make the people renounce joy and persecuting those who provided it. Slowly society would assume the mantle of the new morality; like the cock-fight and the bare-knuckle encounter, the pleasures of amatory dalliance would go underground, a clandestine undertaking. The drabs touting in the streets might be reviled by that society, but their services were yet furtively enlisted by the respectable clerk or City gent hurrying home for the leafy suburbs; the titillation of pornography was still available for those whom time and long dissipation had jaded.

An age of unbelievable hedonism excused by its style and splendour was making its exit. For two centuries the capital had indulged itself with every form of pleasure, gross and refined – the aristocracy in particular. Their day was paling

The impressive entrance to the Great Exhibition of 1851, portal to a new age. (Museum of London)

as they adopted the façade, at least, of a respectability that echoed that of their monarch, who, unusually in a crowned head, kept the pleasures of love – which she was said to enjoy – to the marriage bed. Victoria and her consort Albert, by example, would set the tone for a life more dutiful and moral – if just a little dull. The strictness of their creed was laid at Albert's door. But the climate was set: with them Puritanism would make a raging return, sometimes to a preposterous degree. Even as the wretched of the Haymarket lifted their linen nightly, the immodesty of the naked legs of tables and pianos must be covered in singular pantaloons. Decorum was everything. The royal couple's dignity transformed a visit to the theatre, now to be taken seriously and no longer merely an occasion on which to flaunt one's charms in the latest *décolletée* gown.

Pleasure moved from the subtly sensual towards the cerebral and cultural, losing its sophisticated elegance. After the wild days of the Regency all that followed would be drab; the capital would lose its savour, its inspiration, its eccentricity. An era of great and wonderful achievements in many fields would be brought brutally to a close by an industrial boom that helped to sponsor the capital's sprawl, with great speed, into what had been appealing countryside – the green world its crowded populace had escaped to. Developers crammed bricks and mortar on to every available inch of land they could lay hands on. It may have been necessary, heaven knows, for the city's slums were still awesome and vile, but after the years of fastidious Georgian taste it was a reversion to what was fast and functional. A pleasing aestheticism had fled the public mind. Elegance was no more. Through the capital's congealing, amorphous mass, in the lust for progress, would be driven railroads that bisected communities and cultures. Their vast termini would link it firmly to its hinterlands, diminishing its magic. A greater means of access and egress, a new importance, would be created, along with the change in character.

Puritanism would re-establish itself strongly in the code of the worthy folk who adopted the so-called Victorian values of the work ethic and a sober gentility in grinding out the country's wealth from the grim mills that crushed their lives. Pleasures would become correspondingly muted. There was a determined – and perhaps overdue – suppression of the wildest excesses of society. The old fairs, occasions often of depraved amusement no longer countenanced by the decent-thinking sector of the hoi polloi, were quashed one by one by magistrates who had long awaited the day. Cremorne was the last of the great pleasure gardens and latterly a rendezvous for prostitutes and a bawdy clientele. Shrieks and cries rent the night air to the annoyance of Chelsea's residents, who managed to have it suppressed in 1877. The Theatres Act of 1843, soon after Victoria's accession, had de-licensed the playhouse, but the Lord Chamberlain continued to demand a seemly restraint. The music-hall, still naughty, would slowly re-invent itself for a wider, more genteel audience, and was careful not to give too much offence, though there would be the delight still of a shapely chorus leg and the adorable quiver of a plump but graceful thigh. The capital's private clubs, such as the Travellers and the Reform – so different from the rakes' rendezvous – became truly bastions of class and privilege but also sanctuaries of the new respectability where rank remained uncompromised.

Newspapers of some quality fed the capital's (and the nation's) appetite for intelligence. In 1702 the *Daily Courant* had begun disseminating such information as came its way from Ludgate Hill, starting an industry that would move fractionally with the years to find its centre of gravity in Fleet Street. Alas, no longer; the circus has moved on. Mudie's lending library, like that of his rival Smith, might impose a censorship on what it considered its lady subscribers (at a guinea a year) might read, while the market for what was then thought *risqué* had been only slightly inconvenienced by the passing into law in 1857 of the Obscene Publications Act, intended to crush the flow of pornography from its main source in Holywell Street – this at a time when the capital's newspapers, *The Times* included, faithfully reported every prurient detail of the society cases that came to the divorce courts. Holywell Street, once famous for its holy spring, was a fount of filth which *The Times*, notwithstanding its own daily revelations on human behaviour, called 'the most vile street in the civilised world'. It ran parallel with the Strand; its uncrowned prince was the publisher William Dugdale, who went repeatedly (as is the wont of such men) to prison and died there without slowing production. His volumes sold at two guineas.

Still openly displayed in tobacconists' windows were rows of the fashionably indecent snuff boxes imported from Paris, their interior cameos designed to titillate and amuse, or possibly arouse. From the same source about mid-century there came the naughty slides, plain or coloured, allegedly taken in the bagnios of the French capital, that could be slipped in front of the lenses of the popular stereoscope for late-night, three-dimensional viewing. They showed images of ladies invitingly *en déshabillé* (or worse). A set of twenty plain (i.e. monochrome) cost four guineas.

Blood would still count. But not, perhaps, for much longer. The select echelons of society were losing their fizz, their *élan*. While the clubs of St James's were black-balling the upstart maverick (and places like Almack's, now in decline, sought still to exclude the *nouveaux riches*, censoring its guest-lists), the middle classes were marching on the broadwalks of Kensington Gardens. The upper crust had begun to lose its wealth, and with it power and position, to the new industrial entrepreneurs whose mills were making the land hideous. They would be further hit – along with the countryside – by the collapse of English farming in the mid-1870s, as the rich harvest of the American prairies started to erode their land-owning supremacy.

From 1829 horse buses had been 'opening up' the city, unifying and consolidating its larger identity. That same year Peel's band of blue-coated, top-hatted bobbies began to exert their control. The age of steam was nigh – and indeed had already begun. The links with the continent had been strengthened from 1821 with the start of a steam-vessel passenger service between Dover and Calais, now less than four hours away in reasonable weather. And the country's southern seaside resorts were clamouring to build piers to accommodate the capital's weekend trippers arriving by a growing fleet of paddle-steamers.

Better roads, better communications generally, and the railways in particular, notably expanded the social options, with all that implied for the as yet unstructured leisure industry, and gave a fresh impetus and a wider audience to sporting events such as boxing (now regulated and legitimised) and horse-racing, both of which still united the classes, as did cricket. Heavy wagers, as in the past, however, still rode on the result in all of them. Cricket, that rural game that had first come up from the West Country, had, even by 1743, become the pleasure also of nobles and gentlemen and divines only too happy to enlist the prowess of village tradesmen and gardeners, butchers and cobblers (and defer to them), and to spread its hegemony through the land. (As the wise Trevelyan has succinctly said: 'If the French *noblesse* had been capable of playing cricket with their peasants, their chateaux would never have been burnt.') Football, from its ragged and ruffianly origins, with the formation of the Football Association in 1863 would begin to mould itself into a competitive and near-professional structure with a national profile, its players the new heroes of the working classes. It would emerge as the popular sport of the people, exciting fierce loyalties as the all-encompassing focus of the working man's week. The brutal old sports – the bull- and bear-baiting, the cock-fighting, the prize-fights (which would continue until the end of the century) – would die reluctantly, giving way to the passion for dancing, the circus and all the seemlier pursuits. Life for the many would become more wholesome – and healthier.

The aristocracy would become respectable – on the surface at least, their peccadilloes under wraps, their scandals mainly muted. Imperceptibly they would lose their once inviolable political clout to the emerging middle classes with their rising standards and high expectations. By the time of the Great Exhibition – the event which so successfully show-cased the thrusting new Britain – half of the country's population would be urban. The countryside was about to start its long retreat. Industrialisation would divide the people, emphasising the social divisions as England found her soul slowly submerged in a blight of black factories, back-to-backs and a dreary uniformity. Unquestionably the merry rout had ended. There must have been occasions when the capital, like a raddled old dowager, looked back nostalgically on better times – to that heady and flamboyant past when men played for the highest stakes and women recklessly risked all on the glances of love.

Further Reading

Altick, Richard D. *Shows of London: a Panoramic History of Exhibitions, 1600–1862* (Belknap Press/Harvard University Press, 1978)

Armitage, John. *Man at Play: Nine Centuries of Pleasure Making* (Frederick Warne, 1977)

Bell, Leslie. *Bella of Blackfriars* (Odhams, 1961)

Best, Geoffrey. *Mid-Victorian Britain 1851–75* (Fontana, 1985)

Borer, Mary Cathcart. *The City of London* (Constable, 1977)

Boswell's *London Journal 1762–1763* (Yale, 1950)

Boswell, James. *Life of Johnson* (Panther, 1961)

Burford, E.J. *Royal St James's: Being a Story of Kings, Clubmen and Courtesans* (Hale, 1988)

Burford, E.J. *Wits, Wenchers and Wantons: London's Lowlife: Covent Garden in the Eighteenth Century* (Hale, 1992)

Butler, Frank. *A History of Boxing in Britain* (Barker, 1972)

Cameron, David Kerr. *The English Fair* (Sutton, 1998)

Childs, J. Rives. *Casanova* (Allen & Unwin, 1961)

Defoe, Daniel. *A Tour through the Whole Island of Great Britain* (Penguin, 1986)

Dickens, Charles. *Sketches by Boz* (Penguin, 1995)

Disher, M.Willson. *Pleasures of London* (Hale, 1950)

Erickson, Carolly. *Our Tempestuous Day: a History of Regency England* (Robson, 1996)

Evelyn, John. *The Diary of*, selected and edited by Guy de la Bedoyere (Boydell Press, 1995)

Foreman, Amanda. *Georgiana: Duchess of Devonshire* (Flamingo, 1999)

Green, Benny. *The History of Cricket* (Barrie & Jenkins, 1988)

Gronow, Captain. *The Reminiscences and Recollections of* (Bodley Head, 1964)

Haydon, Peter. *The English Pub: a History* (Hale, 1994)

Hickey, William. *Memoirs of*, edited by Peter Quennell (Hutchinson, 1960)

Latham, Robert. *The Shorter Pepys* (Bell & Hyman, 1985)

Leapmann, Michael. *London's River* (Pavilion, 1991)

Lilleywhite, Bryant. *London Coffee Houses* (Allen & Unwin, 1963)

Low, Donald A. *The Regency Underworld* (Sutton, 1999)

Margetson, Stella. *Leisure and Pleasure in the Eighteenth Century* (Cassell, 1970)

Margetson, Stella. *Leisure and Pleasure in the Nineteenth Century* (Cassell, 1969)

Margetson, Stella. *Regency London* (Cassell, 1971)

Masters, Brian. *The Mistresses of Charles II* (Constable, 1997)

Morrah, Patrick. *Restoration England* (Constable, 1979)

Pearl, Cyril. *The Girl with the Swansdown Seat* (Signet, 1958)

Picard, Liza. *Restoration London* (Weidenfeld, 1997)

Plumb, J.H. *England in the Eighteenth Century* (Penguin, 1950)

Plumb, J.H. *The First Four Georges* (Fontana, 1966)

Porter, Roy. *London: a Social History* (Hamish Hamilton, 1994)

Prebble, John. *Culloden* (Secker & Warburg, 1961)

Rude, George. *Hanoverian London, 1714–1808* (Secker & Warburg, 1971)

Stow, John. *A Survey of London, 1598* (Sutton, 1994)

Trevelyan, G.M. *Illustrated English Social History:3* (Pelican, 1964)

Trevelyan, G.M. *Illustrated English Social History:4* (Pelican, 1964)

Uglow, Jenny. *Hogarth: a Life and a World* (Faber, 1997)

Walpole, Horace. *The Letters of*, selected by W.S. Lewis (Folio Society, 1951)

Weightman, Gavin. *London River: the Thames Story* (Collins & Brown, 1990)

Weinreb, Ben and Hibbert, Christopher. *The London Encyclopaedia* (Papermac, 1983)

White, T.H. *The Age of Scandal* (Penguin, 1962)

Wilkinson, George Theodore. *The Newgate Calendar* (Cardinal, 1991)

Wilson, John Dover. *Life in Shakespeare's England* (Penguin, 1964)

Wilson, J.H. *The Private Life of Mr Pepys* (New English Library, 1962)

Wilson, Harriette. *Selections from the Memoirs of*, edited by Max Marquis (Bestseller Library, 1960)

Index